Muhammad I. Ayish
The New Arab Public Sphere

Medien und politische Kommunikation – Naher Osten und islamische Welt /
Media and Political Communication – Middle East and Islam, Vol. 15.
Edited by Prof. Dr. Kai Hafez, University of Erfurt
(Volume 1–10 at the German Institute for Middle East Studies/
Deutsches Orient-Institut, Hamburg 2000–2005)

Muhammad I. Ayish

The New Arab Public Sphere

Verlag für wissenschaftliche Literatur

ISSN 1863-4486
ISBN 978-3-86596-168-6

© Frank & Timme GmbH Verlag für wissenschaftliche Literatur
Berlin 2008. Alle Rechte vorbehalten.

Das Werk einschließlich aller Teile ist urheberrechtlich geschützt.
Jede Verwertung außerhalb der engen Grenzen des Urheberrechtsgesetzes ist ohne Zustimmung des Verlags unzulässig und strafbar.
Das gilt insbesondere für Vervielfältigungen, Übersetzungen,
Mikroverfilmungen und die Einspeicherung und Verarbeitung in
elektronischen Systemen.

Herstellung durch das atelier eilenberger, Leipzig.
Printed in Germany.
Gedruckt auf säurefreiem, alterungsbeständigem Papier.

www.frank-timme.de

Dedication

To my Wife Halima whose enlightened vision in life has always been a source of inspiration and support

Acknowledgements

The author would like to thank the University of Sharjah for providing the appropriate research environment that made this work possible. It is the author's personal hope that this book would contribute to developing clearer visions about communication and politics in the Arab World and enriching ongoing dialogue between Arabs and the West in the spirit of mutual respect and peaceful co-existence. In carrying out this work, this author is inspired by the ceaseless endeavors of His Highness Sheikh Dr. Sultan bin Mohammed al-Qassemi, Member of the UAE Supreme Council, Ruler of Sharjah, whose devotion to the pursuit of global and human dialogue has been globally-recognized. My sincere thanks also go to Prof. Dr. Kai Hafez of the University of Erfurt in Germany for his valuable comments.

INTRODUCTION 9

CONCEPTUAL FRAMEWORK 32

II.1. The Public Sphere: A Conceptual Definition 34

II.2. Transitions in the Public Sphere 37

II.3. Universalizing and Globalizing the Public Sphere 40

II.4. Critiques 43

II.5. An Arab Public Sphere in the Making? 45

II.6. Proposed Framework 55

II.7. Summary & Conclusions 56

NORMATIVE ARAB-ISLAMIC TRADITIONS 58

III.1. Historical Arab-Islamic Political Experiences 60

III.2. The Arab-Islamic Symbiosis 63

III.3. Normative Islamic Components 69

III.4. Corollary Concepts 71

III.5. Normative Islamic Communication Principles 78

III.6. The Dichotomous Nature of Classical Arab-Islamic Discourse 84

III.7. Summary & Conclusions 93

THE MODERN ARAB PUBLIC SPHERE 94

IV.1. The Arab World Media Scene: 1798-1990 96

IV.2. Summary and Conclusion 125

THE ARAB WORLD IN THE AGE OF GLOBALIZATION 127

V.1. The Arab World in the Eye of the Globalization Storm: Emerging Political Contexts . 129

V.2. U.S. Spearheading Reform 133

V.3. Arab Responses 136

V.4. The Unfolding Political Scene 140

V.5. Implications for the Public Sphere 148

V.6. Summary and Conclusion 149

THE EMERGING ARAB PUBLIC SPHERE 150

VI.1. Defining the Arab Public Sphere 152

VI.2. Components of the Arab Public Sphere 153

VI.3. Summary and Conclusion 183

TOWARDS AN ARAB-ISLAMIC PUBLIC SPHERE 184

VII.1. Islam and Democracy: The Ongoing Debate 187

VII.2. A Proposed Arab-Islamic Public Sphere Perspective 195

VII.3. Arab-Islamic Public Sphere Features 199

VII.4. Components 203

VII.5. Realizing an Arab Global Constructive Engagement 206

VII.6. Summary & Conclusion 212

CONCLUDING REMARKS 214

REFERENCES 230

I
INTRODUCTION

When the idea of this book was floated some two years ago, the author initially thought that it would be just another Arab World media survey of recent communications developments in a region extending from the Atlantic Ocean in the west to the Arabian Gulf in the east. It is a huge area of land with diverse sub-cultural and ethnic entities; yet, with significant common features of language, religion, and history. For hundreds of years, this area, referred to in this book as the 'Arab World', had experienced similar conditions of Arab-Islamic rule, Ottoman domination, European colonialism, and post-independence development. As the 21st century dawned on the region, the Arab World, more than ever before, has continued to grapple with inherited, yet more complicated, political and cultural ferment, centering on the evolution of its unique identity in the ages of both modernization and globalization. At no point in the region's history had political disintegration and cultural disorientation been as acute as in the first decade of the 21st century when state authoritarianism, religious fundamentalism, Western imperialism, and socio-economic under-development have converged to carry conditions into new appalling frontiers. Sadly enough, national and global power politics rather than public diplomacy and human dialogue, has become the key to defining the region's destiny. A prime backlash outcome of those historical tensions and their early 21st century culminations is clearly visible in the region's hurried search for common solutions to its complex woes in parochial nationalism, Islamic fundamentalism, or pragmatic alignment with Western-style socio-economic modernism.

In the midst of those scenarios, the development of modern communications institutions in the Arab World has also exhibited identical features relating to media role in national liberation, cultural integration, sustainable development, and political democratization. As in other world regions, mass and Web-based media have increasingly turned into central players in the evolving public sphere, defined here as the virtual incubator of diverse political and social views pertaining to society and the state. The modern Arab mass-mediated public sphere has traditionally mirrored not only the unidirectional, authoritarian, past-oriented, and exclusivist public discourse in the region, but has also exhibited the complexity of political and cultural norms and values giving rise to such discourse. Arabic, as a language of modern political discourse, has been viewed as 'inherently predisposed' to delivering rosy images of highly sentimental and detached realities. In the age of globalization, this emerging Arab public sphere has been hailed as heralding the region's transition into a more egalitarian phase of development. For the first time in their contemporary history, Arabs have found themselves face to face with a wide range of cross-road challenges arising, among other things, from the information and communications revolution and the expanding American influence around the globe. Governments no longer have the final say in deciding national agendas as more indigenous and exogenous voices seem to gain more ground in the struggle for the hearts and minds of the region's population. In this respect, the author cautions, the evolving public sphere should not be uncritically taken for granted as it could prove to be no more than an arena of 'creative communications chaos', to borrow Condoleezza Rice's reference to the state of political and military confusion in the Middle East. The mass-mediated public sphere could neither be a function of 'coercive democratization', nor a product of imported high-tech media structures. It is rather a reflection of the community's evolution of genuine social visions drawing on a synthesis of the best and the brightest of its cultural heritage and of modern cultural and political practices.

The employment of the notion of the pubic sphere in the Arab political communications context dictates going further beyond traditional descriptions of media landscapes. It rather involves the analysis of moral, cultural, and political foundations that seem to give the evolving Arab public sphere its unique identity. If one claims that the public sphere is traditionally a product of specific European historical experiences, then its investigation within an Arab World setting would likely be plagued by serious conceptual and methodological tensions. But since the public sphere in the age of globalization is no longer viewed as a monopoly of a Western invention, but rather as a universal ingredient of national and global democratic politics, its use for understanding the communication-politics nexus in the Arab World seems highly relevant. In recent years, the issue has come to gain some vogue in the region as some Western, especially American intellectual voices embedded in global politics, have euphemistically described current media and political transitions in the Arab World as bearing seeds of a new public sphere. This optimistic intellectual tradition obviously seems to run counter to yet another stream of Western thinking that perceives the Arab World as a cultural wasteland, a breeding ground for hate and bigotry, with no relevance for contemporary democratic politics. From an intellectual point of view, both views concur in viewing the Arab Middle East as a source of global evil that could be redressed through democratization. In addressing this two-fold perspective, this book strongly argues that the Arab World could bring its rich cultural heritage to bear on contemporary political discourse through a process of creative synthesis that neither divorces itself from core Arab-Islamic values and norms, nor disengages from global political and cultural practices. The key to success in this endeavor is the evolution of a new understanding of both Arab-Islamic morality and global political realities as two mutually-inclusive intellectual domains with promising implications for the region's development for decades to come.

The challenge facing the author in reconciling moral Arab-Islamic traditions and contemporary social and political imperatives of the public sphere has been the subject of a two-century old debate centering on the notion of *Nahda* (Renaissance). Lewis (2005) notes that in the aftermath of Napoleon's expedition to Egypt in 1789, a profound sense of puzzlement dominated the intellectual atmosphere in the country over what seemed to be irreconcilable Islamic and

Western cultures. The puzzlement had continued until the answer was found by Sheikh Rifa'a al-Tahtawi, a very remarkable Egyptian scholar who had spent seven years in France as part of a scientific mission dispatched by Muhammad Ali, the Egyptian ruler at the time, to look into French technological and scientific advancements and harness them to Egypt's benefit. In his truly fascinating book about post-revolutionary France, al-Tahtawi pointed out that when the French talked about freedom, what they meant was what we Muslims call justice. He was quoted as saying that 'just as the French, and more generally Westerners, thought of good government and bad government as freedom and slavery, so Muslims conceived of them as justice and injustice', (Lewis, 2005). When considering how such bold and far-sighted interpretations of Arab-Islamic morality managed to surface in the region's public intellectual discussions two centuries ago, our spirits get surely dampened by the failure of current reconciliatory endeavors to deliver bright thinkers of Tahtawi's caliber at a time when they are most urgently needed.

As much as modern Arab-Islamic reconciliatory traditions were cognizant of significant common grounds shared by both Arab and Western cultural and political orientations, they seemed also conscious of their moral and philosophical disparities. Conceived and carried out within the 'dialogue of civilizations' traditions, Arab World -based efforts to harmonize Arab-Islamic and mainly Western worldviews have come some way, especially in the post-September 11 era. The whole issue of the 'dialogue of civilizations' has been intrinsically about creating and expanding common grounds; establishing bridges; and yet, recognizing diversity. Within that same tradition, this work is meant to be an intellectual exercise in cultural and political reconciliation. This synthetic approach suggests neither appeasing the West nor pushing Islamic norms beyond their prescribed limits by suggesting some illusive common grounds on both sides of the divide. It rather draws more on proven historical evidence that great ideas often derive their viability and sustainability from their dynamic assimilative potential and their built-in propensity to expand their boundaries to accommodate other great ideas and practices with profound moral redeeming values. This was exactly the essence of sustainability in Islamic civilization in different phases of history when Arabs, as bearers of the Islamic message, found themselves face to face with foreign civilizations in alien lands (Bliwi, 2005). Islam possesses a limitless assimilative capacity drawing on a comprehensive conception of the Universe as fully harnessed to the benefit of Man within an elaborate system of morality that embraces a great deal of diversity. It is a central theme of this book that because the two sources of Islamic morality, the *Qur'an* and the *Sunna* (Prophet Muhammad's traditions) flow from a Divine source; the legitimacy of their status as terms of reference could never be questioned. However, our interpretations of those references are always subject to scrutiny since they reflect imperfect human comprehensions of the scriptures as defined by social time and space contexts giving rise to those interpretations. Hence, religious knowledge, as derived from the *Qur'an* and the *Sunna*, within varying historical and cultural contexts, could take multiple forms. It is within this diversity that Arab-Islamic history has seen the evolution of intellectual pluralism as evident in different schools of philosophy, jurisprudence, and politics. The Arab-Islamic community (*Umma*) began to dive into the abyss of darkness only when varying understandings of Islamic morality began to take on authoritarian, domineering and exclusivist tones that discounted other views as heresies. Knowledge in Islam is an open resource and nobody could claim monopoly of its acquisition and interpretation.

The use of the public sphere as a conceptual framework for addressing Arab media role in the region's politics as well as in the Arab-Western dialogue is justified on numerous grounds. First, the dramatic development of media in the Arab World in the past two decades has brought about new communications realities unprecedented in modern history. The information revolution seems to have expanded Arabs' media reach and opened up promising windows of opportunity for the emergence of new local and global players with unorthodox cultural and political views. The introduction of satellite television and the World Wide Web has enabled broader popular access to information in different areas of relevance for both official institutions and private individuals and groups. Second, political and social transformations sweeping the region have created an unprecedented mobility in Arabian societies as marked by the introduction of broader participatory arrangements and more open social and cultural orientations. To a large extent, the ongoing political transition has been induced by both global and local players with vested interests in the region both as a homeland (local players) and as a strategic asset (global powers). The process of change has spawned complex tensions between the modern and the traditional; the dominating and the marginalized; and the local and the global. The implications of how to deal with 'the other' in this highly-charged political transition have been quite immense. In one way or another, the interplay of both new communications and democratic developments has served as an impetus for accelerating the emergence of a new public sphere believed to carry both formidable challenges and bright opportunities for the region's population in the 21st century.

The emerging public sphere, as a prime function of this technological and political confluence, reflects a basic human penchant for social survival (since communication is the building bloc for human communities); and hence, it is not a Western-specific concept despite its historical European inception. In its basic configuration, the public sphere revolves around the broad communication phenomenon which furnishes the adhesive social foundations for community development and sustainability. In the age of globalization, the public sphere has become an indispensable pillar of public life, a benchmark for societies' political and cultural mobility, and more importantly, a corollary component of participatory politics. This book is not intended to question the relevance of the public sphere for contemporary Arab societies, but rather to define conditions for enhancing its standing in an Arab cultural and political context. In this context, the writer argues that a solid and sustainable public sphere has to be based on a sound political conception of society and the state whereby a range of actors with varied rational understandings of reality seek to evolve consensus on how to best serve the interests of their communities. Because it is hard to conceive of the public sphere apart from a political perspective, the author puts forward the notion of 'Islamocracy' or Islamic democracy as the basic conceptual foundation for theorizing about the public sphere in the Arab World. 'Islamocracy' suggests significant compatibilities between Arab-Islamic morality and democratic structures and practices, and hence would provide a fertile ground for the sustainability and enhancement of a public sphere in 21st century Arabian societies. Islam, by default, promotes a public sphere-oriented congregational life-style whether in spiritual rituals or temporal social and political activities despite misunderstandings of its obsessive private sphere prescriptions relating to women and the family.

For many years, Jürgen Habermas' book on *The Transformation of the Public Sphere* (1989) has informed a huge number of scholarly works and public discussions across a range of social science disciplines. As much as this work has generated positive reactions from researchers with varied political, cultural and sociological orientations, it has also spawned detailed critiques and discussions of corollary political concepts like liberal democracy, civil society, public life, public opinion, cultural empowerment, and social emancipation in the 20th century and beyond. In its original form, the public sphere was conceived by Habermas to describe a critical moment in human history, marked by the emergence of a new discursive arena in 18th and 19th century bourgeoisie Europe. In that era, coffee houses, cultural societies, and political salons were at the forefront of a new wave of popular enlightenment allowing for individuals' access to political, social and philosophical debates on issues of public concern. In that context, the concept of the public sphere was used to denote opportunities for individual empowerment and emancipation as well as for community welfare. The public sphere was never meant to describe the mere existence of communication channels accessible to community members. It rather reflected a state of community power relations conducive to free, rational, and critical exchanges of information among individuals and groups with diverse interests and orientations with a vision to achieving a good level of public consensus.

In modern sociological and political writings, the public sphere is conceptualized as a central pillar of democracy and intellectual liberalism, drawing on rational engagement in unfettered public debates to evolve better visions for the development and maintenance of social order. Contemporary political writers seem often keen on tracing issues of media, politics, and public opinion to the genesis of the public sphere in the revolutionary liberal changes that had brought an end to centuries-long domination by aristocratic and ecclesiastical institutions in 16th and 17th century Europe. That era was marked by the growth of modernist thinking as evident in the rising centrality of reason and scientific empiricism, free enterprise, secularism, individualism, and popular emancipation. The institutionalization of Western liberal values of freedom and democracy, coupled with the diffusion of knowledge through emerging mass communication channels, brought about a new space in social and political life. For the first time in human history, public opinion became an instrumental factor in defining political changes in Western democracies. Individuals, more than ever before, were able to exercise tangible bearing on public life and public affairs (Garnham, 1986). They were empowered to do so by the diffusion of new media of communication and the institution of progressive social and cultural values and practices in their societies (Werbner, 1996). It is in this regard that the public sphere has been elevated to higher status in contemporary politics, viewed both as the incubator of public sentiments and concerns and the basis for decision-making.

The evolving arena of rational and critical information exchanges in contemporary times has led several scholars to conceive of the public sphere as the social space where participatory politics is bound to prosper (Benhabib, 1992). As such, the public sphere has turned not only into a significant mirror of public opinion trends, but into an indicator of how sustainable democratic practices could be. Researchers in modern political history argue that societies with limited public spheres are often steered by authoritarian orientations and their media are dominated by commercial and political interests (Lynch, 1999). Actually it was Habermas (1989) who bemoaned the deteriorating state of the public sphere in 20th century democracies as they came under increasing commercial and political influences. For Habermas, the public sphere in the West was losing its rationality and vigor as media institutions increasingly caved in to political and commercial interests. According to Habermas, freedom was losing ground as voices with legitimate concerns found themselves excluded from what seemed to be demagogic and propagandistic political and social debates, bound to generate skewed public opinion trends, and hence disastrous policies on major domestic and global issues. The most cited example in recent years has been the case of the public sphere in the United States on the eve of the Anglo-American invasion of Iraq in late March 2003. The U.S. administration's claims about Iraq's links to al-Qaida and possession of nuclear weapons of mass destruction were rarely questioned in public sphere discussions; often taken for granted as warranting the invasion and even the destruction of another country.

The fact that the notion of the public sphere originated in a specific moment of Western history clearly adds up to its ethnocentric coloration. If the concept was originally meant to describe a state of liberal democracy in modern European times, how valid is it to apply it to non-European settings? In other words, if the notion of the public sphere bears the seminal modernist features of Western enlightenment in the liberal sense of the word, how universal could it be in its relevance for non-Western cultures? Is it possible for non-Western societies to evolve their own versions of the public sphere as distinct from their European and North American counterparts? In consensus-based societies with a collective sense of community affiliation, could the notion of the public sphere generate some workable mechanisms for managing political communications in a manner conducive to social advancement on community-prescribed terms? Other than the concepts of individual empowerment and the realization of sound governance, what are the goals of the public sphere as an umbrella for public political interactions? To make the question more relevant for the theme of this book, how valid is our argument about applying the Western notion of the public sphere to contemporary Arab world settings marked by deep social, political, and cultural disorientations and consensus-based traditions? Is Arab-Islamic culture compatible with the Western notion of the public sphere or should we search for a culture-specific conceptual framework for the development of an 'Arab public sphere'? These are some of the questions this book seeks to address by noting significant harmonies between Arab-Islamic morality and public sphere imperatives. 'Islamocracy' or Islamic democracy is employed in this work to suggest not only how national or pan-Arab public spheres promote sound governance, but also how Arabs could engage with other nations in global public sphere contexts. An important point to be noted is that in a world of diminishing physical boundaries, theorizing about an Arab- public sphere is rather difficult outside the parameters of globalization.

A major question motivating the author to carry out this research project relates to the fact that while the notion of the public sphere is intrinsically Western in its historical genesis and contemporary applications, its manifestations are generally universal and human. Since communities could not survive and develop in the absence of public communications, it is impossible to speak about social and human development outside the confines of public arenas. In ancient times, tribal societies managed to develop their own public sphere systems by allocating physical spaces for regular meetings between leaders and subjects on issues of interest to their communities. When the authoritarian state began to take shape as the defining form of government, channels of communication were evolved to ensure the flow of information on issues of relevance to running citizens affairs, albeit from a domineering state perspective. As modern participatory and democratic forms of government started to evolve in the late 17th century in Europe and North America, the public sphere became more decentralized, tapping on a wide range of non-state actors to serve as 'building blocs' for democratic communities. This transformation in the human public sphere at that moment in history seemed to have inspired Habermas' commentary on the concept as the ideal mechanism for achieving maximum consensus on community issues. It should be noted here that a sphere turns truly public in Habermasean terms only if it induces rational and critical discussions in which the majority of community members could engage. An arena that fails to exhibit these features is normally billed undemocratic, authoritarian, and inhibitive, not bound by all means to lead to true governance and community welfare.

The employment of the notion of the 'Islamocracy' as a conceptual tool for understanding Arab media contribution to the development of the national and transnational public sphere raises some questions that need to be properly addressed in this work. First, the author argues that despite the legacy of misconstrued political and cultural Arab-Islamic traditions and thought systems, the Arab World heritage, with its secular and religious components, possesses moral values that, when eclectically synthesized with contemporary political practices, would allow for the institution of a viable Arab public sphere in the age of globalization. Without a coherent Arab-Islamic political perspective, it would be impossible to conceive a public sphere model that adequately responds to evolving Arab societal needs in contemporary times. Second, this book argues that Islam, as a central source of contemporary Arab morality, possesses the capacity to accommodate significant features of modern democratic practices without compromising its basic intellectual premises. 'Islamocracy' or Islamic democracy draws on the moral values of Islam as a comprehensive way of life to produce a new perspective that embraces key contemporary social and political practices. Third, throughout this book, the author intentionally steers off the concept of secularism in describing Islamic political theory simply because Islam is intrinsically about both temporal and spiritual life matters. This feature of the Islamic worldview offers scholars ample opportunities to expand the realms of Islamic political theory to embrace relevant contemporary practices. The Arabian component of 'Islamocracy' emanates from secular Arab values like solidarity, dignity, honor, and community cohesion. Islamic components, on the other hand, include *Ibadah* (worship in its broadest spiritual and temporal sense), justice, equality, freedom, responsibility, and peaceful co-existence. Arabs' contemporary associations with Western norms and practices as evident in intellectual and political traditions dating back to Napoleon's expedition to Egypt in 1798, are often seen as reflecting renewed centrist understandings of the assimilative nature of their heritage. It should be noted here that 'Islamocracy' is presented here as reflecting Arabs' keenness on preserving their moral identity as the soul that gives life to their imported Western political practices and structures.

Although this book offers significant normative prescriptions pertaining to classical visions of politics and communication in Arab-Islamic history, political and media realities in the modern and globalization eras constitute the major bulk of discussions in this work. The proposed 'Arab public sphere' perspective is inspired by normative moral considerations; yet, it lends itself very much to media and political practices in the age of globalization. In this case, what counts is not the literal translation of normative heritage into concrete practices, but the enlightened employment of the moral foundations of Arab-Islamic culture to evolve new visions for community development and sustainability in the midst of complex world transitions. As al-Jaberi (2003) notes, Islam's assimilative capacity has always been a driving force for the survival of Arab-Islamic civilization. When that feature failed to accommodate arising competing social and political choices, it was bound to run into historical impasses in different eras of Islamic history. The issue here is neither political, nor social, or economic, but intrinsically cultural, echoing stagnated initiatives on the part of religious and secular intellectual and political communities to evolve appropriate visions for the *Umma* (Community or Nation). To some extent, as noted earlier, this intellectual debate on reconciling tradition with modernity runs deep in modern Arab history as evident in the 19th and early 20th centuries' discussions of Arab *Nahda* (Renaissance) in the contexts of foreign domination of Arabian lands. The question of *Nahda,* as deriving from both tradition and modernity, has continued to define intellectual debates throughout the post-independence period, well into the current age of globalization with very minor tangible results realized.

A major portion of the emerging Arab public sphere in the early years of the 21st century lends itself to both traditional and modern political and communication practices and norms. Hence, to grasp the full dynamics, substance, and parameters of this public sphere, it is vital to survey and identify classical and modern features of communication patterns as well as cultural and political traditions in the Arab World. This historical continuity in Arab World's political and communication traditions stands out as the defining feature of the evolving public sphere of the early 21st century. In the same way, this historical continuity also provides the conceptual foundations for developing a more genuine public sphere perspective that adequately responds to both indigenous political needs and global imperatives. This book argues in fact that the emerging public sphere in the Arab World is seriously flawed primarily because it has failed to take account of and creatively apply and synthesize the rich moral values and traditions in Arab-Islamic history. Likewise, it has also failed to provide clear Arab-Islamic interpretations of contemporary media and political realities, drawing more on a sweeping transfer of Western political and media practices without proper consideration for their relevance. In this case, the public sphere has been a casualty of both fundamentalist interpretations of heritage as well as liberally-unfettered inclinations towards Western-oriented views of society and the state. Sadly enough, the development of a genuine Arab-Islamic public sphere has also been adversely affected by imperialist Western (especially American) interventionist policies either as part of the defunct Cold War politics or the current so-called global war on terror.

From a liberal Western point of view, the notion of the public sphere, as a vibrant arena of rational and critical information exchanges on issues of concern to

Arab societies, has been a rare commodity in a region long marked by authoritarian politics. Until the early 1990s, public opinion in the Arab World had been of ancillary importance in the minds of domestic and foreign policy makers as state-controlled media dominated the communications scene (Hamada, 2000). Since the inception of the Arab press in the aftermath of Napoleon's expedition to Egypt in 1798, a systematic trend of information monopoly and intellectual unilateralism has contributed to the emergence of an official-elitist public sphere that promoted state-sponsored discourse as the only viable option to be reckoned with. During Ottoman, colonial, and independence eras, Arab world media systems exhibited varied degrees of discounting public opinion as a reliable factor to be considered in public policy formulation. The main assumption in the 1960s and 1970s was that since Arab societies were engaged in nation-building as a prime post-colonial goal, issues of democratization and liberalization had to take a back-burner position on national agendas, often subordinated to the central questions of national development, Palestine liberation, pan-Arab unity, anti-imperialism struggle, national integration, socialism, and cultural revival. Guided by the Western-inspired modernization paradigm, Arab media demonstrated little propensity for creating a genuine public sphere in the absence of institutionalized participatory practices and structures. That situation reflected markedly on state-oriented media discourse as dominated by past-orientations, emotional appeals, personality cults, and dull formalities.

The 1990s were a revolutionary decade in post-modern Arab World history. The 1991 Gulf war, coupled with the end of the Cold War and the ensuing global technological revolution have sent out deep shockwaves throughout the Arab region. At the turn of the 21st century, the 9/11 terrorist attacks on the United States and the 2003 Anglo-American invasion of Iraq have brought about new shifts in Middle East political and cultural realities as the United States embarked on what was described as a 'global war on terror'. Since 9/11/2001, the U.S. strategy in the Arab World has generally followed a two-pronged track: fighting what is sweepingly perceived as 'Islamic terrorism' through numerous means, including military intervention, and promoting 'democratic reform' as a basis for prosperity and stability in the region. By mid 2007, the U.S. failure to bring about both promised democratic reforms and an end to *al-Qaida* threats, in addition to aggravated impasses in Iraq, Palestine, and Lebanon, have all deepened Arab mistrust in U.S. reformist initiatives. The democratization-based discourse advanced by the Bush administration on the eve of the Anglo-American invasion of Iraq began to lose its glamour on two grounds: first, spiraling violence in Iraqi, Palestine, and Lebanon has fostered long-held popular suspicions in the U.S. strategy in the region where people have to choose between bloodshed and 'American democracy'. Second, U.S. hostility to democratically-elected governments in Palestine, Iran, and Venezuela, in addition to sustained American support for the suppression of Islamic voices in Egypt, Jordan, Yemen, Morocco, Algeria, and Lebanon seem to have reinforced anti-

Americanism within the 'Arab street', which denotes grassroots-based public opinion (Pollock, 1992).

In the meantime, the media scene in the region was cautiously responding to surrounding political and military developments at structural and professional levels. For the first time in recent Arab history, traditional state media domination, especially in broadcasting, was challenged by the launch of private communications outlets and the realization of broader public access to information resources through satellite television and the World Wide Web. A good deal of conventional religious and political wisdom has been contested in Arab media by new enlightened indigenous voices pushing for broader political and social reforms on the basis of both secular and Islamist platforms. The introduction of the World Wide Web, new telecommunications systems, and satellite television have created more vigorous arenas for public political exchanges enabling individual citizens' exposure to information from a wider range of local and international sources. New media outlets have been viewed by Western writers as empowerment tools allowing for the exchange of information not only among elitist and official institutions, but also among members of the general public as evident in the region's fast-growing online blogs. These technological developments have been received with much fanfare by Western scholars and media observers, lauding them as 'the seeds for a new Arab public sphere'. As noted earlier, some Western writers have used the concept of 'the Arab Street', to describe the growing role of public opinion in shaping domestic and foreign policies in the region. But as political developments in the region have come to suggest, the long-preached public sphere has proven to be less attainable in the context of pervasively crude power politics as practiced by state authoritarianism, global imperialism, and religious fundamentalism. This undeclared alliance of the three orientations is bound to stifle the development of a genuine public sphere in a region that continues to grapple with serious socio-economic underdevelopment challenges.

Another central theme addressed by this book is that while the Arab region has seen significant media transformations marked by U.S.-sponsored 'democratic reforms', political and media realities on the ground do not yet warrant any development of a genuine public sphere. What is described by Western researchers as a 'public sphere' is no more than a politically-detached public arena operating in a constitutional vacuum with minimal effects on national or pan-Arab politics. Although the public sphere has traditionally contributed to sustaining liberal democracy for decades, its existence does never precede it. Because the public sphere is an aspect of participatory politics, its survival is highly contingent on setting up more egalitarian structures and instituting more symmetrical political practices. An important feature of the emerging Arab public sphere is the clear overlap of national, pan-Arab, and global public arenas. What looks like a local debate in one national Arab public sphere turns out to have both regional and global manifestations. Whether it addresses conditions in Iraq, Lebanon, or Palestine, the public sphere discourse always involves regional and global players with significant stakes in those local issues. This suggests that the Arab political and cultural discourse has to address both the regional and the global, yet on different fronts. In the age of political transparency and cultural consistency, what counts here is not the evolution of specific local or global discourse strategies, but rather the institution of sound cultural values and practices that creatively promote Arabs' intellectual engagement in the age of globalization. Because national and regional issues are turning increasingly global, a major thrust of this book is the development of what the writer describes as 'constructive engagement' of Arab media in the global discourse through the realization of a genuine public sphere that serves to achieve Arabs' aspirations for political and cultural fulfillment while enriching their contribution to universal values of peaceful coexistence. The author argues that the Arab World holds a good promise to evolve its own sustainable public sphere on the basis of its development of an indigenous political and cultural system drawing on a creative synthesis of traditional and contemporary traditions. In a globalized political and economic system, Arabs have no choice but to engage in this process. Yet, to make such engagement highly constructive, Arabs need to produce their genuine vision of communication and politics through the integration of their cherished moral traditions into contemporary political practices.

From a contemporary political perspective, the view of political and social changes in the region as converging on a Western-style model of the public sphere seem to demonstrate a sweeping obfuscation of the varied cultural, cognitive, religious, and intellectual mosaic that gives Arab societies their unique identity. Lack of recognition for cultural variations between Western and Arab world societies was bound to generate serious misconceptions about how the public sphere should be instituted in non-Western settings. Two-century long endeavors to forcibly impose external values and lifestyles on Arab and Muslim communities have often been received with deep misgivings, leading to backlash outbursts, ranging from fierce media expressions to horrendous acts of terror. The self-prescribed patriarchal nature of the Western drive to 'liberate and reform' the Arab World has always been viewed with profound cynicism across the region which strongly believes that its survival and prosperity does not hinge on relinquishing its cherished cultural heritage, but rather on synthesizing its secular and Islamic moral values into significant features of contemporary political and cultural practices. This argument actually strikes at the very question of *Nahda* (Renaissance) which has informed intellectual debates across the Arab World since the landing of French expeditionary forces on Alexandria beaches in July 1798. Two centuries later, this very historic question remains as much significant as ever before as Arab societies continue to grapple with a widening cultural divide marking their relations with the West in the 21st century. Sadly enough, the prevailing mutual mistrust on both sides of the divide seems to suggest a raging war of civilizations marked by spiraling anti-Western (especially anti-American) sentiments and violence against Western interests in the region. On the other hand, one could also see rising anti-Islamic orientations marked by a series of developments all targeting the Prophet and religion of Islam as manifested in the offensive Danish cartoons, the insulting comments made by the Pope of the Vatican, the Knight Medal conferral on Salman Rushdi by the Queen of England, and the banning of head covers for Muslim women in government workplaces and schools in France. Such attitudes have been tragically unleashed in the midst of an Anglo-American military occupation of Iraq and systematic support for aggressive Israeli policies in Palestine, thus feeding into well-entrenched anti-Western sentiments.

Although this book takes up the issue of the public sphere in the Arab World as the conceptual framework of analysis, the main focus will be on the media landscape as the backbone of the emerging public sphere in the region. This suggests that other pubic arenas like cultural centers, professional associations, religious platforms, and educational institutions will not receive the same level of attention in the analysis. The writer believes that the proliferation of new communication outlets in the region warrants an exclusive investigation of mass-mediated spaces as showcases for the emerging public sphere. In this mass-mediated arena, a range of actors in nascent Arab civil societies do contribute to initiating a more meaningful political and cultural discourse; albeit in recent years, their role seems to have receded in the face of more powerful state-controlled and commercial media orientations. Even though this work addresses media as prime institutions of the emerging 'Arab public sphere', there will be frequent references to what could be termed as the global public sphere that overlaps with national and pan-Arab media landscapes. The fact that traditional boundaries between the global and the local are being gradually eroded by transnational political and economic forces seems to warrant the investigation of how global political agendas shape local media handling of international issues and events. In fact, as noted by many scholars, the locus of control inducing media transformations (as well as political trends) in the Arab world is largely global as local arenas continue to play reactive functions (Ayish, 2003a). As the United States, with its military might and political clout continues to push for the 're-invention' of a new Arab World, whether as part of the Broader Middle East and North Africa Plan, or as part of other strategic visions, media institutions in the region would always take the brunt of coercive changes. The stakes get higher for media players as the United States seems bent on extending its domination to the evolving Arab World public sphere by forcing its agenda on mass-mediated discussions. In many instances, the U.S. government was not hesitant to show hostility towards some media institutions in the region for what was perceived as their role in promoting 'an ideology of terror and hate'. President G. W. Bush's reported threat to bomb the Qatar-based al-Jazeera Satellite Channel, revealed in

November 2005, underscores the bitter realities of how global factors bear on the Arab World media scene.

On the other hand, it might be an oversimplification to describe ongoing transformations in the Arab World public sphere as mere responses to global stimuli. Situating national transformations in external settings goes counter to the thesis of this book that only a synthesis of indigenous religious and cultural traditions with contemporary democratic practices would give rise to a sustainable public sphere in the Arab World. If it is true that Arab national politics is exogenously driven, it is primarily because political processes have reached an impasse with viable local players constantly subdued by authoritarian state machinations, religious fundamentalist tendencies, and domineering global power orientations. In the final analysis, global players could launch the process of change drawing on their own political, economic, and communication resources; but who would give such a change its concreteness and sustainability on the ground? It is the very governments, business sectors, civil society groups, and media institutions who are entrusted with redefining their own missions and goals to fit in with the new metamorphosis in global relations. Those local players, be it official figures, media practitioners, businessmen, religious scholars, political and professional leaders, or other members of the grassroots communities are the ones who will either make or break the promised public sphere. Those are the national players who are bound to generate new social choices for their societies to follow. Hence, local players are accounted for as viable partners in intellectual and political endeavors to construct a genuine Arab-Islamic public sphere drawing on both indigenous traditions and contemporary practices. From a practical point of view, the argument about domestic players as possessing the capacity to evolve their distinctive visions to stand up to external competing strategies has been untenable. It has been observed that influential local players have generally drawn on foreign policy agendas in their struggle against other competing local forces espousing more balanced synthetic schemes of governance for their communities.

The past few years seem to demonstrate that the process of establishing a new public sphere in the Arab World could never be viewed as an easily-accomplishable mission, especially when it involves players with radically-diverse cultural and political norms and values; eventually giving way to a rather coercive public arena mirroring the discourse of the 'powers that be'. This suggests that the institution of a new public sphere in the Arab World is not about business investments in new digital technologies, but more about cultural opportunities and limitations; creative compromises; visionary leaderships; and clear socio-political-horizons. In other words, though the emerging public sphere has initially gained momentum by officially-declared U.S.-driven democratic reforms and the diffusion of new communications technologies, its long-term sustainability has yet to be based on a sound convergence of key traditions and contemporary norms and visions. Its realization draws more on society's propensity to understand, extract and digest the new values of change and synthesize them into indigenous social and cultural systems without risking the loss of their originality. Sadly enough, since the early 1990s, the new public sphere in the Arab World has been evolving as a problematic phenomenon primarily because it has existed outside local democratic arrangements (which are virtually absent), markedly in response to global political and technological developments. The missing indigenous variable will always make the promised difference in either stifling or empowering the institution of a sound public sphere in the region.

It is not the mission of this book to posit global and local social choices as two mutually-exclusive cultural entities that defy intellectual and practical synthesis. Arab-Islamic civilization is rife with a wide range of unique cultural and political experiences drawing on constructive engagement with other cultures (al-Jaberi, 2003). Contemporary Arab intellectual and political communities need to sift through both their accumulated traditional heritage, on the one hand, and modern cultural, political, and philosophical traditions, on the other hand, to generate new perspectives of governance, social relations, and economic welfare. Globalization as a Western undertaking has already taken root in the contemporary Arab World, creating, to Arabs' detriment, serious threats to their cultural identity and societal fabric. An eclectic pragmatic approach to globalization based on values of co-existence rather than confrontation would ensure the development of more viable social choices for Arab societies in the 21st century and beyond (Hamada, 2004). Both Arabs and Westerners are not facing a shortage of moral values on both sides of the divide, but they are in dire need for the goodwill to integrate those values into workable visions of cultural coexistence. Arab-Islamic heritage prides itself on generating a unique universal moral system that does not simply mesh with contemporary human morality, but also contributes to its enrichment and further perfection. A subsidiary stream of Islamic *Fiqh* (Jurisprudence) called *Maqasid Shari'a* (Ends of Islamic Law) has been harnessed by contemporary Islamic thinkers to generate more constructive interpretations of Islamic teachings based on outcomes rather than on procedural formalities. As long as arising practices do not contravene the pillars of Islamic law (*Shari'a*), and as long as they contribute to community advancement, they would be instituted as integral parts of the envisioned Arab system.

Although this work addresses a wide range of questions relating to the very notion of the public sphere and its manifestations in different non-Western settings, the central theme taken up by this book relates to the extent to which an Arab concept of the public sphere, drawing on the notion of 'Islamocracy', could be evolved in the 21st century. This issue seems to take on additional significance as it directly pertains to ongoing post 9/11 debates about the relevance of Arab-Islamic political culture in the age of globalization (Hamada, 2004). In other words, the long-term value of the study lies not only in scrutinizing what is termed as an emerging Western-style Arab public sphere, but rather in reinforcing convictions in the plausibility of developing a public sphere model drawing on the eclectic synthesis of both contemporary and classical Arab-Islamic traditions and practices. This integrationist approach derives its conceptual and practical strength from the assimilative capacity of Islam, as a comprehensive way of life, to accommodate contemporary universal values that seek spiritual and temporal human advancement. In general, the thesis of this book may be broken down into the following components:

1. Since the early 1990s, the Arab World has experienced major political and technological transformations that warrant a legitimate discussion of an 'emerging public sphere.'
2. Aforementioned political and media transformations have been accompanied by a resurgence of what amounts to be a Western 'neo-Orientalist' tradition based on a sense of American-style 'democratic determinism' in an Arab World often viewed as an intellectual wasteland.
3. There is a strong historical continuity shaping Arab political and media landscape of the 1990s and beyond. To understand this historical legacy, we need to study communication patterns in classical and modern eras of Arab World history.
4. A genuine public sphere would be realized in the Arab World when indigenous and modern communication and political traditions are synthesized into a new perspective drawing on the notion of 'Islamocracy'. The proposed framework harnesses the best and the brightest of Islamic moral values to confer a unique identity on modern political institutions and practices. It draws on representative participation, written constitution, and power separation.
5. The 'Islamocratic' mass-mediated public sphere bolsters a synthetic political culture drawing on justice as a pivotal concept for community welfare. It promotes centrist orientations based on freedom, diversity, equality, accountability, respect, and co-existence.

A major argument offered in this book is that the 'Islamocratic' public sphere is an important and an indispensable arena for the re-production of 'life world' political actions on the ground. It is a social space needed by a wide range of actors affiliated with different political and cultural orientations in the community to present their views, debate rival perspectives; and justify their actions. As an imperative of national and global politics, the 'Islamocratic' public sphere is a window from which communities judge the relevance of 'life world' actions and formulate their positions on them. As much as this space is needed by political actors, it is also of paramount importance for stimulating national and global communities' inputs into political processes. In the age of globalization, it would be quite unthinkable to imagine national and international affairs being run outside public sphere boundaries. The information and communications revolution has made it incumbent on political actors in the region to seek out media outlets to present their views to a global public opinion on rational and open grounds. Likewise, such communications developments have attracted increasing interests among different actors to be part of this emerging arena that is taken as an opportunity for greater political participation, and hence, for greater impact on decision making processes pertaining to national and global affairs.

Chapter Review

The second chapter addresses the notion of the public sphere in its ideal Habermasean and realistic universal manifestations. It discusses the historical context in which the public sphere came to rise and how it has varied across different times in modern history. The chapter also notes that as a West European concept, the public sphere was traditionally associated with ethnocentric and culturally-biased conceptions of governance, society, freedom and individuals' rights to democratic participation. As noted earlier, the relevance of applying such a concept to non-Western settings has remained a rather enduring intellectual question in academic and political discussions in modern sociology, political science, literary criticism, feminist research, and media studies. If the public sphere, as opposed to the private sphere, is an imperative concept of any democratic community system possessing a certain level of public life, then we are not simply talking about the mere existence of this public space, but rather about the quality of its political discourse. Most thinkers seem to concur that the notion of the public sphere should be tied in with the ideal of realizing some sort of an egalitarian, liberal, and democratic entity that draws on rational and critical public discourses. In this sense, a public sphere that is detached from community realities is most likely to be culturally and politically deadlocked. It is this quality of public discussions that has created rather heated debates on how the public sphere needs to be investigated. This argument has been contested in particular by opponents of rational public debates, who note that rationality in modern democratic politics is often eclipsed by commercial interests who serve to obscure constituents' visions about the relevance and moral value embedded in issues addressed in public arenas (Murdock, 1992).

The theory of the public sphere has been applied in humanities and social sciences in tune with evolving ethnic, social, gender-based and cultural diversities in modern communities. Hence, one could speak of a public sphere for women, for ethnic groups, for the young, for liberals or for conservatives. In this sense, it could be possible to identify multiple sub-public spheres exhibiting significant variations within a single community. Yet, it should be noted here that faulty elements in sub- public spheres are likely to bear negatively on the overall composition and performance of the broad 'umbrella public sphere' which constitutes the total sum of sub-spheres. Sometimes, one might find a vibrant and high-quality sub-public sphere operating alongside a more restrictive sub-public sphere of some type. An example of this schizophrenic feature of the public sphere in the Arab World is the proliferation of 'ultra-liberal' entertainment television shows alongside a far more inhibitive political news environment. Policy makers in this case seem to draw short-sighted demarcations between political content as directly addressing specific political events, personalities or issues and cultural/social content as dealing with social values and norms, generally intended for entertainment. They take a more strict approach to the former simply because they believe it has a more direct damaging impact on existing political systems while the latter is perceived to be less directly related to politics. This double-faced approach to the public sphere content as marked by the understatement of entertainment effects on audiences seems to reflect a myopic view of social change as embracing independent political dynamics that could be conveniently controlled or engineered. But as recent research on social development has revealed, it is not possible to break up social and cultural values into smaller particles and control them according to our perceptions of their potential risk. We could not expect individuals to undertake liberal orientations in their social and cultural lifestyles while curbing their political rights to free speech and expression and to participatory governance. In the Arab World, this feature has never been more conspicuous than in 'reality television' as an extra-liberal ingredient of the emerging cultural public sphere (Kraidy, 2006; Lynch, 2006a). In criticizing Western promotion of the evolving Arab public sphere as a promising sign of a new democratic era, the author argues that this sphere is flawed on four grounds: it draws on exclusively Western intellectual traditions; it lends itself to global political and technological developments; it sits on alarmingly-shaky economic foundations; and it continues to be shaped by national authoritarian and global power politics.

The third chapter discusses the normative underpinnings of Arab-Islamic morality as the defining framework for political and cultural values in classical Arab history. The writer notes that historical political traditions in the Arab-Islamic heritage reflect both tribal orientations and tailored interpretations of the *Qur'an* and the *Sunna* (Prophet's traditions). Although this chapter surveys both tribal and Islamic moral values and experiences in classical Arab-Islamic history, it is only normative Islamic components that will be harnessed for the development of the concept of 'Islamocracy' as the political foundation for the public sphere. But in developing the concept of 'Islamocracy', this work focuses exclusively on the Islamic components primarily because they are elaborate enough to fit into a broad vision of communication and politics in the contemporary Arab World. Secular and Islamic premises underlying the Arab-Islamic Worldview include secular components like *Nasab* (lineage), *Sharaf* (Honor), *Abawiya* (Paternalism) and Fasaha (eloquence) and Islamic components like *Tawhid* (Monotheism), *Umma* (Community), *Adl* (Justice), *Ilm* (Knowledge), *Shura* (Consultation), *Hurriya* (Freedom), *Mas'uliya* (Responsibility) and *Musawa'a* (Equality).

Because of its complex structure, the Islamic worldview has come to define specific perspectives on politics despite the clear permeation of tribal traditions into Arabs' political experiences in classical history. In its basic configuration, the normative Islamic political theory provides that though sovereignty belongs solely to Allah, it is the *Umma* (Community) who is entrusted with devising mechanisms and practices for realizing such sovereignty. The Caliph or leader is entrusted with applying the principles of Islamic justice in the community (*Umma*) and beyond. The leader is morally accountable to Allah, but the community has the right to rectify his erroneous path through *Shura* before resorting to other means should wrong conduct persists. In a sense, the leader is accountable to the Community in carrying out his mission of safeguarding sound understanding and practice of religion, protecting subjects, and enhancing community welfare. In Islamic political theory, there is heavy emphasis on justice as the anchoring moral value for sustaining community welfare and development. It should be noted here that tribal and Islamic political and cultural underpinnings of Arab political thought and practice in classical history seemed to have generated a flawed public discourse plagued by four dichotomies: rational-intuitive, individual-conformist, transcendental-existential and egalitarian-hierarchal.

The fourth chapter traces the development of the modern Arab public sphere from the introduction of the first rudimentary newspaper during Napoleon's expedition to Egypt in 1798 to the late 1980s. It is argued here that the Arab mass-mediated public sphere in the modern period (1798-1990) evolved in two broad political contexts: direct foreign domination and Cold War politics. In both contexts, Arab media echoed nationalist ambitions for liberation and independence (first context) and nation-building and modernization (second context). In both contexts, however, media continued to serve as public arenas for debates of broader intellectual questions relating to Arab renaissance (*Nahda*) and the modernity-tradition nexus. The writer notes that the diffusion of print and broadcast media in Arab societies during Ottoman, colonial, and independence periods was instrumental for the institution of the foundations of the modern Arab political discourse. Yet, the chapter argues that since a genuine public sphere could not be induced by the mere establishment of media structures, the absence of participatory and egalitarian political and social traditions in modern Arab societies rendered the public sphere a hollow arena of public noise with little tangible effects on political realities. The chapter provides an extensive review of the post-colonial media discourse, often characterized as patriarchal, politically inhibitive, and monologist.

The fifth chapter surveys major political transformations in the Arab World since the early 1990s with a focus on what have been termed as 'U.S.-induced democratization trends'. The main thesis of this chapter is that the Arab World has been on the defensive regarding the re-structuring of its political system, always taking up a rather reactive posture to global political reforms. The writer argues that although the region has witnessed significant shifts in its political orientations, it still has to come a long way in achieving Western-style democratic reforms. It is noted here that as globally-inspired political recipes in the Arab World continue to ignore the region's indigenous cultural and political traditions, reform would remain an illusive goal to achieve. Whether carried out through the use of crude force, brutal economic sanctions, or soft educational and religious system revisions, political reform in the region has been rendered more a mirage than a reality in the absence of uniform and consistent American drives to bring about real political transformations based on justice and mutual respect. To a large extent, this murky political reality is bound to adversely affect the realization of a genuine Arab public sphere whose sustainability in the first place has to draw on a synthesis of both traditional and contemporary political systems of thought (Islamocracy) that recognize Islamic political morality while accommodating relevant aspects of modern democratic politics.

The sixth chapter investigates the development of the so-called emerging public sphere in the Arab region since the early 1990s. The writer notes that in the aftermath of the Cold War and in the midst of an unprecedented revolution in communication technologies, the Arab World found itself in the middle of a global storm marked by the 1991 Gulf War, the September 11, 2001 terrorist attacks on America, and the 2003 Anglo-American invasion of Iraq. The media and other forums of public discourse were never off-reach for the rough waves of change. Western researchers have noted an expansion in the number of media outlets made available to Arab audiences, prompting them to speak of a public sphere in the making. Satellite television and Internet-based media outlets are seen as the main pillars of the 'so-called public sphere'. These communications developments have been promoted as vanguards of a new public arena holding the promise of setting the ground for more democratic, liberal and egalitarian public discourse, commensurate with the institution of a more sound political and social order. The author describes features and components of the Arab public sphere in terms of actors, institutions, discourse quality, and potential effects. It is argued here that the widely-celebrated Arab public sphere could not be conceived outside the boundaries of political reforms in the region. The author notes that the appalling Arab public sphere in the region is most likely to remain hostage to state authoritarianism, global imperialism, and narrow-minded fundamentalism.

The seventh chapter answers the central question posed in this book: if the Arab political experience of the past 20 years, contrary to Western analyses, has failed to produce sound democratic political manifestations on the ground, then the existing media landscape could not be claimed to have produced a solid public sphere to reckon with. As noted earlier, what we are witnessing is the emergence of media institutions evolving outside the existing political and constitutional boundaries of Arab societies, though they have become integral parts of the media mix accessible to Arabs on a daily basis. In this chapter, the writer argues that flawed political arrangements in contemporary Arab societies are bound to generate a problematic public sphere. Before we could speak of an Arab public sphere, we need to ensure the development of conceptual foundations for sound political practices not dictated by global powers, but rather evolving from combined indigenous traditions and contemporary political practices. In this sense, the author proposes a broad normative political Arab-Islamic public sphere framework drawing on the concept of 'Islamocracy' as a synthesis of Islamic and contemporary values and practices. The proposed framework envisions a range of public spheres accounting for local, regional and global variations among players, political orientations, and audiences. The author elaborates four conditions for the institution and development of the proposed Arab-Islamic public sphere: it has to be indigenously-based (reflecting Arab-Islamic traditions), Islamically-inspired (emanating from broad Islamic morality), democratically-oriented (empowering community members' participation in shaping their future), and economically sustainable (drawing on transparent and solid funding). In addition, the author suggests that Arabs' constructive engagement with the global public sphere is contingent on the institution of a genuine 'Islamocratic' discourse that promotes a broad-minded universal vision; projects a well-defined Arab-Islamic identity; and draws on solid pan-Arab political and economic power.

The eighth chapter outlines prospects for the emerging public sphere developments in the Arab World in the 21st century. In this chapter, the writer notes that the concept of the public sphere should no longer be cynically viewed as a Western invention promoted to sow seeds of evil in Muslim and Arabian lands. As we get more inundated by the rough waves of Globalization, we in the Arab World seem to be running out of time in catching up with the fast-moving global bandwagon. In order to be part of that bandwagon, Arab societies need to rethink their conventional wisdom not only about politics and the state, but also about the notions of public debates, discourse construction, and community participation in public affairs. Obviously, these are key ingredients of Western civilization; yet, they are not its exclusive monopolies. The new realities of globalization dictate that we generate new creative ideas for addressing a fast-growing Arab society, trying to survive in the midst of a far diverse and more complex global community. This is not a call for casting off our cherished moral values and systems, but rather for stimulating our brains to evolve new formulas for empowering those values and systems to better address contemporary problems facing our societies in the 21st century and beyond. For over two centuries, Arab societies have been adamant in defying foreign drives to absorb them into alien cultural 'black holes', and thanks to our religious and intellectual resilience, we have managed to hold on (as was the Algerian case during French colonial rule). In the 21st century, things are different and the enemy is no longer hiding behind steel walls to take us by surprise. The enemy is already settled within us as well as among us, increasingly eroding our self-confidence to rise up again and systematically eating up our dissolve to lead a dignified and honorable life. The 'Islamocratic' public sphere as a discursive social space drawing on the institution of social justice and human freedom within a synthesized Islamic and contemporary morality through constructive engagement with 'the other' offers a gleam of hope for a way out of this debacle!

II
CONCEPTUAL FRAMEWORK

> The concept of the public sphere was developed not simply to understand empirical communication flows, but to contribute a normative political theory of democracy. In that theory, a public sphere is conceived as a space for the generation of public opinion to assure a minimum level of moral-political validity. Thus, it matters who participates and on what terms. In addition, a public sphere is supposed to be a vehicle for mobilizing public opinion as a political force. Thus, a public-sphere is supposed to correlate with a sovereign power, to which its communications are ultimately addressed. Together, these two ideas–the validity of public opinion and citizen empowerment vis-à-vis the state–are essential to the concept of the public sphere in democratic theory. Without them, the concept loses its critical force and its political point.
> (Fraser, 2005)

Since its inception in the early 1960s, the concept of the public sphere has informed research in a wide range of humanities and social science disciplines like sociology, politics, linguistics, literature, architecture, media and arts. Traditionally associated with German philosopher Jürgen Habermas (1989), the theory of the public sphere has received a wide range of praise as well as critical scrutiny from diverse political, sociological, and philosophical orientations. In its basic configuration, the concept metaphorically describes a social space bustling with rational and critical exchanges among individuals and groups seeking to reach consensus on issues central to the realization of democratic governance. In developing the concept of the public sphere, Habermas was capturing a critical moment of 17th and 18th century European enlightenment history, marked by the proliferation of public salons, clubs, cafés and newspapers. In that era, European societies were experiencing significant transitions from the private spheres of the family into the public spheres of the state as marked by more substantive inputs into discussions of public affairs. However, in his historical account of the public sphere, Habermas, as a critical Frankfurt School thinker, noted a marked decline in the quality of public discourse in the commercial mass media of the 20th century. In the era of the welfare state, Habermas observed a marked rise in the promotion of consumerist patterns and a unidirectional perpetuation of dominant political and cultural ideologies (Habermas, 1989). Such transition, according to Habermas, has turned the public sphere into an arena of political and ideological manipulation inhospitable to serious national discussions of issues impinging on community life.

In the age of globalization, the public sphere has experienced major transformations in scope, players, discourse, and form. With the gradual obliteration of political, geographical, and cultural boundaries characterizing modern national political communications, the notion of the public sphere has acquired new global and trans-national dimensions. New communications technologies, exemplified by satellite television and the World Wide Web, are allowing for global discussions of issues and problems confronting societies in the post-Cold War era. In its structural development, the public sphere has therefore turned increasingly transnational, embracing multinational players, addressing global issues; drawing on diverse channels of communication; and targeting worldwide audiences. Intellectual debates on this transition have generated interest in what have been termed as 'national or regional sub-spheres' within which more specific arenas relating to women, culture, religion, ethnicity, politics, and economic development have developed. Although the public sphere reflects peculiar historical Western political experiences pertaining to the practice of democratic politics, the writer argues that the concept needs to be reconsidered to accommodate sweeping global transformations, on the one hand, and national aspirations for cultural and political fulfillment, on the other hand. Among other things, rethinking the concept of the public sphere within non-Western settings requires a re-conceptualization of the intellectual and philosophical premises underlying classical liberal democratic politics and its relevance for non-Western cultures. But regardless of how critically addressed the public sphere is, it is indisputable that its theory continues to be influential in different disciplines, especially politics, where the quality of the public discourse has been taken as a significant barometer of the quality of political values and practices. Boyd-Barrett (1995: 231) suggests that the weight public sphere theory gives to the everyday culture of a social class and its use of the media confers on it an impressive sociological authenticity which underlines the dearth of equivalent work for other media in other historical and social contexts.

II.1. The Public Sphere: A Conceptual Definition

For many years, the public sphere has been a defining concept for a plethora of research works and discussions in politics, sociology, literature, arts, cultural studies, and communication. Kellner (1997) notes that Jürgen Habermas's classic *The Structural Transformation of the Public Sphere* has received detailed critiques and promoted extremely productive discussions of liberal democracy, civil society, public life, and social changes in the 20th century. Intrinsically engrained in continental European philosophical traditions as well as in general critical theory, the 'public sphere' metaphorically denotes some sort of a public social space posited against the 'private space'; it is the public part of life in which the individual interacts with others and with society at large in fulfillment of constitutionally-provided democratic rights. Among other things, the concept of the public sphere in Western democracies refers to the capacity of civil society members to coordinate their common affairs through a collective discourse which transcends private and narrow individual interests. Thornton (1996) remarks that Habermas developed the normative notion of the public sphere as part of social life where citizens could exchange views on matters of importance to the common good, so that public opinion can be brought to bear on political and social processes. In its basic form, the public sphere involves open discussions of all issues of public concern, whereby discursive argumentation is employed to ascertain general interests and the public good. The public sphere presupposes freedom of speech and of assembly, a free press, and the right to freely participate in political debate and decision-making. Its main function in democratic contexts is to contribute to the development of a solid public opinion to achieve maximum consensus for shaping national and foreign politics. The aforementioned references to the public sphere are nowhere clearer than in Habermas' definition of the concept as:

> 'a realm of our social life in which something approaching public opinion can be formed. Access is guaranteed to all citizens'. A portion of the public sphere comes into being in every conversation in which private individuals assemble to form a public body. They then behave neither like business or professional people transacting private affairs, nor like members of a constitutional order subject to the legal constraints of a state bureaucracy. Citizens behave as a public body when they confer in an unrestricted fashion -- that is, with the guarantee of assembly and association and the freedom to express and publish their opinions -- about matters of general interest' (Habermas 1974: 49).

In less abstract terms, the public sphere may be described as the site and subject of liberal democratic politics; hence, the study of the public sphere is the study of the history of democracy. In theory, it is posited as that space within which people rationally discuss matters of common concern about which it seems necessary to reach a consensus. Calhoun (1992) defines the public sphere as a 'contested participatory site in which actors with overlapping identities ... engage in negotiations and contestations over political and social life, the public sphere is that site of interaction in which actors routinely reach understandings about norms, identities and interests through the public exchange of discourse'. Dean (2001) notes legal distinctions between public and private spheres, where 'public' refers to the state and 'private' refers to the market and the family. Arendt (1958) offers a notion of the public sphere rooted in her understanding of the politics of ancient Greece as marked by the 'Agora' or marketplace. For her, what is important about the public sphere is that it is a space of freedom and contestation that needs to be separated from the demands of work and the necessities of bare life (Arendt, 1958).

The historical roots of the public sphere are located within ancient and modern Western political traditions. Although some scholars like Arendt (1958, 1960) ground the genesis of the public sphere in ancient Greek political debates and Roman legal provisions, the major bulk of research takes the European Renaissance as the defining historical moment for this phenomenon. As such, most writers note that the public sphere describes a critical moment of human history, drawing on how coffee houses, societies and salons in 17th and 18th century bourgeoisie Europe turned into centers of enlightened debates on public issues of the time. The bourgeois public sphere, which began appearing around 1700, according to Habermas's historical account, was to mediate between the private concerns of individuals in their familial, economic, and social life, on the one hand, and the demands and concerns of social and public life, on the other hand (Habermas, 1989). At that time, the public sphere drew on a range of information and political communication tools such as newspapers, as well as institutions of political discussion like parliaments, political clubs, literary salons, public assemblies, pubs, coffee houses, meeting halls, and other public spaces where socio-political discussions were made possible. For the first time in history, individuals and groups could play a substantive role in shaping public opinion; giving direct expression to their needs and interests while influencing political practices. The bourgeois public sphere made it possible to develop a realm of public opinion that opposed excessive state power along with the powerful interests that were coming to shape nascent bourgeois society at the time.

The historical development of a bourgeois public sphere required more than launch of public discussions; it demanded a fundamental shift in the conditions of public discourse. Habermas articulates this shift in terms of the emergence of more self-assertive individuals who had been previously confined to private spaces. This emphasis on the significance of the private nature of the individuals constituting this public arena dominates the early sections of Habermas's account, which outlines the preconditions of a bourgeois public sphere. It is here that Habermas recognizes Arendt's contributions to the conceptualization of the public sphere in her book *The Human Condition*, first published in 1958. In that remarkable study, Arendt praised the former integrity of the *Greek polis*, which was achieved through the rigorous subordination of the private world of the household, defined by its association with women and slaves (Pask, 2004). For Arendt, the loss of the demarcation between the two spheres is characteristic of the modern world, as borne out in a spectacular fashion in American politics of recent years. Habermas revises Arendt's account to produce a very different evaluation of what she terms the social, or the new public relevance of what was formerly a mere private arena (Habermas, 1970). The concept of the bourgeois public sphere is believed to give a local habitation and name to something Arendt is less concerned to specify historically, in addition to providing the bourgeois public sphere with a positive political and cultural vocation (Arendt, 1958).

In today's political discussions, the public sphere is often positioned at the heart of any re-conceptualization of democracy. Poster (1995) notes that contemporary social relations seem to be devoid of a basic level of interactive practice which, in the past, was evident in a range of loci of democratizing politics such as the Agora, the New England town hall, the village Church, the coffee house, the tavern, the public square, a convenient barn, a union hall, a park, a factory lunchroom, and even a street corner. From a philosophical perspective, the concept of the public sphere is founded on a set of norms that seem to reflect classical European visions of liberal democracy drawing on at least four distinctive features: (1) any and all individuals come together (in principle), (2) around issues of general interest, (3) without concern for social status, and (4) in order to achieve rational consensus by means of critical discussion (Calhoun, 1992; Fraser, 1993). Furthermore, conceptions of the public sphere presuppose the institution of a set of basic rights. To achieve a rational-critical debate, the public sphere needs constitutional foundations of freedom of opinion and speech, freedom of the press, and freedom of assembly and association. As Benhabib (1992) observes, to realize the transactions of the private owners of property in the sphere of civil society, individuals need equality before the law and protection of private property. From a Western liberal democratic point of view, the conditions for making a public sphere possible include a political environment providing for freedom of speech and assembly, a free press, and the right to freely participate in political debate and decision-making. Following the democratic revolutions in modern Europe and North America, Habermas (1989) suggested that the bourgeois public sphere was institutionalized in constitutional orders which guaranteed a wide range of political rights, and which established a judicial system that was to mediate between claims of various individuals or groups, or between individuals, groups, and the state.

II.2. Transitions in the Public Sphere

As much as Habermas idealizes the bourgeois public sphere of 17th and 18th century Europe, he also demonizes 20th century media as undermining the spirit of the public debates. Kellner (1997) notes that the main thrust of Habermas' work is the degeneration of an idealized bourgeois public sphere into a low-quality media landscape dominated by an expanded state and a press representing organized corporate interests. The role of media has shifted from building up a healthy public sphere based on reasoned discussions into a process of a 'refeudalization' of the public sphere marked by a structural fusion of state, commercial, and media interests (Habermas, 1989). The media turned from forces of democratic enlightenment into manipulators of public opinion, conditioning the public into the role of passive onlookers and consumers (Habermas, 1989). Elliot noted that in the 1980s technological and economic developments in Britain were promoting a 'continuation of the shift away from involving people in societies as political citizens of nation states towards involving them as consumption units in a corporate world'. This suggests that the 'fourth estate', as a guardian of the public sphere, became increasingly fused into new industries wholly oriented towards the profit-making motive underlying any other business. In Habermas's view, the media output was no longer contributing to rational discourse in the public sphere, but rather served to entertain and turn the potential participants in the public sphere into mere passive consumers (Garnham, 1986).

The transition from the liberal public sphere of European Enlightenment into 'welfare state capitalism and mass democracy', according to Habermas, is grounded in Horkheimer and Adorno's analysis of the culture industry. Both thinkers, echoing critical Frankfurt School orientations, argue that giant corporations have taken over the public sphere and transformed it from an arena of rational debate into one of manipulative consumption and passivity (Kellner, 1997). In this transformation, 'public opinion' has shifted from rational consensus-building based on well-informed debates to a manufactured opinion generated by polls, media experts, or 'spin doctors'. Rational debate has caved in to managed discussions and manipulations by the machinations of advertising and political consulting agencies. Habermas observed that 'publicity loses its critical function in favor of a staged display; even arguments are transmuted into symbols to which again one cannot respond by arguing, but only by identifying with them' (Habermas, 1989: 206). The value of this Habermasean historical account lies not in its lyrical descriptions of the formative years marking the emergence of public sphere, but in its critical bemoaning of the transition of the liberal public sphere into a mass-mediated one. Garnham (1986: 45-53) identifies tendencies towards media internationalization as a further threat to the ideal public broadcasting service model. This observation highlights the paradox that while media ownership, control and (entertainment) content become increasingly internationalized, it cannot be said that the media (yet) function to develop an international public(s) nor even a European public the way that the BBC once created a national public for the United Kingdom.

Although 20th century media transitions have done serious damage to the role and status of the public sphere in the Habermasean sense, some scholars continue to see opportunities for re-defining relations between media and democratic politics. Curran (1991) outlines ways in which traditional media could contribute to democratic functions by acting as 'an agency of representation'. He suggests a reorganization of media to allow diverse social groups to express their views, calling on the media to 'assist the realization of common objectives of society through agreement or compromise between conflicting interests'. According to Curran (1991: 103), the media should contribute to this process by facilitating democratic procedures for resolving conflict and defining collectively- agreed aims'. Other scholars see a promising role for traditional media in bringing about a genuine public sphere by living up to the ideals that conferred on the modern press its watch-dog characters and gave it the 'fourth estate' status. Some scholars like Hartley (1997) have gone far enough to boldly argue that the media of the late 20th century are the public sphere on their own right. He notes that 'television, popular newspapers, magazines and photography, the popular media of the modern world, are the public domain, the place where and the means by which the public is created and has its being'. He believes that the Habermasean notion of the public sphere is clinically dead as mass media create their own public arenas in the form of 'popular readerships', and media audiences for which they produce meaning as a replacement for the discourse communities of the Enlightenment. Kellner (1997) argues that despite the potential media role in manipulation, social control, promotion of conservative positions, and intensifying differences between 'haves' and 'have-nots', new media have produced new public spheres and spaces for information, debate, and participation that contain both the potential to invigorate democracy and to increase the dissemination of critical and progressive ideas.

The introduction of the World Wide Web has fueled further discussions on how new interactive technologies promote or inhibit the realization of a global public sphere. There is a growing body of sociological literature that is attempting to address such an issue (Ess, 2001; Poster, 1995; Schneider, 1997; Toulouse and Luke, 1997; Thornton, 1996; and Ward, 2001). But despite the fine quality of this research, the overall focus is confined to discussing the Internet as an emerging public sphere. The overriding theme is defined by debate on whether the Internet-induced public sphere can foster democratic communication and a newfound political awareness that would enhance democratic government. It has been argued that the new communications technologies, especially the Internet, with its global reach and interactive capability, carry the potential for reinstating a serious discourse among diverse players in the global arena. Habermas himself thinks that 'the phenomenon of a world public sphere' is today 'becoming politically a reality for the first time in a cosmopolitan matrix of communication (1989). Kellner (1997) argues that in the contemporary high-tech societies, there is emerging a significant expansion and redefinition of the public sphere beyond Habermas as a site of information, discussion, contestation, political struggle, and organization that includes the broadcasting media and new cyberspaces as well as the face-to-face interactions of everyday life. Rheingold (1994) observes that the Web has a democratizing potential in the way that alphabets and printing presses had', stressing the importance of active participation embedded in online communications. Castells (1997: 351), in his discussion of the supposed democratizing potential of the Internet, picks up on the term 'Athenian democracy', which the cyber-democrats sometimes use to define their vision, pointing out that this could turn out to be an unwittingly accurate description of a future. Fernback and Thompson (1995) believe that the virtual public sphere brought about by computer-mediated communication will serve a cathartic role, allowing the public to feel more politically involved.

But despite the huge euphoria associated with the introduction of the World Wide Web, some researchers argue that new media allow for public sphere venues, but not for the realization of tangible political effects. Dahlberg (2000) compared Internet practices, particularly focusing upon publicly-oriented online deliberative forums, with a model of the public sphere developed from Habermas' theory of democratic communication. In his essay on Cyber democracy, Poster (1995) contends that Habermas's idea of the public sphere is 'systematically denied' in the Internet medium. He calls for abandoning the concept of the public sphere when studying the Internet. Ward concludes that the possibility of rational discussion on the Internet is a dubious claim. This conclusion is not surprising given her assumption that 'connecting people via electronic networks and giving them information will not necessarily lead to a more democratic society any more than connecting students via computers in our classrooms necessarily leads to frank open discussion' (Ward, 2001). Katz notes that cyber-discourse also shows that 'confrontation, misinformation, and insult . . . characterize many public forums on the Internet' (Katz, 1997). Fraser (2005) argues that Internet communications would hardly be viewed as building blocs in the emerging public sphere primarily because they do not reflect institutionally-recognized players engaged in rational discussions and seeking to advance the practice of democratic politics. An interesting comment by an Arab blogger posted on an Egyptian site notes:

> I think the Internet is great, it's a great medium of communication and propagating information, but not in reform or democratization. Real freedoms and democracy are built on the ground, not in virtual spaces. That would be asking too much from the Internet (Mohamed, 2005).

II.3. Universalizing and Globalizing the Public Sphere

Garnham (1986) notes that universalism is one of the strengths of the public sphere concept. Yet, discussions of the public sphere show that the notion continues to remain hostage to its Euro-centric theoretical premises as they pertain to the ideas of democratic politics and the individual's relationship with the public arena. Although critics have raised serious questions about the relevance of the public sphere for non-Western settings where rationality seems to be a minor feature in defining public discourse and national politics, the diffusion of democratic culture in countries of the former Soviet Union and the Third World since the early 1990s seemed to have given impetus to serious investigations of the public sphere beyond Western settings. Some researchers have questioned the validity of applying public sphere theories in countries with authoritarian, centralized, and less rational modes of expression where public opinion has minor impact on national politics. In countries with state-dominated media, the concept of the public sphere seems a stranger to local political and cultural norms, and hence, has been precluded as irrelevant to scholarly investigations. But how valid is this argument about the relevance of the public sphere to less democratic social and political systems? The writer argues that traditional barriers to the development of a genuine public sphere in post-modern societies seem to be on the wane with the circumvention of state media censorship and the growing abundance in media outlets. However, the replication of this concept in non-Western settings without consideration for indigenous cultural variables is bound to produce flawed intellectual recipes for media role in national and global politics. The challenge facing researchers in the area of a global public sphere is how to evolve a universal public sphere paradigm that draws on multicultural perspectives to generate a global social space capable of accommodating public debates with diverse cultural orientations.

The problem associated with a global public sphere mostly relates to the absence of a concrete and accountable political system that is expected to be bound by public debates. If the national public sphere is situated within a well-defined political and social system drawing on clear-cut constitutional mechanisms, then how do we envision the development of sound expectations about global public sphere efficacy? McDonagh (2003) notes that the first problem one must overcome in applying the concept of the public sphere to the analysis of international political discourse is where exactly to situate the public in the global. In other words, are we talking simply about communication between states or is there room for other actors? A major issue for the characterization of the global as made up of a set of public spheres is that Habermas himself regarded constitutional democracy as something of a necessary prerequisite for an active and effective public sphere. As he puts it himself in a discussion paper on the need for a European constitution, 'democratic legitimation in complex societies derives from the interplay of institutional consultation and decision-making operations with informal, media-transmitted, opinion formation processes within a public sphere of communication' (Habermas, 1989). Lynch (1999) observes that the international public sphere serves as a location for norm formation and for deliberations over the shared interests of international communities, but in the absence of an authoritative political subsystem, the public sphere is bound to be less sustainable. Hence, without centralized political institutions to act, the creation and manipulation of a public consensus in an international public sphere seems significant. On the other hand, the absence of a central decision-making body to influence public discussions could suggest that public sphere deliberations are less weighty, since in the end every state maintains it sovereign decision-making capacity and can reject an international decision. This tension between international deliberations and formal anarchy, in which deliberations can produce only a non-binding consensus, stands at the heart of the international public sphere theory.

If the classical Habermasean public sphere was meant for societies with distinct political and cultural identities and institutions, then how could this concept be applied to a wider level of interstate-entities? As noted earlier, the proliferation of online communications has made it possible to speak of 'transnational public spheres' in the same way we speak of 'sub-public spheres' (diasporic public spheres, regional public spheres) and even of an emerging 'global public sphere'. A growing body of media research is noting the evolution of discursive arenas that overflow the bounds of both nations and states. As Fraser (2005) puts it, numerous scholars in cultural studies are ingeniously mapping the contours of such arenas and the flows of images and signs in and through them. But the conception of the public sphere in global terms seems to raise a theoretical problem as the notion was developed not simply to understand empirical communication flows, but to contribute a normative political theory of democracy. In this regard, the public sphere was viewed as a social discursive space in which rational-critical debates take place to optimize democratic practices. Public opinion is the mechanism through which public sphere's effects trickle down to political realities on the ground. As such, the public sphere is expected to empower the citizenry vis-à-vis private powers and permit it to exercise influence over the state. In this sense, the public-sphere is supposed to correlate with a sovereign power, to which its communications are ultimately addressed. As Fraser notes (2005), these two ideas – the validity of public opinion and citizen empowerment vis-à-vis the state – are essential to the concept of the public sphere in democratic theory.

The trans-nationalization of the public sphere seems also destined to stumble into a major obstacle, as public sphere theory from its inception has always been implicitly Westphalian and/or nationalist; it has always tacitly assumed a Westphalian and/or national frame' (Fraser, 2005). Critics argue, however, that the increased salience of transnational phenomena associated with 'globalization', 'post-coloniality', 'multiculturalism', etc. have made it possible – and necessary – to rethink public sphere theory in a transnational frame. These developments, Fraser argues, force us to face the hard question: is the concept of the public sphere so thoroughly national-Westphalian in its deep conceptual structure as to be unsalvageable as a critical tool for theorizing the present? Or can the concept be reconstructed within a transnational frame? In the latter case, our task would not simply be to conceptualize transnational public spheres as actually existing institutions; but would rather involve the formulation of a critical theory of the public sphere to illuminate the emancipatory possibilities of the present 'postnational constellation' (Fraser, 2005). According to Fraser, then, the public sphere theory empirically highlights historic processes, however incomplete, of the democratization of the Westphalian-national state, thus representing a contribution to Westphalian-national democratic theory. Van Dijk (1999) distinguishes three conditions of the public sphere that are likely to disappear in the new media environment of a trans-national society: 1) the alliance of the public sphere with a particular place or territory diminishes: 'Members of a particular organic community or a nation are no longer tied to a given territory to meet each other and build collectivities'; 2) the unitary character of the public sphere is transforming into an amalgam of different 'sub'-spheres as the distinction between public and private spheres is blurring; and 3) the conventional notion of a single, unified public sphere is likely to disappear in favor of a more segmented, pluralist model, something like a 'complex mosaic of differently sized overlapping and interconnected public spheres'.

II.4. Critiques

By the end of the 1980s, Habermas became cognizant of the serious flaws embedded in his concept of the public sphere as defined within Frankfurt School orientations. His latter reformulation of the concept culminated in his book *Between Facts and Norms: Contributions to a Discourse Theory of Law and Democracy* (1992). This work reflects a more optimistic turn in Habermas' writing and thought, indeed in his intellectual trajectory that could be seen as something of mirror image of that of Adorno, Horkheimer and the other Frankfurt school theorists. As a result, he turned from public discourse to the use of language to explain transitions into democratic realities in what he described as a theory of the 'communicative action' (Habermas, 1992). Habermas argues that language and communication are central features of the human 'lifeworld' that can resist the systemic imperatives of money and power which undermine communicative structures. His shift to language and communication enabled him to evolve a solid tool for social critique, and to establish critical theory on more solid foundations to overcome the impasse that he believed the Frankfurt School had become trapped in (Fraser, 1993). Habermas's argument is that language itself contains norms to criticize domination and oppression and a force that could ground and promote societal democratization. In the capacity to understand the speech of the other; to submit to the force of a better argument; and to reach consensus, Habermas argued that 'communicative action' could generate norms to criticize distortions of communication in processes of societal domination and manipulation. Cukier et al. (2004) notes that Habermas has come to give a grand name (the Ideal Speech Situation) to the operation of the public sphere as based on 'four validity claims' to comprehensibility, truth, appropriateness, and sincerity. Ideal speech is inconsistent with an intention to distort, or to use overweening power or wealth purposely to manipulate. In a latter phase of his intellectual career, Habermas experienced yet another major shift in the opposite direction – from a pessimistic view of a public sphere dominated by commercial media and professional opinion makers towards a more optimistic view where 'under certain circumstances civil society can acquire influence in the public sphere'. In this conception, Habermas has shifted the public sphere away from the notion of Bourgeois society towards a more inclusive definition – 'its institutional core comprises those non-governmental and non-economic connections and voluntary associations that anchor the communication structures of the public sphere in society component of the 'lifeworld' (Held, 1980).

As much as Habermas' *The Structural Transformation of the Public Sphere* has generated positive reactions from researchers with varied intellectual orientations, it has also spawned detailed critiques and discussions of concepts like liberal democracy, civil society, public life, and social changes in the 20th century and beyond. Critiques of this theory have centered on issues relating to its idealization of the Bourgeoisie public sphere; its exclusion of women and minority groups; its myopic view of the ample discourse opportunities generated by modern media institutions; its emphasis on rationality as the sole defining concept of public debates; and its ethnocentric conceptual nature. The major thrust of Habermas' book critiques centered on the peculiarity of the historical moment of the European Bourgeois public sphere as a case to be generalized to contemporary non-Western settings. Some researchers have argued that Habermas was over-idealizing the public sphere of 17th and 18th-century Europe as if it were reflecting some sort of perfect critical and rational processes of public discourse. By making the British 18th century history 'the model case' for the emergence of the public sphere, Habermas seemed to exempt earlier epochs and other nations from contributing to the development of modern public debates. Some researchers give strong credence for public sphere development to 18th century republicanism and to the political theory and practice of renaissance in Florence, republican Rome, and 5th century Athens (Arendt, 1958). In this regard, Fraser (1993) outlines four assumptions underlying the Habermasean public sphere that are especially suspect: 1) that it is possible for actors in the public sphere to bracket their differences in status, in other words that societal equality is not a necessary condition for free and un-coerced communication; 2) that a proliferation of multiple publics is necessarily a step away from democracy rather than towards it; 3) that discourse in the public sphere should necessarily be disinterested and that the appearance of private interests and issues is always undesirable; and 4) that a functioning democratic public sphere requires a sharp separation between civil society and the state.

Feminist researchers and activists take Habermas's public sphere to task for excluding women from public life by subordinating them to the will of a male-dominated community. As noted earlier in 17th and 18th century Europe, a major part of the criticism pertained to whether the classical public sphere model systematically excluded or subordinated women, working class subjects, and blacks from consequential contributions to the formation of public opinion. In the 1980s, Lyotard's critique was expanded by feminists like Nancy Fraser who demonstrated the gender blindness in Habermas' position (Fraser, 1990). Habermas conceded that he presented a 'stylized picture of the liberal elements of the bourgeois public sphere' (Habermas 1989: xix), and should have made it clearer that he was establishing an 'ideal type' and not a normative ideal to be resuscitated and brought back to life (Habermas 1992: 422f). In commenting on the anti-feminist biases embedded in Habermas's public sphere, Felski (1989: 167) notes that 'unlike the bourgeois public sphere, the feminist public sphere does not claim a representative universality, but rather offers a critique of cultural values from the standpoint of women as a marginalized group within society. In this sense, it constitutes a partial or counter public sphere.... Yet, insofar as it is a public sphere, its arguments are also directed outward, toward a dissemination of feminist ideas and values throughout society as a whole'. In addition, non-Europeans saw in it some ethno-centric approaches to the investigation of political and social relations, while others argued that the whole concept drew on a historical moment of European development that may not be replicated elsewhere. Furthermore, there have been several different kinds of intellectual challenges to the centrality that Habermas ascribes to rationality in democratic politics. Some researchers questioned the extent to which modern capitalist politics is shaped by rational appeals, rather than by self-interest, passion, riots, or some more obscure cultural motivations. Hence, they have noted that the critical rationality of the bourgeois part of the public sphere was mostly a normative ideal rather than a description of bourgeois practices (Lyotard, 1984).

In media studies, the public sphere has been criticized for idealizing and perhaps romanticizing what was in fact not only a very elite world, but also a male-dominated mass communication sector around the world (Boyd-Barrett, 1995: 230). In this regard, the public sphere theory has been taken to task for overlooking the history of the working class press and for being over-pessimistic in its assessment of the rise of the mass media (Curran and Seaton, 1988). The press and broadcast media clearly do still serve as a forum for discussion of issues of public interest among people who are knowledgeable, interested, and able to speak on behalf of broader social interests and whose discussions have the potential of being politically influential. Modern media, it is argued, while they no longer feed in directly to face-to-face group discussions of public affairs in the manner described by Habermas, have instead invented their own publics and public forums for discussion. The view that any broadcast programs in particular only function to 'consolidate consensus' is commonly rejected as far too simplistic. It is true that the mass media of the late 19th and 20th centuries were influenced by commercial forces of a range and magnitude not in evidence before that time. 'But the smaller media which oiled the conversations of the bourgeois coffee house public sphere were tied to the interests of a relatively privileged elite in defining what were the issues most worth talking and thinking about at that time' (Boyd-Barrett, 1995: 231).

II.5. An Arab Public Sphere in the Making?

As noted earlier, the public sphere, as an integral ingredient of democratic politics, has been a central concept in Western commentaries about the evolving Arab World media landscape in the post-modern era. Most researchers and media analysts seem to promote a Western-style version of the public sphere as the defining feature of the unfolding political and communication scene in the region. However, this conception of the public sphere as reflecting Western political orientations seems to be problematic primarily because it fails to account for indigenous Arab-Islamic norms and principles that govern political and communication practices in the region. In addition, references to emerging media developments in the Arab World as reflecting true public sphere trends are quite misleading because the basic political foundations of a genuine public sphere in the region have not come yet to materialize. Propagating an aura of realism and legitimacy around evolving media developments would not be helpful in grasping the real nature of change in the Arab World's political and media landscape. What we are witnessing is a media phenomenon that has come to evolve primarily in response to a convergence of U.S.-driven political reform initiatives and the global information and communication revolution. We have not yet seen real public spheres reflecting genuine indigenous political and media transitions in an Arab region that continues to be hostage to political uncertainty, intellectual ambivalence, and cultural stagnation.

This book seeks to define the substance and delineate the parameters of the 'Arab public sphere' from a synthesist traditional and contemporary perspective in the age of globalization. This area of research takes on critical significance not only for the investigation of political discourse in the new era, but also for the practice of politics in its classical and contemporary manifestations. As noted earlier, the development of a solid Arab-Islamic perspective of the public sphere should be given top priority in the Arab World simply because battles in a globalized world are increasingly waged more in intellectual than in military arenas, especially in the post-9/11 era. The battle for the hearts and minds of people has become the defining feature of relations between nation-states in the age of globalization. The writer argues that building an Arab public sphere is viewed as a collective effort to be exerted by all parties: religious institutions, universities, think tanks, political establishments, and media practitioners. Because a viable public spheres seems unthinkable in an authoritarian environment, an Arab-Islamic theory of politics that draws on moral traditions and contemporary political practices, referred to as 'Islamocracy' or Islamic democracy is presented here as furnishing the intellectual foundations of the proposed Arab public sphere perspective.

The emerging media scene in the Arab World has attracted a growing body of Western (especially American) research that glorifies current communications transitions as heralding the advent of a more democratic public sphere (Hudson, 2003; Anderson, 2003; Lynch 1999, 2003, 2005; Alterman, 2004; Eickelman, and Anderson, 1999, Eickelman, 2002b). Lynch (1999: 5) carried out a study on Jordan's identity in multiple public spheres, noting that tensions between *Qawmiya* (Arabism) and *Wataniya* (nationalism) in Arab political thought and practice have structured underpinnings in the public sphere. The Arab state system, he argues, possesses a public sphere that transcends state borders and which often trumps domestic public spheres. Eickelman and Anderson (1999) promote a new sense of public as emerging throughout the Muslim-majority states and Muslim communities elsewhere, shaped by increasingly open contests over the authoritative use of the symbolic language of Islam. New and increasingly accessible modes of communication have made these contests increasingly global, so that even local disputes take on transnational dimensions. These increasingly open and accessible forms of communication, according to Eickelman and Anderson (1999), play a significant role in 'fragmenting and contesting political and religious authority'. To an extent, Western writings about the emerging public sphere seem to be based on views of Western-style television talk shows with critical discussions of political and religious taboos. According to some writers, those programs are reframing local issues in terms of a wider Arab narrative, 'so that a Jordanian clampdown on press freedoms and a Syrian campaign to arrest political dissidents cohere into a single story of the absence of Arab democracy' (Lynch, 2004).

Hafez (2006) suggests that in principle, television, in the absence of effective partisan mechanisms in contemporary Arab World politics, can take over some functions of political parties. According to Hafez, 'television can integrate, aggregate, and articulate the political will of the people; it can mobilize people for non-parliamentarian political action; and while it might not be able to work out political program, it can help a society open up a dialogue on democratic reform'. Lynch (2006) observes that al-Jazeera and other Arab satellite television stations have transformed Arab politics over the last decade. Shattering state control over information and giving a platform to long-stifled voices, these new Arab media have challenged the stagnant status quo by encouraging open debate about Iraq, Palestine, Islamism, and other vital political issues. Lynch argues that these public arguments have redefined what it means to be Arab and reshaped the realm of political possibility in the Middle East. How Arab governments and the United States engage this newly confident and influential public sphere will profoundly shape the future of the Arab world, according to Lynch. Hawthorne (2004) observes that since 9/11, the question of Arab reform not only has become closely linked in the minds of Western policy makers to the fight against *al-Qaida*, but has also become a dominant theme of discussion in the region itself. On his part, Anderson (2003) notes that the emerging Arab public sphere has allowed for more media discussions of issues that pertain to politics and religion with diverse interpretations being debated for the first time.

This book discounts Western researchers' promotion of the idea of an emerging public sphere in the region as reflecting some ethnocentric visions of Western-style democratic politics and as precluding viable indigenous social alternatives. The writer agrees with the thesis presented by Zayani (2005) that Arab transnational broadcasters are helping to shape a new Arab public opinion that will support the political status quo, not undermine it, as many Western scholars believe. The author argues that the basic premises underlying Western fanfare about an Arab public sphere are flawed at least for four reasons. First, the public sphere is embedded in exclusively-Western intellectual conceptions viewing the emerging social and political arenas as incubators of genuine public opinion. In the Arab World, public opinion is normally discounted as a basis for policy making. Second, the public sphere is emerging in the region more in response to global political and technological developments than to indigenous trends. This would not allow for the integration of social or cultural variables that define Arab notions of politics and communication. Third, the evolving public sphere has shaky economic foundations that are likely to bear negatively on its sustainability as an independent arena. Most media in the region survive on state subsidies or as part of larger business corporate interests. Fourth, the emerging public sphere remains hostage to national authoritarian and global power politics as well as to fundamentalist religious orientations.

II.5.1. The Intellectual Roots of the Arab Public Sphere

Most writers on the emerging Arab public sphere describe it as an arena for unfettered, democratic, critical and rational debates of issues of interest to Arab communities around the world (Eickelman and Anderson, 1999; Anderson, 2003; Lynch, 2003; 2006a). In one way or another, the notion of the public sphere as applied to the emerging Arab communications and political scene seems more or less to echo classical Habermasean concepts of media as independent fourth-estate players in democratic societies. As a corollary concept of democratic politics, the public sphere is an intrinsically Western ideal type that has evolved in purely Western social and political contexts to serve diverse interests arising in specific moments of European history. As noted earlier, the rise of the bourgeoisie class was accompanied by the evolution of liberal social and political values that provided the driving force for public enlightenment in 17th and 18th century Europe. In a sense, the Habermasean public sphere was meant to denote those specific European participatory norms and practices drawing on scientific rationality, critical investigation, freedom of expression and entrepreneurship, and participatory democracy. It actually signified the emergence of an alternative public arena characterized by critical, rational, diverse and free exchanges of ideas to induce the formation of public opinion as the encapsulation of the best achievable consensus on pressing issues of the time. As a 'free marketplace of ideas', the classical European public sphere epitomized the liberal Western values of freedom, individualism, participation, diversity, and rationality in running public affairs.

The intellectual fanfare accompanying the diffusion of the notion of the Arab public sphere is rooted in the neo-conservative liberal ideology that takes free markets of goods, services as well as ideas as key foundations for democracy in the region. Ideologues of the New American century and the American Enterprise Institute as well as global financial institutions like the World Bank and the International Monetary Fund seem to emphasize political liberalism and free trade as the anchoring points for reform in the Arab World (Sein, 2005). Moore (1994) notes that there seemed to be no answers among policy-makers in Arab states to the question of how to resist International Monetary Fund (IMF) and World Bank prescriptions for minimum state economic management and structural-adjustment programs that insist on the waiving of subsidies. Resistance might be costly as it could place a country on the periphery of the international system; but so can conformism to IMF and World Bank prescriptions, which could bring about a permanent risk of social unrest. An implicit assumption in this orientation is that Western-style democratization has come to take on significant ideological connotations as espoused by major Western players as the sole viable socio-political choice for other nations to undertake.

The promotion of the public sphere in the Arab World on exclusively Western intellectual terms was bound to create tensions in a region with culturally-divergent orientations. In traditional Arab-Islamic societies, divisions between the state and civil society are uncommon within the broad notion of *Umma*, when the state is subsumed under community, and the temporal and the spiritual are highly intermixed. In Arab-Islamic culture, the juxtaposition of the state and non-state sectors as representing two mutually exclusive sets of interests could also be misleading when it comes to consensus-based patriarchal societies that do not always view dissent as a positive political value. In addition, the rules of debate in Arab-Islamic culture are defined by values of respect, humility, kindness, and mercy. On many occasions, the elevation of discussions into broader public scales could be frowned upon as long as problems could be resolved in a 'low-profile fashion'. In developing communities across the Arab World, public statements could degenerate into ethnic, tribal or communal strife with negative consequences for the *Umma*. In a culture that words are often taken for action, the introduction of a public sphere that thrives on sensational and excessively critical debates is potentially dangerous. On the other hand, existing intellectual divergences between Arab and Western conceptions of public debates should never lead us to discount the public sphere as incompatible with Arab-Islamic culture. On the contrary, in the age of globalization, political transparency, and participatory governance, the public sphere has become a central imperative of public life in communities around the world, including the Arab region. As societies lose their ability to shape their public spheres on their own ideological terms, they have no choice but to reconcile the values of free, rational and critical public discussions with their cultural norms to allow for balanced debates that are neither detached from traditions nor alienated from modern discourse practices. This is basically the prime thesis advanced in this book.

A key question raised in this book relates to the relevance of applying the purely Western-oriented concept of the public sphere to non-Western settings, namely the Arab World, which had experienced varied historical social and political experiences drawing on distinctive religious and secular moral values. As noted earlier, the public sphere is an imperative feature of public life, without it societies would be virtually unable to function as democratic entities. So, the writer does not contest the relevance of the concept of the public sphere per se, but the relevance of its Euro-centric intellectual percepts as based on values of 'unfettered freedom', individualism, and the state-civil society division. It is argued here that societies with limited or poor public spheres are those marked by autocratic authoritarianism, and are likely to be doomed in this age of open space communications. But given its Western intellectual foundations, the concept of the public sphere, when applied to the Arab World setting, would likely produce some sort of dialectical situations embracing dual paradoxes embedded in Western and Arab-Islamic intellectual traditions. It is noted in Chapter III that communication in Arab-Islamic traditions is viewed as a social phenomenon embracing distinctive dualities in its intellectual and epistemological theses. The ethical boundaries of communication in Arab-Islam heritage are defined by Scriptures and historical Arabian traditions that place high value in words both in spoken or written forms of communication that need to be governed by decency, respect, rationality, piety, and concern over private and public community interests. Public debates in Arab-Islamic culture are important features of historical experiences and normative traditions; yet, debate needs to be based on reasoning, adherence to Islamic beliefs, and the safeguarding of individuals' decency and reputation as well as protecting community interests on the basis of established facts rather than rumors and unverifiable statements. Once debates are unleashed on certain issues, they should demonstrate the minimum conditions for respect, rationality, responsibility, and balance.

II.5.2. The Global Genesis of the Arab Public Sphere

Like other world regions, the Middle East has been at the center of the global technological and political transformations defining the new post-Cold War World order. From a technological point of view, the introduction of new information and communications technologies has been viewed as an outstanding feature of globalization. Because technological innovations were initially introduced in Western societies, the convergence of broadcasting, telecommunications, and computer industries has been instrumental in the expansion of Western economic and cultural influence around the world. The information and communications revolution sweeping the Arab World since the early 1990s has generated a media-rich landscape with significant regional and global extensions as evident in satellite television and the World Wide Web. Among other things, this revolution has also been accompanied by a mainly U.S.-driven democratization effort mounted in the post 9/11 era as part of the global war on terror. The convergence of the information and communications revolution and political reform in the Arab World has been a major force behind the emerging public sphere. This new political and communications transformation has been taken by Western writers as a foundation for a new wave of political discourse that would facilitate Arab World's transition into a democratic phase of its contemporary development.

The defining feature of the Arab mass-mediated public sphere in the 1990s and beyond has been its reactive attitudes towards global communications trends rather than to indigenous initiatives. It is understandable that Arabs do not possess the technological know-how that would qualify them to be leaders in the global technological bandwagon. It is also understandable that Arabs, more divided than ever before, are not in a position to preach alternative political schemes for other societies because they themselves have failed to evolve their own political vision for the future. But to confer a sense of determinism on the evolution of Arab media in the age of globalization suggests an obfuscation of the intellectual and cultural dynamics of Arab societies by reducing them to mere passive recipients of external media technologies and political ideologies. In this sense, one has to distinguish between nations' desire to join bandwagons as mere passengers or as leaders with a say in defining the final destination of such a trip. A survey of the evolving Arab media scene over the past 15 years shows that Arabs were no more than bandwagon passengers sitting passively as they waited to reach a destination set for them by others. The Arab media terrain is full of modern institutions with 'flashy' digital technologies that match the best in the world; but they carry either rigid or outdated discourse, or excessively liberal content modeled on global media formats.

The reactive nature of the Arab public sphere development since the 1990s suggests its disengagement from indigenous political, social and cultural settings. The emerging public sphere as a globally-induced political space is expected to be steered by global rather than by local agendas. It is a sphere that reflects exogenous priorities rather than endogenous concerns. Because it operates in a legal and constitutional (global) vacuum, its impact is perceived to be disruptive for both state and community spheres. In the short run, state-dominated public spheres are most likely to be adversely affected by the emerging global sphere, especially on matters pertaining to day-to-day policies. In the long run, the absence of a meaningful community input into the global public sphere would adversely affect cultural spheres embracing social traditions and religious norms. On the other hand, one should not be oblivious to the fact that the rise of a 'pan-Arab' audience made possible through technological advances, as mentioned earlier, has allowed for the reintegration of diaspora Arabs into trans-Arab life and society. No longer detached from their homelands, many Arabs living in the West read Arab newspapers (in print or on the internet), watch Arab television (there are over 50 Arabic satellite channels that are available in the UK) and actively seek out Arab sites on the internet (Ermes, 2004).

II.5.3. The Economic Foundations of the Arab Public Sphere

The fact that the public sphere, in its historical development, emerged mainly in conjunction with the rise of the Bourgeoisie class in 17th and 18th century Europe carries more than a political connotation. In the outgoing feudal and Church-based system of Medieval Europe, it was impossible for the public sphere to survive in the absence of solid economic support as authoritarian controls over information flows precluded any subsidies of opposing views. But when the new class of free entrepreneurs began to establish itself as a central player to reckon with in the evolving European political arena, governments were no longer able to control the proliferation of salons, cafés and printed publications as new arenas for the discussion of political issues bearing on community life. The new Bourgeoisie class, with its ample economic resources, was willing to support the institution of channels of public debates as part of emerging democratic enlightenment. Hence, the press and other public forums were born in a private economic context to serve the mission of democratic rule. An important implication of that development was embedded in constitutional provisions relating to the press in Europe and the United States, affirming freedom of the press and its rights to be protected against government encroachments. Not only did those constitutional terms contribute to shielding the public sphere against state intrusion, but they also empowered the press to operate on a commercial basis within well-defined freedoms. In 18th and 19th century Europe, the freedom-commercialism nexus was well-maintained in Europe and the United States, even in contexts of political turbulence. But as the 20th century dawned on Europe, excessive commercial interests were apparently brought to bear on media performance. As noted by Habermas, the prime loser of this arising disequilibrium was the public sphere.

In the Arab World, as will be observed in Chapter IV, media traditionally did not develop in a context of freedom and enlightenment, but in the context of foreign domination and authoritarian statehood. In the Western media experience, freedom is the rule and restriction was the exception. In the Arab World, restriction was the rule and freedom was the exception. The major implication of this historical legacy is that Arab media could not develop work traditions of independence from a paternalistic authority. As will be noted in the modern phase (Chapter IV), Arab media grew and developed as part of state or partisan structures, serving as mouthpieces for official policies within the euphemistic 'developmental communication' paradigm. Heavy dependence on a paternalistic authority contributed to depriving media of their economic sources of survival, and consequently of their independence vis-à-vis the state. The same principle applies to other potential components of the public sphere like cultural clubs, educational institutions, and political forums. Of course, the absence of real participatory political institutions in the Arab World and the diminution of the middle class have stifled the emergence of an independent press. Sakr (2006) notes that after a decade of satellite television, the Arab broadcasting landscape was in need for major restructuring to allow for a greater degree of competition. The cliché 'Those who pay the piper decide the tune' was the best defining statement to describe media economic relations with the state in the modern era.

The question that needs to be addressed here relates to the viability of an Arab public sphere surviving on its own economic resources and shielding itself from state intrusions as the Western media situation presumably suggests. Realities on the ground show that private media in the Arab World, especially television, hardly make viable profit as they operate as part of broader corporate structures with huge financial resources to draw on. It is clear that as they operate within huge corporate structures, private media are not expected to make financial profit per se, but to diffuse a specific ideology that fits within existing mainstream cultural and political orientations (Ayish, 2003a). An important point to be raised here relates to the fact that some of those owning private media outlets are either part of state apparatus or have some vested interests in state policies. Hence, one could not speak of well-defined boundaries between private media and state-controlled media as both seem to be engaged in common pursuits and orientations in political and economic arenas. In addition, we should note the expanding role of multi-national corporations as sources of media subsidies in the Arab World. In many ways, multi-national advertisers seem keen on dealing with pan-Arab media that are more aligned with established state and global policies. In light of these limitations, the Arab public sphere is defined by state and globally-oriented actors; hence, its ability to sustain its independence by drawing on self-generated economic revenue seems limited.

II.5.4. The Authoritarian Nature of the Arab Public Sphere

Despite the diverse political transformations witnessed by the Arab World since the early 1990s mainly in response to U.S.-induced reform pressures, the Arab authoritarian state continues to be the dominant player in national and to some extent regional politics. Nawar (2003) noted that the Arab state has been converted into a 'Black Hole', devouring all forms of opposition either through coercive accommodation or voluntary domestication. More than ever before, the state security apparatuses have been brought to bear on top decision-making positions, especially with the heightened U.S.-waged global war on terror. As will be noted in Chapter IV, the historical perpetuation of authoritarian practices in Arab countries has seriously militated against the institution of civil liberties and the initiation of more pluralistic visions of the social order. Even when parliamentary bodies were established through free public elections, the state always found ways to promote its policies and programs through subtle 'stick and carrot' systems that rendered national representative assemblies of minimal values. Under special emergency laws, the state has been able to stifle genuine political diversity and to pre-empt the emergence of more viable social options in society. The prime casualty of these authoritarian trends is civil society which has been turned into formalistic structures with minimal input into policy making. Political commentators blame successive U.S. administrations for condoning and even encouraging authoritarian state practices, especially when it comes to repressing opposition voices labeled as 'Islamist'. Such tendencies, from the United States perspective, perfectly fall within its global anti-terror drive and need not be contested.

The institution of a genuine Arab public sphere is bound to be hampered by an increasingly more powerful state authoritarianism that derives its survival from a strong security machine as well as from Western support. Western writers about the emerging media scene note that Arab governments continue to bloc real reforms in the communications sectors in areas relating to freedom of expression, human rights, fair trials, and personal safety. Many of them heap blame on Arab governments for failing to carry out American-style political reforms to allow for a more diverse and liberal media environment. Governments, on their part, continue to have a final say on licensing new media outlets, introducing constitutional amendments conducive to media freedom, providing protection to journalists, and enabling their citizen's free access to information sources within their borders. Zaine (1992: 516) notes that authoritarian government control has been reflected on the media scene by the application of censorship. To a large extent, media laws in the Arab world seem not only to favor government interpretations of national interests, but are also vulnerable to frequent government revisions. For example, the 1993 Jordanian press law was hailed as a liberal attempt to institutionalize a greater margin of freedom; yet its May 1997 amendment requiring the press to maintain a minimum $450,000 capital led to the closure of ten weekly publications and to widespread protests from the journalistic community. The early 2007 revision of the Jordan Press Law providing for tougher penalties on convicted journalists and for the inclusion of online communications under its jurisdiction has also generated further discontent. As the editor of a Jordanian daily newspaper notes, the press in the country's democratic phase continues to be hindered by legal restrictions and lack of structural changes in ownership patterns (Hourani et al., 1998). To some extent, government monopoly of public media has been brought to bear on the practice of democratic politics as evident in the cases of Egypt and Algeria.

Since the dawn of the 21st century, the media milieu in the Arab World continues to be stifled by heavy-handed state controls despite some minor advancement. All Arab constitutions embody explicit references to freedom of the press and of speech; yet, the way legal provisions are interpreted seem to suggest skewed visions of the practice of freedom. Although the subject of press freedom in the region has been an occasional topic of debate in political and media circles at national and global levels, the author will refer her to two reports published by two think tanks, one local and the other international to describe the aggravated nature of the problem. The (2006) study published by the Amman Center for Human Rights Studies relied on direct monitoring of violations of press freedom in the Arab countries in 2006 through the accurate survey of online document on press freedom, such as the 'Arab organization for the Freedom of the Press', 'Reporters without Borders', and the 'International Committee for the Freedom of the Press' websites. Killings of journalists and media workers reached its peak in 2006 with Iraq topping the list (88.57%), followed by Somalia (5.71%). Kidnapping of journalists was noted in Iraq (50%) and Palestine (25%) while the highest rates of assaults on media workers reached (13.98%) in both Iraq and Yemen. Arbitrary arrests of media workers were noted in Yemen (17.59%), Algeria (12.04%), and Iraq (10.19%). Trial of media workers was also reported in Algeria (50.68%), Egypt (13.51%), and Yemen (8.78%). Closure of newspapers was noted in Iraq (38.46%), Yemen (30.78%), and Algeria and Egypt each (7.69%). The other document is published by the International Research and Exchange Board (IREX) (2005) and provides details about the Middle East and North Africa Media Sustainability Index. Index components include freedom of speech, journalistic professionalism, and plurality of news sources, business management, and supporting institutions. The average scoring for all index objectives in the Arab countries ranged from 0.31 for Libya to 1.08 for Syria, to 1.27 for Yemen to 1.87 for the UAE, to 1.88 for Egypt to 2.16 for Jordan and Lebanon each to 2.48 for Qatar. Those scoring below 1.0 were virtually unsustainable while those above 2.0 and below 3.0 were classified as enjoying near sustainability.

II.6. Proposed Framework

Because alternative media initiatives would be based on new political visions of governance, they are most likely to face outstanding threats from at least three sources: the West, namely the United States, because experience over the past few decades has shown that strategic security and political considerations always take precedence over real democratic reform concerns; the authoritarian state, because new visions of participatory governance undermine the legitimacy of its long media control traditions; and Islamic militant groups, because the amalgamation of traditional and contemporary communication norms and practices is wholly discounted within fundamentalist interpretations of the Scriptures. Because authoritarian practices continue to mark Arab political life, and while Western-inspired formulas are offered as the sole panaceas for our communication woes, the current fanfare about an Arab public sphere in the making does not seem to lend itself to reality, at least in the short run.

Islamocracy	
Islamic Morality: *Ibadah*, Justice, Equality, Freedom, Responsibility, Honesty, Peaceful Co-Existence	**Democratic Procedures and Structures** Written Constitution, Representative Bodies, Power Separation
Islamocratic Public Sphere	
Diversity, Freedom, Accountability, Decency, Equality, Respect, Centrism, Identity	

Grounded in Islamic Morality
Reflecting Indigenous Community Concerns
Drawing on Sustainable Economic Resources
Framed by Democratic Practices
Goal
To Sustain Islamocratic System

II.7. Summary & Conclusions

Although the concept of the public sphere has spawned a wide range of critical analyses across a wide range of disciplines, it has been widely viewed as one of the most useful conceptual tools for understanding how public discourse bears on contemporary political and social life. As a corollary concept of democratic politics, the public sphere has been taken as one significant barometer of how politically and culturally vigorous a society is. In the age of globalization, the public sphere has taken on further significance as it turned more transnationalized with manifestations in different non-Western communities. From the original Habermasean concept of 18th and 19th century Bourgeois Europe's public salons and coffee houses, the public sphere has seen dramatic transitions in its substance and parameters, serving as an indispensable arena of communicative actions that shape and get shaped by political realities on the ground. These transitions have presented scholars and media commentators with new intellectual challenges pertaining to the relevance of this intrinsically-Western concept for societies outside the boundaries of Western political and cultural traditions. It has been noted that the public sphere has increasingly become an indispensable ingredient of contemporary politics without which the survival of any community seems unthinkable.

On the other hand, the writer argues that while recognizing the centrality of the public sphere for contemporary national and trans-national politics, one needs to re-think the concept when applied to non-Western settings like the Arab World. It has been noted that while Western intellectual traditions in the age of globalization shown optimism over an emerging Arab public sphere, the writer argues that the new public arena is seriously flawed for four reasons. First, it is inspired by Western intellectual traditions about liberal democracy while obfuscating the indigenous cultural and political heritage that has defined Arab communities' life for centuries. Second, the emerging public sphere draws more on global technological and political developments than on indigenous transformations. Third, the economic viability of the new public sphere is still murky as media institutions continue to get their sustainability from state subsidies or unpredictable finances. Fourth, despite the fanfare about real democratization in the Arab World, the emerging public sphere remains grounded in state authoritarianism. The prime theme of this book is that a genuine Arab public sphere holds a good promise for Arab World politics in the long run; however, it needs to be grounded in both indigenous traditions and contemporary political practices to secure its survival. The author suggests 'Islamocracy' or Islamic democracy as a defining political concept for the development of a genuine Arab public sphere that draws on cherished moral Arab-Islamic values and contemporary political traditions. The writer reiterates that we are never in short of intellectual schemes for media development, but rather of good intentions to empower communications to play their roles as tools of intercultural understanding and political democratization.

III
NORMATIVE ARAB-ISLAMIC TRADITIONS

> *Ye are all guardians; and ye will be asked about your subjects: the Imam is the guardian of the subjects; and a woman is guardian to her husband's house and children; and a servant is a shepherd to his master's property. Ye are all guardians; and ye will be asked about your subjects.*
> *(Prophet Muhammad)*

Long before the emergence of Islam in the mid 7th century, Arabs had inhabited areas extending from Yemen in the south to Mesopotamia in the north, living in rival tribal communities affiliated with two imperial powers: The Persians to the east and the Romans to the west (Hitti, 1963). The Arabian Peninsula in particular had known the growth of scattered tribal settlements in Mecca and Medina where local people made a living from trading with neighboring non-Arab communities; raising cattle; doing primitive agriculture; and carrying out custodianship of the Mecca sacred sites. With the rise of Islam as a comprehensive way of life, the face of Arabian communities was changing from local tribalism to universal statehood as Arabs expanded their territorial gains to include new lands in Africa and Asia. By all standards, Islam was considered a revolution in human history, encompassing both a spiritual religion and a material way of life, based on the ideology of *Tawhid* (monotheism) and the servitude of man to Allah *(Ibadah)*. Arabian tribes were moved from rival groups engaged in frequent infighting to an *Umma* (Community or Nation) bonded by 'brotherly' rather than blood relations. It was noted by many historians that the power of Islam to assimilate other non-Arabian social and cultural traditions was instrumental for Arabs' survival and development in different lands.

According to Muslim beliefs, Islam, as a universal and comprehensive way of life, preaches high moral values like justice, mercy, freedom, cohesion, and equality. Among other things, it also embeds a specific theory of governance to lead the *Umma* into further welfare and prosperity in tune with the Divine Scheme of *Ibadah* (Worship of Allah in its spiritual and temporal forms: *Ibadat & Mu'amalat*). A normative classical Islamic political theory, based on the *Qur'an* and *Sunna*, draws on the concept of *Khilafa* (Caliphate) with the Caliph serving as Allah's vice-regent on earth, who is entrusted with establishing *Adl* (Justice), *Ihsan* (Kindness), community cohesion, and good doing[1]. *Shura* (Consultation) has been defined as community input into the political process in the Islamic state on matters not specifically addressed by the *Qur'an* and *Sunna* (Prophet's traditions). *Shura* is viewed as the essence of the Islamic political system and its expanded interpretations have spawned a wide range of modern perspectives relating to modern perceptions of democracy in the Muslim World.

In this book, the notion of *Shura* is taken as an explicit reference to community participation in running its own affairs and to more restrained authoritarian tendencies. From a normative perspective, *Shura* also carries significant connota-

---

[1] Qur'an (16:90).

tions for the proposed Arab-Islamic public sphere theory. In certain ways, the parameters of the Arab-Islamic public sphere are defined by some researchers on the basis of both Scriptures and historical experiences. However, because political traditions in Arab-Islamic history (except for the era of the Prophet and the Rightly-Guided Caliphs (632-661 AD) did not yield a single concrete experience to reckon with, this chapter focuses more on identifying normative principles of governance as evident in the *Qur'an* and the *Sunna*, on the one hand, and Arabian tribal traditions, on the other hand. This chapter also seeks to shed light on classical historical and normative Arab-Islamic perspectives of politics and communication in order to understand contemporary public sphere realities in the region. The author argues that while there is no single Islamic theory of politics and communication in Arab-Islamic history, normative and historical evidence is rife with a range of moral values that could be integrated into a contemporary perspective of the public sphere with a broader theory of democratic politics referred to here as 'Islamocracy'. Available evidence shows that intellectual and practical political and communication experiences in the modern Arab World derive their sustainability from a strong historical continuity. The writer believes that an understanding of the normative and experiential foundations of politics and communication in classical Arab-Islamic history extending from 650-1798 would be significant for grasping the basic features of Arab public sphere realities in the 21st century.

III.1. Historical Arab-Islamic Political Experiences

Classical Islamic affirmation of the theory of politics is evident in several works by Arab and Muslim authors who described political structures in their times; promoted certain political orientations; or prescribed specific normative political perspectives. Some of these works include '*Imamhood and Politics*' by Ibn Qutaiba, '*Royal Decrees*' by al-Mawardi (d. 448H, 1058 C.E), and by Abi Yaala al-Firaa, '*Shari'a Politics in Reform of Ruler and Ruled*' by Ibn Qiam al-Jaouzia, '*The Enlightenment of Kings*' by al-Tartouchi, '*The Refined Gold in Kings' Advising*' by Abu Hamid al-Ghazali, '*The Honourable in Royal Literature*' by Ibn Taqtaqi, and '*The Finest Practices in Royal Customs*' by Ibn al-Azraq. Ibn Rushd's rational approach to political philosophy won him widespread acclaim while Ibn Khaldun's *Muqaddima* (Introduction) represented the first systematic interpretive study of the rise and fall of political systems in human civilizations. Al-Jaberi (2004) notes that Ibn Rushd's description of politics in the Arab-Islamic world as a combination of 'virtue, dignity, freedom and domination', while Ibn Khaldoun describes it as based on *Shari'a* laws, ethical rules, natural laws of association, and tribal power'. As much as those writings on Islamic political traditions were marked by intellectual abundance, they also embraced diverse schools of thought, perspectives, and interpretations. Religious and philosophical variations among Arab-Muslim scholars regarding the nature and function of the political system reveal a deeply-engrained diversity in political analyses and commentaries. From infallible *'Imamhoods'* to 'powerful leaderships' to 'chosen caliphs', political theories in Islam have spawned notable debates in classical times that have continued into the contemporary phases of Arab history (al-Khayyat, 2004).

Classical Arab-Islamic political traditions draw on diverse historical tribal experiences as well as on normative principles embodied in the *Qur'an* and the *Sunna*. Some writers argue that except for that of *Khulafa Rashidin* (Rightly-Guided Caliphs (632-661 AD), political experiences in classical Arab-Islamic history were heavily imbued with tribal colorations on matters of leadership choice and succession, community role, and political structures and mechanisms (Mady, 2004). Ghazali (2004) notes that the institution of hereditary Caliphate in Islamic history 'was a mistake for which Muslims paid a heavy price'. He believed that the tribal spirit among Arabs was behind this downfall, in the past and the present, calling on Arabs to respect Islam rather than manipulate its teachings to fit their traditions. The significance of political practices instituted by Arab-Muslims in different historical periods later derives from their uses as models or normative frameworks for political theorization. This historical continuity seems to inform significant ingredients of contemporary Arab political practices in the 21st century as debate on political reform in the Arab World continues to generate wide-ranging views of how Islam could respond to contemporary political challenges facing the *Umma*.

This section surveys basic features of the classical Arab-Islamic political experiences as conceived by diverse schools of thought. The writer argues here that variation in Muslims' conceptions of *Khalifa* (Caliph or Imam) appointment; defining his qualities and mandate; and elaborating a role for the community in public affairs has generated debates among political historians with diverse ideological orientations. Some intellectual traditions have explicitly embraced issues like the subject of the Caliphate, the choice of a ruler, and the inherent debates and differences associated with political practices on the ground. Debbagh (2004) notes that political theory in Islam has received varied conceptions in mainstream *Sunni* and *Shi'a* Islamic traditions. In mainstream *Sunni* traditions, this theory is based on the fact that the Prophet did not name a Caliph to succeed him, leaving this to the discretion of the *Umma*. The *Khalifa* (Caliph) is the ruler entrusted with enforcing Islamic *Shari'a* and guarding religion; and he could not carry out such a mission unless he enjoys real full powers. Debbagh identifies three theories of appointing political leaders in *Sunni* traditions: Theory of *Ahl al-Hal wal-Aqd* (those empowered to take decisions, including the decision to appoint a leader); theory of *Wilayat al-Ahd* (legacy of outgoing *Khalifa* pertaining to succession and inheritance); and theory of *Ghalaba* (Overpowerment and usurpation). While the first theory confers full legitimacy on the *Umma* (as represented by *Ahl al-Hal Wal-Aqd*) to appoint leaders, the two other theories grounded legitimacy in tribal or crude power politics. *Shi'a* sect followers, on the other hand, believe that the Prophet derived his legitimacy from Allah who chose him and gave him the mandate to be His Messenger on earth. According to *Shi'a* beliefs, the Prophet named 12 *Imams* to serve as guardians of Islam as both an *Aqida* (ideology) and *Shari'a* (Law).

The historical political experience in Islamic traditions has been a subject of investigation by scores of contemporary Arab and foreign scholars. The problem with such works is that they sought to apply modern criteria to classical Islamic political practices applied 14 centuries ago. Ibrahim (2004) identified what he described as the 'despotic elements' of contemporary Arab politics as rooted in historical experiences of government. He noted that while philosophy in ancient Greek communities promoted public discourse about politics and democracy, it was poetry that defined the discursive public arenas in Arab history. He identifies unity of leadership and community as central features of political theory in Islam, which implies that a tyrant, yet powerful Caliph capable of applying justice in the community and safeguarding its religion, would make an ideal leader. Within this context, obedience to the ruler was promoted as a noble compulsory social and political value in the *Umma's* struggle to ensure its survival and safeguard its religion on earth. Ibrahim's claim that rulers were not accountable to the community, and therefore developed the propensity to be despots lacked specific historical support as it was based on general observations or selective evidence. Some writers take evidence of compulsory community obedience to the Caliph from scattered anecdotes that promoted despotism as the basis for the classical Arab-Islamic political experience. For some contemporary political thinkers, the absence of clear-cut consensus regarding the appointment of the Caliph and the definition of his mandate as well as the role of the community in the Islamic political system was bound to produce despotic political traditions (al-Wali, 2006; Abd al-Rahman, 2006; Khlify, 2004).

Critical writings about classical Islamic political practices have also taken concrete Arab-Islamic political experiences (From the *Umayyads* onward) to task for perpetuating tribal political traditions with respect to the Caliph and the community (Ghazali, 2004). However, the fact that Islamism and tribalism carry consensus-based orientations should in no way connote a uniformly submissive political heritage for the Arab World throughout history. Historical evidence shows that the application of Islamic and tribal political theory was neither smooth nor consensual. On many occasions, political differences arising from divergent interpretations of Scriptures or from tribal alliances gave rise to diverse communal tensions that culminated in major bloodsheds. The conflict between Ali and Muawiya was the first major confrontation in Islamic history over the political legitimacy of the *Wali al-Amr* (Ruler). Though some historians attributed that conflict to divergent interpretations of the Prophet's political legacy, others grounded it in competing tribal political ambitions (*Bani Hashim* versus *Bani Umayya*) (Abd al-Rahman, 2006). In her study of Islamic political systems of thought during the first six centuries of Islam (the 17th to the 13th centuries AD), Crone notes that the pre-eminence of the Prophet and the four-Caliph thesis created a consensus among the community of believers, the *Umma*. Further dissent came along with the first civil war, *fitna* between Ali and Moawiya. By transforming the Caliphate now acquired by force into a quasi-hereditary monarchy, the *Umayyads* voluntarily set themselves apart from the early Caliphs. When the 'Abbasids came to power after a bloody revolution in 750, they were among the last Caliphs to claim legitimate descent from *Quraysh*, the most powerful tribe in Mecca to whom the Prophet belonged.

The problem of basing analyses on individual Arab-Islamic historical political experiences does not derive from their fluidity, but from the limited public debates they had generated in different phases of Arab-Islamic history. Apart from the aforementioned works dealing with political practices and norms, political discussions were shrouded in limited philosophical and communal spheres. Greek-inspired Islamic philosophy was bound to clash with sophist schools of thought as well as with orthodox interpretations of Islam. That conflict gave rise to divergent perspectives regarding the centrality of *Aql* (reason) and *Naql* (revelation) in shaping the Islamic worldview (al-Jaberi, 1982). While religious scholars with conservative orientations like al-Ghazali concluded that reason is too limited to comprehend the true nature of the Universe and the Creator, rational philosophers like Averos (Ibn Rushd) promoted greater trust in human reasoning. The *Mutazellites* were a splinter group which rationalized religious views, while *Ashaarites* brought Islamic thinking to a more orthodox track. On the other hand, mainstream Islamic thought also came to be based on a new branch of jurisprudence called '*Maqasid al-Shari'a*' (Ends of Islamic Law) which seeks to deduce the intended goals and ends behind Islamic laws in their temporal (*Mu'amalat*) manifestations. Although the prime areas of *Shari'a* ends started with preserving five things: religion, self, offspring, reason, and wealth, latter scholars restructured them to accommodate more priorities arising in different Islamic phases of development. In addition, the rise of *Shi'a* as a new religious and political orientation in 8th century Islamic history had a significant bearing on key premises and practices regarding political theory in Islam. Most recently, *Shi'asm* has given rise to a new Islamic political theory called *velayat-e faqih*, or 'rule by jurisprudence' (Westerners call it 'Islamic Republicanism') viewed perhaps as the most important Islamic innovation of the 20th century (Crone, 2004).

III.2. The Arab-Islamic Symbiosis

An enduring question marking public debates in Arab-Islamic history pertains to the embryonic relationship between Arabs and Islam. Duri (2005) noted that Islam and Arabism 'were closely linked at first, but subsequently followed separate courses'. Arabs' interaction with new foreign civilizations in Asia, Africa and Europe provided new perspectives into public discussions, especially in areas of philosophy, literature and pure arts. Arab Caliphs in the *Umayyad* and *Abbasid* periods patronized literary and intellectual works by poets, men of letters, scientists, and religious scholars. Proponents of pan-Arabism, in response to the emergence of Islamic fundamentalism, continue to assert the complementarity, if not the synonymy, of Islam and Arabism. For example, Duri (2005) has concluded that 'Islam unified Arabs and provided them with a message, an ideological framework, and a state'. He also noted that 'the Islamic movement came about as Arab in its environment and leadership', and that Arabs in the formative era of Islam had 'a strong sense of their unity and distinctiveness, for the state was Arab, the language was Arabic, and Arabs were the carriers of the message of Islam'. In different phases of Arab-Islamic history, political traditions came to take on significant tribal colorations as manifested in patriarchal family-based hereditary schemes. This feature was central in numerous writings that invoked secular-tribal variables assumed to have shaped Arab-Islamic political traditions. Barakat (1992) notes that tribalism continues to undermine the unity of *Umma* in both its Islamic and secular nationalist manifestations. As Lebanese scholar Muhammed Mahdi Shamsuddin pointed out, Islam has 'attempted to destroy tribal solidarity by diverse means in order to establish a community based on unity of belief' (Shamsuddin, 2000). The triumph of Islam in unifying conflicting tribes into an *Umma* of believers does not mean that it has managed to completely flush out tribalism as tribes themselves managed to use Islam in diverse ways. Tribal structures and relations continued to mark Arab communities throughout history. The following section reviews basic Arabian tribal moral values believed to have permeated the Arab-Islamic political experience.

III.2.1. Lineage (*Nasab*)

Although Islam endeavored to combat *Asabiya* (tribal solidarity) as a social and political deficiency in the *Umma* by fostering *Ukhuwa* (brotherhood), this pre-Islamic feature of social life seemed to have persisted into the Islamic phase of Arabs' history. Blood relationships based on male-line kinship furnished the adhesive element in internal tribal organization in Arab society. Abu Lughd (1990: 94) notes that while scholars see lineage or segmentation as a description of the socio-political organization of tribal groups, others see it as an ideology through which the social system is maintained. As a criterion for individual social standing and tribal affiliation, genealogy was an important theme of poetic jousting in Arab history. Jarir (d. 729), a well-famed Arab poet during the Umayyad period (661-750) vilified the descent of his rival poet, al-Farazdaq (d. 732) by saying:

> Turn down your eyes (because) you are from Numayr
> You have attained the status of neither Ka'b nor Kelab
> (Both Ka'b and Kelab were two large Arabian tribes)

Al-Farazdaq's response to Jarir was:

> And those who challenge Tamim shall know
> Those fated to sink when the surge rolls on
> (Tamim was also a large tribe)

Quraish was the largest tribe in Mecca and two of its tributary clans were *Bani Hashim* from whom the Prophet descended and *Bani Umayya* to whom Caliph Muawiya belonged. While *Bani Umayya* rose to prominence in the Islamic era of Arab history after they had established the *Umayyad* Caliphate in Damascus (661-750), *Bani Hashim* were associated with the establishment of the rival *Abbasid* Caliphate in Baghdad (750-1258). The dynastic pattern as based on hereditary blood relations continued to mark the Arab World's socio-political landscape for centuries to come. The *Fatimites*, descending from Fatima, daughter of the Prophet established a state in Egypt, while the Ottomans dominated the whole Arab world as part of the Turkish Empire for over five centuries. In the contemporary Arab World, lineage-based social relations continue to shape contemporary social structures. Barakat (1985) points out that the family is the nucleus of social organization and the center of economic activities in ancient and modern Arab society. For Barakat, the family serves as an intermediary between the individual, society, and the institutions through which individuals inherit socio-cultural and political allegiance (1985: 171). A major implication of a lineage-based society has been the rise in individual vis-à-vis collective orientations in Arab communities throughout history. The availability of a horse or camel in the desert made an Arab independent; he could disappear at any time; and he could even join another tribe (Patai, 1969). On the other hand, although pre-Islamic Arabs derived their status on the basis of individual values (lineage), they seemed to have found a good deal of solace in tribal rather than institutional or national affiliations. *Asabiya*, or tribal solidarity, was the mechanism through which a person expressed his individualism in the context of the collective tribal ethos. This spirit of *asabiya* is best expressed in the Arabic proverbs: 'blood is thicker than water' and 'I and my brother against my cousin; I and my cousin against the stranger (or against the world)'. Reflecting a 'magnified individualism' of the tribe, *asabiya* connoted independence, self-sufficiency, and dignity. Ibn Khaldoun (2002), in his *Muqaddima*, provided detailed elaborations on the notion of *Asabiya* as a major seed of state disintegration.

III.2.2. Honor (*Sharaf*)

In pre-Islamic Arab communities, the cult of honor, more than the cult of gods, was the real religion, the real social bond (Rodinson, 1981: 165). The concept of honor originally derived from a person's lineage, implied courage, the capacity and the will to defend the independence of the group, and the chastity and freedom of its women and dependents. It is also a derivative of the broad concept of dignity (*karama*), a highly charged emotional frame through which the individual determines the worthiness of his/her life. A special code of honor is applied to women and is termed *ird*. It emphasizes women's adherence to a strict code of conduct and dress. Violation of this code would call for revenge by death penalty to cleanse shame (*arr*). In recognizing the importance of safeguarding *ird*, a woman is referred to in secular Arab traditions as *hurma*, a concept that connotes a person who enjoys a respectable status that should not be desecrated. To avoid incurring *arr*, pre-Islamic Arabs had developed the inhumane habit of burying newly-born females alive (*wa'd*). Islam prohibited this obnoxious practice. For Arabs, the maintenance of honor as an important component of dignity deserves the sacrifice of one's life. This in fact is one of the key concepts inherited in Islam. The Prophet was quoted as saying that a Muslim getting killed in defense of his *Ird* is considered a martyr. While honor is conducive to recognition by others, shame leads to disrespect if not avenged. The famous Arab poet al-Mutanabbi (915-965) emphasized this in one of his verses:

> High honor is not safe from injury
> Until blood is spelt over its flanks

III.2.3. Paternalism (*Abawiya*)

Paternalism is the interference of a state or an individual with another person, against their will, and justified by a claim that the person interfered with will be better off or protected from harm (Arenson, 1989). This feature was characteristic of the Arab patriarchal social systems at micro and macro levels (Sharabi, 1988, Barakat, 1985; and Patai, 1971). Sharabi notes that patriarchy is a term that essentially defines a special kind of sociopolitical structures, with a specific value system, and forms of discourse and practices, based on a distinctive mode of economic organization (1988: 15). In Islamic political theory, the Caliph is also *Wali al-Amr*, a person in charge of subjects or *Raiya* as noted in the Prophet's statement: '*All of you are shepards (Roa'a) in charge of your subjects. Man is in charge of his household and so is a woman...*' In a sense, this feature seems to reflect some enduring hierarchical structures in family and state relations whereby authority is centered on an individual, usually a male, with exceptional traits who serves as an exclusive source of inspiration for the family and the community at large. This patriarchal feature was occasionally abused throughout Arab-Islamic history as it came to connote absolute empowerment of individuals in running family and community affairs.

In the Arabs' pre-Islamic era of inter-clan rivalry and conflict, paternalism was perceived as vital for consolidating political control and fostering collective cohesion. The patriarchal social structure of the tribal Arab society placed high value in collectivity, allegiance, obedience, harmony and oral modes of expression. The tribal chief generally was the sole source of commands, and his orders were binding on all members of the tribe, albeit occasionally he would seek the advice of a council of elders on matters of public concern. The chief was a leader in conflicts, a source of assistance to his tribe's people, and a symbol of tribal valor, wisdom, generosity, and forgiveness. His role was asserted in the midst of common consciousness of helplessness in the face of a stubborn and malignant nature. This view of a patriarchal leader as powerful and just, yet despotic, has been carried into late 20th century Arab world political practices with the rise of personality cults in different communities around the region. A tribal leader, according to Arabian traditions, deserves full loyalty and support because he is the symbol of the tribe's unity and honor.

III.2.4. Eloquence (*Fasaha*)

Although poetry has been historically recognized as a form of expression around the world, it is the Arabs who have elevated poetic productions to a highly sacred status. In pre-Islamic period (*Jahiliya*), poets were influential players in tribal communities. In the Islamic era, poetry, as practiced in the *Jahiliya* times was discouraged; thus giving way to other oral traditions like oration. Yet, whenever tribal features of community life were visible, poetry was always at the forefront of public life. This oral potential was decisive not only in asserting the deeply-ingrained individualism in Bedouin society, but in determining the status of the tribe with whom the poet or speaker was associated. Arabs' appreciation of eloquence was intrinsically derived from the versatility and musical beauty of Arabic, an offshoot of the Semitic family of languages, which include among others Hebrew and Amharic. One of the main characteristics of Arabic is the morphological structure of its root patterns. This means that the vast majority of Arabic word stems are constructed from roots, each of which usually consists of two consonants, and form patterns (consisting of vocalic as well as consonantal elements) with which the roots inter-digitate. For example, the word *ilm*, meaning knowledge, is derived from the root three-letter verb *a-l-e-m-a*, which means knew or got informed. In addition to its high derivative potential, Arabic also possesses an elaborate system of affixes, which allows the language to be both rhymic and rhythmic, making it strongly conducive to poetry and rhymed utterances. Arabic also consists of numerous stylistic variations drawing on rhetorical devices capable of delivering precise shades of meanings, be it praise, derogation, emphasis, or simple descriptive utterances.

Throughout the classical history of the Arabian people, language was central to the definition of their collective identity. Jabra (1988: 260) points out that it may seem like an oversimplification to say that one of the operative definitions of an Arab in the last 100 years has been 'anyone who speaks Arabic as his or her own language and consequently feels as an Arab'. Bishai (1973: 66) notes that Arabic, especially its literary style, has been and still is to the Arabs not only a vehicle of expression, but also a religious symbol, a national identity, and an articulation of their achievements. The Prophet was quoted as saying: 'I love Arabs for three things- because I am an Arab, the *Qur'an* is in Arabic and the language of those in Paradise is Arabic' (Jameelah, 1967: 7). Rugh (1979: 20, 21) notes that Arabic carried special meanings for Arabs because it is the language of the *Qur'an*, accepted as the highest linguistic achievement, and because of its intrinsic beauty quite apart from the meaning it conveys. Hitti (1963: 21) noted that 'no people in the world have such enthusiastic admiration for literary expression and are so moved by the word, spoken or written, as the Arabs'. In the 21st century, Arabic continues to define the cultural identity of the Arab people in the face of global hegemony (Suleiman, 2003).

Written in rhymed form, the Arabic poem *qasida* amounted to a policy statement for the tribe or the Caliph. It covered three distinctive areas: lampoon or satire *Hijaa* which owes its development to inter-tribal conflicts; the *Marthiya* dirge or burial song which was originally associated with pagan mourning cults; and the *Madih* panegyric or praise poem which was used as a means of winning the favor of powerful tribal chiefs. Authors of lampoons used to vilify and mock enemy tribes by reviling their descent or detracting from the virtuousness of their ancestors. In this case, poets were acting as if they were mouthpieces for their tribes in times of peace and war. In a dominantly oral Arab culture, the spoken word had magic effects on audiences who were easily moved by poems delivered in public places. Words were taken as equivalent to action; hence, it was incumbent on poets to choose emotionally-charged words and statements to boost their messages. This feature is significant in contemporary analyses of Arab communications in light of Habermas's notion of 'the communicative action'. In the Islamic era, the oral nature of Arab culture was emphasized. The *Qur'an*, in Arabic meaning 'something being recited', was revealed to the Prophet who had to read it loud to his scribes to be able to memorize it. The first *Sura* (chapter) of the *Qur'an* started with the imperative verb 'Read...'. The Prophet, being illiterate himself, relied heavily on his oral means of expression to disseminate the word of Allah. In addition, the oral character of Arab-Islamic culture was manifested in Islamic religious rituals: call for prayers from mosque minarets, *Qur'anic* recitations, pilgrimage rituals, individual and congregational ritualistic prayers, *Jum'a* (Friday prayer) sermons, and so on.

III.3. Normative Islamic Components

According to the Islamic scholar Abu Ala al-Maududi, the political system in Islam, in its basic normative configuration, is based on four values: *Uluhiya* (emanating from Allah), *Tawhid* (Monotheism), *Risala* (Message) and *Khilafa* (Caliphate) (Nabhan, 1974). The *Uluhiya* principle suggests that the source of Islamic law (*Shari'a*) on this earth is derived from Allah; it is not man-made (*Wadei*). Qutb (1966) notes that Islam is a system that reflects a divine scheme for the *Umma;* a system that liberates individuals from servitude to human mortals to the servitude of Allah. Hence, Islam is a liberating *Ilahy* (divine) system that is not supposed to change across time as it is capable of accommodating new developments within its spiritual and legal principles. It is the duty of Muslim scholars of jurisprudence to keep abreast of new developments in this world and to extract the appropriate Islamic norms that make them acceptable to Muslim communities *(Ijtihad)*. It is in this area that the aforementioned *Maqasid al-Shari'a* (Ends of Islamic Law) principle seems relevant, especially on matters pertaining to political governance. In echoing his conservative interpretations of Islam, Qutb noted that because the Islamic system is intrinsically emanating from Allah, the Rule (*Hakimiya*) belongs solely to Him; thus ruling out alternative forms of governance like Western democracy (Tamimi, 2001).

According to *Tawhid* principle, Allah alone is the Creator, Sustainer and Master of the Universe and all of its components. Our organs and faculties are the bountiful provisions of Allah and have been bestowed on us by Him alone. According to al-Maududi (2004), the principle of *Tawhid* renders meaningless the concept of the legal and political sovereignty of human beings. The concept of *Tawhid* emphasizes the oneness of Allah, the Creator, and the Omnipotent who is the only one worthy of worship. Belief in the existence of partners to Allah is termed *shirq* or association, an unforgivable sin in the Islamic faith: 'Allah forgiveth not that partners should be set up wit Him, but He forgiveth anything else to whom He pleases).[2] The overriding importance of *Tawhid* was meant to obfuscate all types of polytheistic creeds that had dominated the pre-Islamic era in Arabia. The concept implies, among other things, man's exclusive servility to Allah. It also precludes the location of sovereignty in temporal social institutions as sovereignty and guardianship belong only to Allah.

The concept of *Tawhid* also implies belief in the unity of Allah, man and nature. In the unitary perspective of Islam, all aspects of life, as well as degrees of cosmic manifestations, are governed by a single principle and are unified by a common center. There is nothing outside the power of Allah, and in a more esoteric sense nothing outside His Being, for there cannot be two orders of reality (Nasr, 1981: 7). It is only through *Tawhid* that individuals acquire a sense of be-

---

[2] Qur'an (6:48).

longing to the temporal living reality of which he/she is an important element. *Tawhid* emphasizes the indivisibility of reality in its spiritual and temporal manifestations. The sacred and the mundane, though representing two seemingly antithetical realities, are inseparable in Muslims' individual and collective consciousness. The notion of a Power Transcendental located beyond the boundaries of material reality is unthinkable in Islam. The concept of *Tawhid* implies that Allah alone is Great; therefore no human being is greater than another before Allah.

The medium through which Muslims receives *Shari'a* (law of Allah) is known as *Risala*. Muslims have received two things from this source: the Book or *Qur'an* in which Allah has set out His law, and the authoritative interpretation and exemplification of the Book by the Prophet, through word and deed, in his capacity as the representative of Allah on earth. The Prophet, has also, in accordance with the intention of the *Qur'an*, set exemplary traditions for Muslims (*Sunna*) to follow. The combination of these two elements (*Qur'an* and *Sunna*) is called the *Shari'a*. Jurisprudence (*Fiqh*) is the interpretation of the *Qur'an* and *Sunna* on well-established scientific methodologies. As a science, jurisprudence, is defined as the aggregate legal proofs and evidence that, when studied properly, will lead either to certain knowledge of a *Shari'a* ruling or to at least a reasonable assumption concerning the same. In formulating an Islamic political theory, Islamic scholars have drawn on the *Qur'an* and *Sunna* traditions to spell out the nature and parameters of an Islamic political system.

Khilafa means representation and succession, and according to Islam, Man is Allah's representative on earth; His vicegerent. By virtue of the powers delegated to him by Allah, and within prescribed limits, man is required to exercise some Divine authority (al-Maududi, 2004). The Caliph is the religious and temporal symbol of the Islamic *Umma* and the guardian of its religious values. He is nominated to this post by the endorsement (*Beiya'a*) of selected men (*Ahl al-Hal wal-Aqd*), as noted in the *Beiya'a* of the first Caliph Abu Bakr on following the death of the Prophet in a place called *Saqifat Bani Saida*. In normal situations, the Caliph should be credited for his piety, honesty, and expertise. He is not expected to monopolize power, but to share decision-making on matters not provided for in the Scriptures with qualified members of the community through the practice of *Shura* (Consultation). In order to qualify for the Caliphate, the candidate has to be a male Muslim, knowledgeable in Islam, able to make independent decisions if necessary, just and trustworthy, with good morals, physically able, and politically, militarily, and administratively experienced. The duties of the Caliph include safeguarding Islam; applying Islamic Shari'a; establishing justice; ensuring the protection of the *Umma*; and running the affairs of the community.

A Caliph in Islam is not an absolute ruler, but a person who is entrusted to lead the *Umma* and would therefore be held accountable before Allah and the community for his actions. The first Rightly-Guided Caliph Abu Bakr was quoted on the first day after assuming office as Caliph to the Prophet as saying: 'I have been entrusted to rule you, though I am not the best of you. If you see me doing that on the right track, support me; if you see me going off the right track, rectify me. Obey me as long as I obey Allah in your rule. If I disobey Allah, you show no obedience to me'. The second Rightly-Guided Caliph Omar bin al-Khattab was also quoted as saying: 'Anyone of you who sees me crooked, do straighten me out. Then one of the audiences stood up and replied: I swear by Allah that if we saw that crookedness in you, we would rectify that with our swords. Then Omar replied: praise to Allah that this *Umma* has someone who rectifies Omar by his sword'. Many Muslim scholars have commented that it is permissible to disobey or remove the *Khalifa*, when he is not meeting all his responsibilities under Islam. For example, al-Mawardi believed that if the Caliph has followed the *Qur'an* and *Sunna*, the people must follow and support him. On the other hand, if he becomes either unjust or physically incapacitated, then he must be removed. Al-Baghdadi believed that if the Caliph deviates from justice, the *Umma* needs to warn him first to return to the straight path. If this fails, then he can be removed. Al-Juwayni held that since Islam is the goal of the *Umma*, any Caliph who steps away from this goal must be removed (Debbagh, 2004).

III.4. Corollary Concepts

In addition to the above four ingredients of the Islamic political theory, the writer also adds six more values: *Adl* (Justice), *Umma* (Community), *Shura* (Consultation), *Ilm* (knowledge), *Musawat* (equality), and *Mas'uliya* (Responsibility).

III.4.1. *Adl* (Justice)

Adl is a central concept in Islamic political theory. It is the basis for the perpetuation of good community because it ensures keeping the balance between rights and duties in *Umma*, a balance that is instituted by Allah when He created the Universe. Justice is perhaps the most important of the supreme values of Islam (Qutb, 1949). In fact, it can be said that the main purpose of revelation and the tasks of Prophets has been to establish justice. Thus, one of the early scholars of Islam said that 'where the signs of justice appear and its face is shown in any way, that is where the Law of Allah and His religion are found' (Islamonline, 2003a). As such, justice is the first principle of social life. It defines relations in life: between the ruler and the ruled, the rich and the poor, husband and wife, parents and children. Divine Justice is the backbone of the whole act of creation. The balance and due proportion evident in heavens and the earth are a manifestation of Allah's Justice. Thus in Islam, balance and justice are central to the design and order underlying Allah's creative fiat as also in the ultimate reckoning on the Day of Judgment. It is the consequence of Divine Justice that man has free will because, without free will, man does not merit either reward or punishment for his deeds. For this reason, a wide range of Islamic philosophical writings related the application of justice to freedom of choice in man's actions (Bou leewali, 2005).

III.4.2. *Umma* (Community)

The advent of Islam, a word which means the 'act of resignation to God', brought about a new universal social system, stressing brotherhood *ukhuwa* and piety *taqwa* at the expense of genealogy as a criterion of social status. From divided clans, engaged in inter-tribal conflicts and dependent on foreign powers for survival, Arabs were transformed into an *Umma* or community of believers with a new worldview. In *Umma*, sovereignty belongs only to Allah to Whose Will all human beings, the rulers and the ruled, are subjected. Mowlana (1993: 15) notes that the notion of *Umma* is conceived as universal and not as subject to territorial, linguistic, racial and nationalistic limitations. While Western conceptions of community seem to have placed relationships among community members mostly within a secular frame, Islam considers *Umma* an epitome of the harmony and perfection of Allah's creation, transcending boundaries of time and space. It is described in the Holy *Qur'an as* 'the best *Umma*' sent forth to mankind because it enjoins the right conduct; forbids the wrong; and believes in Allah.'[3] In *Umma*, the individual should dedicate his daily existence to the achievement of a greater ideal: a harmonious community consistent with the vision of the Holy *Qur'an*. Between the individual and his family, there is an obligation of mutual support, and between the individual and his society, there is a bond of cooperation for the benefit of the whole and the protection and well-being of the individual (Boullata, 1985: 61). In the Prophet's words, 'the faithful in their mutual compassion, sympathy, and love, are exemplified by the whole body. If one of its organs falls ill, the remainder will suffer'. As such, a community becomes possible on the basis of its members' commitment and accountability to the public good, as the Prophet said:

> *Ye are all guardians; and ye will be asked about your subjects: the Imam is the guardian of the subjects; and a woman is guardian to her husband's house and children; and a servant is a shepherd to his master's property. Ye are all guardians; and ye will be asked about your subjects.*

---

[3] Qur'an (3: 110).

Community in Islam is not a passive entity; it is the social body to which the Caliph is accountable in running its affairs. An important mechanism for regulating community input into public affairs is *Shura* (Consultation) which has been noted as the Islamic version of modern democracy. *Shura*, as explained below, means that the ruler would not monopolize his decisions and policies and should always seek feedback from the community not as a simple formality that he can do away with, but as a fundamental foundation of the decision-making process. The community taps on a wide range of resources in different fields and has the potential to contribute to decisions bearing on its future. The community also possesses the power to monitor the performance of the ruler to ensure keeping him on the right track of Islam. Hence, the community is not bound to give obedience to a despotic ruler who fails to apply the principles of justice and peace to its members. The Prophet was quoted as saying: 'No creature ought to obey anyone in disobedience of his Creator'. In one sense, the principle of *Shura* was instituted to stifle authoritarianism in public offices and to promote community participation in decisions affecting the *Umma* future.

III.4.3. *Shura* (Consultation)

As noted earlier, the concept of *Shura* (consultation) has been a central component of normative Islamic political theory. Despite the lack of consensus on how binding consultation is on the leader, there is a broad agreement that this practice is instituted to expand the decision and policy making process to embrace a larger number of actors in the community. Although the structure of the group to be consulted has not been well-defined, many Muslim scholars have grounded this practice in a consultative council (*Majlis ash-Shura*) to be either selected by the Caliph or chosen by the community at large on the basis of piety, knowledge, expertise and experience. There is no fixed size for this group, however, it is generally agreed that it should not be too large. Muslim scholars have established some basic prerequisites which the members of the *Majlis ash-Shura* should have to become part of that group. From classical writings, al-Mawardi noted that each member must be just with adequate knowledge of Islam and sufficient wisdom and judgment to select the best leader. Al-Juwayni and Abdul-Jabbar set three conditions that include deep knowledge, distinction, and Islamic faith. Rashid Rida wrote that the *Majlis ash-Shura* should be made up of the best of the *Umma*, composed of the scholars, leaders, soldiers, businessmen, and respected people of the society. All members should have deep knowledge of Islam as a basic prerequisite, and their opinions and decisions are obeyed and respected. The *Majlis ash-Shura* should have people from many fields of expertise to ensure a broad base of support and knowledge (Islamonline, 2003b).

If a government is by the people, then it only makes sense that the people choose or elect those who will govern on their behalf and control their destiny. In contemporary Islamic thought, *Shura* has been closely viewed as a corollary concept of 'Islamocracy', or Islamic governance. In the *Qur'an*, one sees an insistence on using *Shura*, or mutual consultation, in deciding communal affairs[4], which would include choosing or electing leaders to represent and govern on behalf of the community. Interestingly enough, a model already exists in Islamic history for Muslims in using mutual consultation as a process of selecting a new leader. When Prophet Muhammad was on his deathbed, many of his Companions urged him to name a successor who would lead the community, but the Prophet refused to do so – a clear indication that he wanted the next leader to be chosen through mutual consultation rather than be imposed on the community. As such, when the Prophet passed away, the most pressing issue for the community was to choose its next leader. Three Companions were nominated to take the post of *Khalifa* (Caliph), and in the end, the Prophet's closest Companion, Abu Bakr, was chosen to be the community's new leader. Abu Bakr and his three successors, known collectively as the Four Rightly-Guided Caliphs, were also chosen in a similar fashion that reflected popular consent. So the idea of choosing a leader in accordance with popular will is certainly not a new idea in the Islamic tradition.

III.4.4. *Ilm* (Knowledge)

Ilm (knowledge) is a central component of Islamic political theory because it is through an educated and well-enlightened community that a sound political process could be sustained. While the domain of knowledge in the pre-Islamic period was confined mainly to literary and folkloric modes of expression, the advent of Islam heralded remarkable developments not only in the scope of knowledge, but in its epistemology. The *Qur'an* represents a linguistic achievement so high that Arabs were unable to match despite their record of distinguished literary craftsmanship. Baffled by the linguistic miracle of the Holy Book, Arabs were steered by Islam to explore areas of knowledge other than poetry and prose. Arab Muslims were also enjoined to draw on a multiplicity of knowledge acquisition methods other than imagination and oral transmission. An all encompassing scientific and information revolution was unleashed with far-reaching repercussions not only for Arabs, but for other peoples as well.

The concept of knowledge *ilm* has been taken as a point of departure for most theoretical endeavors to elaborate an Islamic communication paradigm. Sardar (1993: 43) notes that:

> Communication in Islam is intrinsically related to the fundamental Qur'anic concept of *ilm*. Often translated as 'knowledge', *ilm* is one of the most frequently occurring terms in the Qur'an. As a defining concept of the world

---

[4] Qur'an (3:159, 42:38).

view of Islam, its influence permeates all aspects of Muslim individual and societal behavior. This is why the pursuit of *ilm* is a religious obligation for all Muslims. For the Muslims of the classical period, Islam was synonymous with *ilm*; without it an Islamic civilization was unimaginable. For a Muslim civilization of the future, it is even more so.

Denoting the realization of an information-rich environment, *ilm* incorporates the substance of knowledge, its acquisition, as well as its communication for the benefit of the community. Sardar points out that the history of communication in Islam is a history of Muslim understanding of the notion of *ilm*, and its actualization in society (1993: 52). The Holy *Qur'an* advises Muslims to pray: 'O, my Lord! Advance me in knowledge'[5]. It also asserts that those who have knowledge are not equal to those who don't[6]; that it is by virtue of knowledge that humans are superior to angels and have been made vicegerent of Allah on earth[7]; and that knowledge links humans to Allah: 'Only the knowledgeable persons.... fear Allah'[8]. Mowlana (1993: 18-19) elaborated an Islamic Community Paradigm, which he argued was responsible for the information, and scientific revolution that characterized the early middle ages. What is known as a dark age of the 7th to the 11th centuries in Western history was the golden age in the Islamic community. During that period, the *Umayyad* (661-750) and *Abbasid* (750-861) states marked the most prosperous and productive periods in the entire Islamic history of the Middle East. Rulers encouraged and promoted creative arts, giving protection and security to scholars and artists of all kinds. Perhaps the greatest contribution that the early *Abbasid* Caliphs made to Islamic humanities and scholarship was their encouragement of the translation of several important Greek books into Arabic. Abbasid Caliphs al-Rashid and al-Ma'moun brought from Asia Minor several Greek manuscripts and entrusted their translation into Arabic to a number of scholars under the leadership of a translator known as Ibn Lu'qa.

The concept of *ilm* implied different, but important sources of knowledge acquisition. The primary source is revelation as in the case of the *Qur'an*. Muslims are enjoined to submit to revealed knowledge by heart-based belief. In the meantime, Islam emphasizes the role of the intellect or reason *Aql* in leading man to the Divine. Mahmoud (1977: 89-90) notes that a good deal of rationality had marked Arab culture as evident in Arabs' approaches to language codification, Islamic jurisprudence *Fiqh*, and receptivity to Greek writings, mathematics and philosophy. Islamic jurisprudence-based works were centered on four schools of interpretation of the *Qur'an* and the *Sunna*: *Shafi'iya*, (after Muhammad ibn Idris al-Shafi'i, d. 820); *Hanbaliya*, (after Ahmad ibn Hanbal, d. 855); *Malikiya* (after Malik ibn Anas, d. 795); and *Hanafiya* (after Abu Hanifa, d.

---

[5] Qur'an (20:114).
[6] Qur'an (39:9).
[7] Qur'an (20:30).
[8] Qur'an (35:28).

767). The philosophical stream of thought was concerned with establishing harmony between reason and revelation. Affected by translated Greek works of Plato and Aristotle, Muslim-Arab thinkers such as al-Farabi, Ibn Sina, Ibn Hazm, Ibn Tufayl, and Ibn Rushd laid down foundations for a new philosophical orientation in which intellect and reason were elevated to a higher status. In his utopia, *The Perfect State*, al-Farabi (d. 950) was greatly influenced by Plato's writings as he elaborated a theory of civil administration based on the concept of emanation of power from an absolute center, namely Allah. In *Hay bin Yaqthan* (The Alive Son of the Awake), Ibn Tufayl (d. 1185) narrated a story about a baby who was left alone on a desert land. From contemplation and observation, he got to know some natural phenomena, and in the end he discovered the existence of Allah together with a large body of ethical values. In other words, he independently reached the main principles of Islam which suggests human mind and divine revelation converged on a single point.

III.4.5. *Mas'uliya* (Responsibility)

In Islam, life is the responsibility of all members of the community, entrusted to them by the Creator, to contribute to the realization of justice and happiness within the confines of *Shari'a*. Man is responsible for his acts before Allah and will be held accountable for the tiniest of actions: 'And who so doeth good an atom's weight will see it then. And who so doeth ill an atom's weight will see it then'[9]. On the other hand, no one will be held responsible for others' mistakes and sins as long as they did not have a part in their perpetration: 'Whosoever goeth right, it is only for (the good of) his own soul that he goeth right, and whosoever erreth, erreth only to its hurt. No laden soul can bear another's load. We never punish until we have sent a messenger'[10]. In Islamic political theory, the Caliph is entrusted with the responsibility of safeguarding the *Umma* and securing its survival and prosperity. Once a person fails to fulfill his/her assigned responsibilities, he/she should not be allowed to be in a position of responsibility because of the dire consequences. Members of the *Umma* share in bearing responsibility by giving advice to the Caliph and contributing to enjoining good doing and combating evil in society. The concept of responsibility was heatedly debated within classical philosophical traditions seeking to identify key ethical values in Islam with some philosophers or *Kalami* members placing all responsibility on the individual, while others spoke of some deprivation of free will. Hence, responsibility for actions is attributed to some force of determinism known as *Qada' wa Qadar* (Judgment by a Power-Transcendental). Contrary to key Islamic concepts affirming the individual's responsibility for his actions, such determinism was sometimes used to justify corrupt or despotic practices.

---

[9] Qur'an (99:6).
[10] Qur'an (17:05).

Responsibility in Islam implies that the individual is also free, otherwise he would not be held accountable for his actions. Freedom in Islam, according to Imam (1985) means that the individual is not overburdened by others' subordination as he claims servitude only to his Creator. The individual, thus, is free to do what he thinks is right in promoting his relationship with Allah by pursuing his own interests or serving the community at large. Once freedom starts to generate harm for the community, then it turns into a threat that needs to be checked. In other words, freedom is not just an individual pursuit, but it also has community components that in Islam outweigh the individual benefits. The individual is free to subscribe to different religions or systems of thought as long as this tendency does not adversely bear on community interests. The notion of free will necessitates freedom of choice, and this is why the *Qur'an* so emphatically states 'There is no compulsion in religion'.[11] The *Qur'an* also encourages the free formation and mobilization of social and political groups when it says 'And let there be a people among you who invite to good and enjoin what is fair, and forbid what is wrong'[12].

III.4.6. *Musawat* (Equality)

Islam has declared all members of the *Umma* are equal in their social status. Before Allah, the most pious are the most honored. Allah says: 'O Mankind! We have created you from a male and female, and made you into nations and tribes, that you may know one another. Verily, the most honorable of you in the sight of Allah is he who has most *taqwa* among of you. Verily, Allah is All-Knowing, All-Aware'.[13] Islam dose not discriminate between two races, or two groups of people, or between two colors. In his historic Farewell Speech (*Khutbat al-Wadaa'*), Prophet Muhammad addressed his followers during his last pilgrimage, saying: 'O People! Your God is one; your father is one; no preference of an Arab neither over non-Arab nor of a non-Arab over an Arab or red over black or black over red except for the most righteous. Verily the most honored of you is the most righteous'. In addition, not only did Islam emphasize the equality principle theoretically, but also practically in some of the worship rituals that translated this principle into a sensible fact that dose not escape people minds, thus: in the mosques where Friday prayer is held once every week, as well as the five daily prayers; equality is exercised practically as all differences vanishes among people. That is, whoever came to the Mosque first, took his place in the front rows despite his social status, and whoever come last, his place is late and if you look at any row among the prayer's rows, you would find in that raw the rich

---

[11] Qur'an (2:256).
[12] Qur'an (3:104).
[13] Qur'an (49:13).

and poor, the knowledgeable and the less knowledgeable, and the Arab and the non Arab.

Based on the above discussion, it appears that political theory in Islam embraces values and practices conducive to the institution of a sound public sphere. Islam, by default, is a community and public-oriented life system in which individuals are encouraged to withdraw from their private family and clannish spheres, but not to relinquish them, to engage in public debates within the broader *Umma* sphere. On the one hand, leaders are accountable to Allah and the *Umma* to honestly carry out the mission of justice that ensures safeguarding community interests. The community, in return, is required to monitor the performance of the leadership to ensure its commitment to the basic interests of its members. The notion of *Shura* suggests sharing information and expertise between the leadership and the community, something that amounts to a participatory decision-making mechanism on matters of concern to the public interest. To reinforce their participation in serving community affairs, community members need to be empowered to voice their concerns to leaders either through *Shura* councils or other platforms. Diversity within unity seems to have been an acceptable practice as long as inputs contribute to community welfare within specified moral frameworks. A whole set of communication ethics defines public exchanges and dialogue that ensure good intentions; demonstrate respect for information sources and audiences; and heed the power of reasoning as a key factor in persuasion.

III.5. Normative Islamic Communication Principles

Drawing on the above precepts of Islamic political theory, communication in Islam, as based on the *Qur'an* and the *Sunna,* is a central part of the human living experience encapsulated in the Islamic concept of *Ibadah* (Worship). *Ibadah* embodies the ultimate goal of life in Islam as to assert man's exclusive servility to Allah: 'I have only created *Jinns* and man, that they may worship Me'[14]. Unlike followers of other monotheistic religions, Arabs came to believe in Islam as more than just a religion; it is a *Din* or a 'complete way of life', deriving its comprehensiveness from the concept of *Ibadah*. Islam considers every virtuous action which is sincerely performed and which aims at carrying out the commandments of Allah, thus seeking His pleasure, an act of worship, for which Muslims will be rewarded. Even eating, drinking, sleeping and such worldly actions which satisfy physical needs and even yield sensuous pleasures, become acts of worship provided they are performed with true religious motives (Zarqa, 1976 :109). As such, to call Islam a religion obscures many of its key aspects, which in the West do not generally fall under the rubric of religion, but which

---

[14] Qur'an (31:56).

nevertheless are critical for a fuller and more adequate understanding of Muslim culture (Pasha, 1993: 63). In addition, the concept of *Ibadah* implies that all events of everyday life are transformed into instances of sacred principles. Classical Arabic has produced no term which is exactly synonymous with the word secularism, or which denotes a distinction between the sacred and the profane. Hence, we notice that daily interactions are colored with religious overtures making speech itself an act of *Ibadah*. To express admiration of a beautiful object, Arab Muslims would exclaim '*Ma Shaa' Allah!*' which means 'Great by Allah's will; to salute others, Arabs say, '*As-Salamu Alaikum wa-rahmatu Allah*' (Peace and God's Mercy be Upon You'); to start doing any work, Arab Muslims start with the *Basmala* statement (In the Name of Allah); to respond to a question about one's health or self, he/she responds, '*al-Hamdu Lillah*' (I am very thankful to Allah). Even names of people are colored with religious symbolism as evident in names starting with the word 'abd' which means servant. Thus we have *Abdulkhaliq* (Servant of the Creator), *Abdulqadir* (Servant of the Omnipotent); *Abdulazim* (Servant of the Great) and *Abdulkarim* (Servant of the Generous), and so on.

According to Islamic beliefs, the Divine revelation of the *Qur'an* was a unique communication experience in which the transcendental came into touch with the existential to promote a universal message to humanity, a message deeply rooted in a grand Divine Scheme of happiness and prosperity for Man on this earth. Communication has been pivotal in Islam's vision of the living experience because it is through communication that the Islamic *Umma* (Community) comes into existence, and it is through communication that the *Umma* keeps its transcendental relations with its Creator. Three 'spheres' of communications are envisioned in Islam: the transcendental sphere, embracing the individual's relationship with his Creator; the public sphere, involving community members' relationships with each others, and between them on the one hand, and the leadership, on the other hand; and finally, the private sphere, covering the individual's relationship with his private family domain (Imam, 1985). Because of its centrality in the human living experience, communication in Islam has been an integral part of community life. The fact that the *Qur'an* was revealed in Arabic to an Arab Prophet was bound to create unique 'communicative actions' that draw both on Arab culture and Islamic morality. Although the main thrust of those communicative actions was orally-based, the introduction of *Tadwin* practice (documentation) into the Arab-Islamic state during the *Umayyad* and *Abbasid* periods marked a significant shift into written communications. Both Islamic and Arabic traditions shared an emphasis on the spoken word though the two diverged on the moral boundaries of communication. Earlier in this chapter, it was noted that pre-Islamic Arab culture highly valued eloquence as a noble personal feature that won the individual or his tribe a great deal of popularity and acclaim as it was employed within the concepts of honor and dignity.

The convergence of tribal and Islamic moral and oral expressive practices produced a range of communication patterns marked by significant dichotomies that adversely bear on expected outcomes. The following section sums up the basic moral components of an Islamic communication patterns as derived from the *Qur'an* and *Sunna*.

III.5.1. Enjoining Virtue & Inhibiting Vice

Within the comprehensive concept of *Ibadah* (Worship), the community of believers carries the Divine mission of establishing a human system based on virtue as defined by Islamic morality. Communicators are expected to be active promoters of good deeds and inhibitors of evil. In this case, there is no room for objectivity in reporting events and issues that carry evil messages harmful to religious beliefs, community security and safety, public decency and individual privacy. Communication in Islam is an instrument for fostering good aspects of community life and combating its evils; thus communicators are not neutral conduits of information, but are integral elements of a committed reporting process. This orientation is very much in line with the advocacy journalism thesis that views objectivity as a hoax. There are numerous verses in the Holy *Qur'an* that substantiate this feature: (Allah does not like talking of evil words in public, except by him who has been wronged; and Allah is Hearing, Knowing)[15]; (Those who love that indecency should spread abroad among the Believers, for them shall be a painful punishment in this world and Hereafter; and God knows but you do not know)[16]; (Hast thou not seen how God has struck a similitude? A good word is like a good tree whose roots are firm and branches are in the heaven)[17]; and (And the likeness of a corrupt word is like a corrupt tree, uprooted from the earth, having no stability)[18].

III.5.2. Addressing Humanity

Though communication in Islam addresses specific contextual situations in certain languages, it carries a message of relevance to mankind because its values and norms are universal. In this case, communicators in Islam are expected to broaden their vision to embrace a universal audience rather than confine their discourse to a certain nationalistic or ethnic group within specific geographical boundaries. Since the message of Islam carries a universal human appeal, it is expected to embrace a communication discourse that finds resonance across a wide range of Muslim linguistic, ethnic or national groups: (And We have not

---

[15] Qur'an (4:148).
[16] Qur'an (24:19).
[17] Qur'an (14:24).
[18] Qur'an (14:26).

sent thee, but to entire mankind, as a bearer of good news and as a warner, but most men do not know[19]. The message of Islam is based on mercy, peace, and justice. These ethical values are the building blocs of communication in the Islamic *Umma*.

III.5.3. Drawing on Reason

Communication in Islam derives from Man's active use of his rational capacities to understand the universe and community relations and actions. In this case, communicators should not be swayed by emotional rhetoric and pompous expression. Communicators are expected to describe and analyze community problems and events in scientific ways and to draw up rational conclusions that could contribute to effective solutions of problems. In the areas of *Mu'amalat* (life affairs), communication identifies human living situations and unravels how things are developing. Information sources used should be factual, reflecting sound and rational judgments of things rather than subjectivist tendencies of individual communicators: (it gives its fruit every season, by the leave of its Lord; and Allah strikes similitudes for mankind that they may pay heed)[20].

III.5.4. Freedom of Religion

Communication in Islam draws on freedom of religion and thought and opposes coercion in this regard. Freedom of thought means that the individual has the right to pursue his/her line of thought or ideology as long as he/she does not intrude on the dominant Islamic ideology. In this case, communicators with non-Islamic ideology should heed the Islamic identity of the community and should show respect for its beliefs: (There is no compulsion in the religion; rectitude has become clear from perversion; so whoso disbelieves in idols and believes in Allah, has laid hold of the most firm handle, which cannot break; and 'Allah is Hearing, Knowing'.[21] On the other hand, within the Islamic faith itself, there is ample room for the pursuit of diversity on matters pertaining to *Mu'amalat* (life affairs), especially when there are no specific Scripture texts addressing those matters. This actually includes a wide range of areas to which members of the community could contribute through their ideas and visions by utilizing *Maqasid Shari'a* (Ends of Shari'a), a branch of Islamic jurisprudence that seeks to extract working principles from evolving situations based more on the original intentions of *Shari'a* than on formalities. In this sense, freedom of expres-

---

[19] Qur'an (34:28)
[20] Qur'an (14:25)
[21] Qur'an (2:256)

sion is allowed in Islam as long as it empowers the individual to promote virtue and curb evil in the community and beyond.

III.5.5. Institution of Justice

Justice, as noted earlier, is pivotal to community survival. It applies to a wide range of personal, political, and social domains. In this case, communication in Islam is a tool for reinforcing justice and combating oppression in the community and beyond. The institution of justice suggests that communicators function as advocates of equity by highlighting positive aspects of just social and political arrangements and exposing areas of injustice and oppression: (Allah enjoins justice, good-doing, and giving to kinsmen, and He forbids indecency, disgusting things and rebellion; He admonishes you so that you may pay heed;[22] and communication in Islam draws on fairness and justice when approaching different issues and personalities: (O' Believers, be your securers of justice, witnesses for Allah, though it be against yourselves or your parents and kinsmen; whether he be rich or poor, Allah stands closest to either; so do not follow caprice lest you deviate from justice; and if you twist or turn aside, Allah is aware of the things you do.)[23]

III.5.6. Bearing Responsibility

Communication in Islam draws on responsibility for expressions and acts: (We offered the trust to the heavens and the earth and the mountains, and they refused to take it and feared it, but man took it; he was surely wrong-doer and utterly ignorant)[24]. While freedom of thought and religion is endorsed in Islam, it is not an absolute right enjoyed by individuals in society. Freedom is defined by responsibility and cannot be conceived outside its boundaries. In this case, communicators in Islam are expected to carry out their mission freely; yet they should not encroach on others' rights through offensive messages. Respect for other religions and intellectual orientations are central to communication in Islam. Violation of others' rights through offensive communications deserves penalty because of the damage inflicted on individuals and communities.

---

[22] Qur'an (16:90)
[23] Qur'an (4:135)
[24] Qur'an (33:72)

III.5.7. Demonstrating Honesty

Communication in Islam is based on honesty and truth-telling. This suggests that communicators should avoid reporting false or unverified information. They should be transparent and faithful to truth with no sense of manipulation: (O Believers, do not betray Allah and the Messenger, and do not betray your trusts knowingly);[25] : (O Believers, fear Allah and be with the truthful);[26] and : (And those who do not testify falsehood, and, when they pass by idle non-sense, pass by it with dignity);[27] and Communication in Islam precludes provocative and propagandistic messages likely to cause problems for individuals and groups: (O Believers, avoid much of suspicion; some suspicion is a sin; and do not spy, nor backbite one another; does any of you like to eat the flesh of his dead brother; you would hate it; and fear Allah; Allah is All-returning, Merciful);[28] (And those who hurt the Believing men and Believing women, without their having earned it, they have surely taken upon them a calumny and a manifest sin);[29] and Communication in Islam promotes verification of information accuracy and precludes making unconfirmed statements and rumors about events and personalities: (O Believers, if a transgressor comes to you with a news, make clear, lest you afflict a people in ignorance, and then repent on what you have done).[30]

III.5.8. Respecting Others

Communication in Islam precludes defamation and mockery of others for the sake of inflicting harm on them or allowing others to make fun of them. Defamation is a big sin in Islam because it causes damage to others' reputations. In this case, communicators should respect the dignity and honor of community members and demonstrate commitment to their respect: (O Believers, let not a people scoff at another people, it may be they are not better than they, nor let women (scoff) at other women, it may be they are better than they. And do not find fault with one another, nor call by nicknames. Giving bad names is transgression after belief, and those who do not repent, they are the wrong-doers).[31] Ridiculing others for the sake of defamation or fun is prohibited in Islamic culture which sees all community members as equal and deserving respect.

---

[25] Qur'an (8:27)
[26] Qur'an (9:119)
[27] Qur'an (25:72)
[28] Qur'an (49:12)
[29] Qur'an (33:58)
[30] Qur'an (49:6)
[31] Qur'an (49:11)

III.6. The Dichotomous Nature of Classical Arab-Islamic Discourse

It has now become clear that a convergence of Islamic political theory and communication perspectives would lead to the emergence of a public sphere bound by the moral foundations of Islam while providing ample opportunities for the *Umma* to debate issues of concern to its realities. Throughout the classical Arab-Islamic history, the concept of the public arena as a social space for the exchange of ideas among individuals and groups on matters of common concern was defined by a broad community affiliation with a single source of political theory as prescribed by the *Qur'an* and the *Sunna*. For 1200 years, Arab Muslims had subscribed to a single ethos that permeated their cultural, political, social and legal institutions, serving their communities in the best way possible. Unlike the ancient Greek philosophers who took politics as a subject of scrutiny, Muslim intellectuals and scientists focused their efforts on pure sciences, literature, religious scholarship, and philosophical ethics. Very few of them took social and political realities as launching pads for new perspectives on how their communities should look like. It is for this reason that this chapter has sought to study the Arab-Islamic public sphere from a normative point of view simply because political practices and traditions on the ground were more or less mirroring the revealed message of Islam rather than the man-made intellectual ferment. This is, of course, understandable in that specific era of Arab-Islamic history; hence, it would be unfair to apply contemporary benchmarks on past political experiences.

On the other hand, the integration of Islamic moral ideals into tribal Arabian values was bound to create serious tensions in the evolving classical Arab-Islamic discourse. Those tensions were reproduced in the form of dichotomies embracing divergent Arab and Islamic moral and cultural orientations that continue to define the Arab public sphere in the age of globalization. These dichotomies include: individualist-conformist, transcendental-existential, intuitive-rational, and Egalitarian-Hierarchical.

III.6.1. Individualist/Conformist

Although individualism is a highly-valued concept in the Arab-Islamic worldview, it is conceived differently in the secular and Islamic contexts of Arab culture. In secular Arab traditions, the concepts of lineage, honor, paternalism, and eloquence were conducive to highly visible individualistic orientations on the part of the Arabs. These concepts were viewed as pillars of the extremely revered notion of the ego-centered dignity. To live and die in dignity is a life pattern held in high esteem in Arab culture. To deprive an Arab of his dignity is to transform his life into a worthless pursuit. Yet, individualism as a virtuous trait, derived its significance from its public manifestations. The tribal poet was always keen on displaying his pride in public arenas like markets, councils, or other meeting places because he was aware that such publicity was conducive to the advancement of his social standing. Giving poetic works in limited or private settings was far less attractive than delivering it in the audience of a Caliph, a tribal chief, or crowds of people in markets or religious places. The individual in secular Arab culture, as noted earlier, could not live on his/her own, outside the boundaries of collective tribalism. When left alone, the individual often feels disoriented and unable to survive n his own. The individual's hopes for strength and power lay in his/her cooperation with, and service to others. Public perceptions of a person's dignity were decisive in shaping the individual self-esteem. For this reason, the individual is keen on attaining a high degree of public visibility in dignifying situations and a low visibility in indignifying situations

Individualism is best expressed in views of the Arab poet al-Thougrai (Ba'albaki, 1980: 52) as follows:

> The most distinguished and outstanding man in life
> Is the one who counts on nobody in this world (except himself).

Another verse by the famous Arabian poet Abu Firas al-Hamadani seems to express the same theme, though with a deep sense of narcissism when he wished that:

> 'No rain would ever fall on earth if he should die in thirst!'

Tribal affiliation gave the individual a sense of security and conferred on him public recognition. On his part, the individual might continue to view his conformity to a tribal code of conduct as an involuntary submission to a higher authority, something abhorred by independence-oriented desert inhabitants. An ideal image of the Arab was that of the rebellious *abi* who would never submit to tyranny and injustice, and would sacrifice his tribal conformity to win personal freedom and independence. To live up to his own code of ego-centered dignity, the Arab would find a great deal of comfort in invoking notions of personal honor, lineage, eloquence, and paternalism as superb combinations of qualities recognized by society (Hitti, 1963). As Durayed bin Assama (d. 8 Hijri), an Arab poet described his tribal affiliation with Ghaziya:

> I am from Ghaziya, if it carries out an invasion, I will do join in
> If it seeks the path of righteousness, I will also go with it

In Islam, on the other hand, a Muslim's personal spiritual relationship with Allah is the basis for his/her conformity to the divine law *Shari'a* of the *Umma*. Individualism in Islam involves endeavors on the part of a believer to 'compete' with others in winning the pleasure of Allah. But this reward cannot be attained solely through devotional rituals, but through accountability and commitment to community affairs. Self-denial might become a viable option since it leads to maximizing believers' individual transcendental gains which have precedence over temporal interests In this sense, though individualism reflects the person's efforts to maximize altruistic benefits (transcendental), it thrives very much on the existence of a collective ethos or bond in the community. The public domain of the *Umma* is transformed into a testing field of individual achievements that originates in the inner domain of the individual. Both domains share symbiotic relationships and are thus viewed as complimentary rather than contradictory.

The individualist-conformist orientations in Arab-Islamic culture produce two distinctive patterns of communication in public arenas. In the first pattern, generally associated with secular Arab traditions, communication is a process of liberating the individual from the shackles of conformity to a collective system and of assisting him/her to assert his/her own code of dignity. Poetry was a powerful tool for achieving this. Though poets were serving as mouthpieces for collective tribal or national entities, they never hesitated to produce ego-centered poems in which one detects an assertive personality rebelling against a larger constraining reality. Going public was perceived by individuals as a means of self-assertion and tribal recognition. Hence, individuals would find it incumbent on themselves to be part of public meetings and councils both to show their tribal conformity and to demonstrate their individual self as a building bloc in the tribal community.

On the other hand, communication in Islam, spiritual or social, is a process of facilitating the individual's integration into the larger *Umma*. It is a process of harmonizing the believing inner self with the collective believing self of the community. Falling within the concept of *ibadah*, all communication acts are used not only as tools of harmonizing the individual self with a collective ethos, but are they elevated to the status of acts of worship in their own right, thus deserving Allah's rewards. Whether it is a call for prayer, a salute, a *Qur'anic* recital, a congregational sermon, or a speech on matters of public interest, communication arenas in Islam contribute to the integration of the believing self into the larger community of believers. As an ultimate goal, it serves to assert Muslim's exclusive servility to Allah. Furthermore, individuals in Islam are ordered to go public to show their attachment to their community concerns. The Prophet was quoted as saying:'Those who do not heed the concerns of Muslims are not part of them'. In this case, an individual would contribute to the welfare of the community to seek rewards from Allah while at the same time he/she proves his/her standing in public spaces.

III.6.2. Transcendental-Existential

Reality in Arab-Islamic culture is conceived as made up of two domains, one belonging to the world of idealist imagination and divine sacredness of a Power Transcendental, the other to mundane matter and the profanity of sensible existence. The first world is perfect and absolute, the second imperfect and relative. We become conscious of the first domain through heart and intellect, while our knowledge of the second domain is based on first-hand encounters. This dual perspective of reality has profound implications for the presence in public arenas in Muslim societies. Muslims may go public in religious rituals like prayers, sermons, and pilgrimage to fulfill their religious commandments; yet they make use of these occasions to address worldly issues of concern to the community. A Friday sermon could address social, political and cultural issues in addition to the spiritual aspects of believers' life. A pilgrimage could be an opportunity for Muslims to meet and discuss non-spiritual and non-religious issues within the umbrella of the Islamic faith.

A thin line seems to separate both spheres (Mundane/Transcendental) as they operate in an interactive fashion. For example, the vision of divine perfection and absoluteness is a guiding principle in Muslims' handling of real life problems. In Islamic teachings, Allah created man to establish the perfect community in an imperfect world, and gave him guidance through revelation. Allah, Almighty, does intervene in the course of world events. In secular or semi-religious intellectual works of utopia, the imagination of an idealist reality standing at odds with the living reality was also a source of inspiration for Arab poets and philosophers in their approaches to worldly matters and issues. The animal story *Kalila wa-Dimna*, authored by Abdullah bin al-Muqaffa who lived in the Abbasid era, and the well-known *One Thousand and One Nights* were two distinguished works of literature in which fiction was used to project real world events. Because the transcendental world is associated with divine absolutism and sacredness, it was natural to view it as far more superior to the low world of relativism and profanity. In different life situations, the transcendental world has become a guiding light for dealing with the mundane world as Mahmoud (1977: 6) notes:
The essence of Arab culture, old and modern alike, is that it distinguishes decisively between Allah and His creatures, between the absolute idea and the universe of change and transience, between the eternal truth and events of history, between the immutability of the Everlasting Being and the dynamism of the ever-changing being. The distinction, however, does not place the modes of existence at one level: it rather makes the world of events a symbol pointing to the world of reality.

Attachment to 'transcendentalism' and detachment from 'existentialism' in the Arab-Islamic culture seems to have given rise to a communication that thrives on the surrealistic, the imaginative, and the metaphysical. In secular and Islamic Arab culture, this feature was nowhere more conspicuous than in the emphasis on form to the exclusion of meaning in Arabic language. The concept of form embraces not only the inflated connotations of words and phrases, but the musical nature of Arabic as a central component of an intrinsically oral Arab culture. Arabic is a language of musical beauty and limitless fantasy. Rhetorical devices like hyperboles, metaphors, and similes produce flowery expressions that outmatch the reality they are supposed to denote. And when they do so, they do it in the least direct and explicit of terms. To describe an average tribal chief as an 'insurmountable lion'; to refer to the lineage of a person as 'descending from the stars'; or to describe the sun as 'feeling shy for not matching the beauty of the beloved', are commonly detected in the Arab-Islamic literature.

Arabic also contributes to this detachment trend by virtue of its oral nature. Words are important not because of the meanings they convey, but because of their musical quality. A sermon, a Holy *Qur'anic* recital, a speech or an interpersonal exchange of information yield far more effective communication in an oral than in a printed form. Listeners may not follow up the communication source as much for the meanings he/she attempts to deliver as for the musical effects of his/her utterances. In the Islamic-Arab culture, the permeation of sacred beliefs into Arabic has been quite profound. As noted in the discussion of the concept of *Ibadah*, names of persons like *Abdarrahim* (servant of the Merciful) or *Abdarrahman* (servant of the Gracious) are common in Arab society. Allah's intervention in the day-to-day affairs of the living experience is also clear in the use of such phrases as *insha'a Allah* (Allah willing) when somebody plans to do something; *Allah Yarzuq* (Allah will provide means of sustenance) for somebody who is looking for a living to earn; or *Allah ma yurid* (Allah does not want this to happen) when somebody plans to do something, but could not.

Sharabi (1988: 86) observes that while all languages structure thought processes, classical Arabic structures them in a decisive way. This is not only because of the ideological character of a language within its rigid religious and patriarchal framework, but also because of its inherent tendency to impose its own patterns and structures on all linguistic production. Arabic is considered a received language, a language of others or as Barakat (1985: 65) puts it, it favors literary over scientific writing, rhetoric over written prose, and speech over writing. If the visual orientations of Western culture are epitomized by such statements as 'more than sees the eye'; 'seeing is believing'; or 'what you see is what you get'; the orally-based Arab communication may be dramatically expressed in parallel statements like 'more than hears the ear', or 'hearing is believing'. As classical Arab poet Bashar bin Burd said: 'The ear, more than the eye, is sometimes infatuated by beauty'. This orally-centered communication suggests a mouth-to-ear-based epistemology of knowledge whereby the spoken word is taken for real, thus granting the source of the message ample opportunities for the manipulation of the listener. This feature also seems to bear heavily on socialization and education. Sharabi (1988) notes that children's first encounter with classical language is through sacred texts which they are often made to learn by heart. From the beginning, a child develops dissociation between learning and understanding as the former is based on memorization, and an absence of all questioning becomes normal in knowledge acquisition. He also remarks that although the Holy *Qur'an* as the path of innovative change affirmed reading, it was not encouraged. It is for this reason that Sardar (1993: 52) claims that 'the introduction of printing into the Arab-Islamic World was frowned upon by traditional *ulama* (religious scholars) because it tended to undermine their orally based expression of authority. '

As a cautionary note, however, it is suggested here that this orally-based epistemology of knowledge did not confer on the word of mouth an unquestionable credibility. Allah warned believers against blindly trusting what is orally conveyed to them without verifying it: 'O ye believers! If a wicked person comes to you with any news, ascertain the truth; lest you harm people unwittingly, and afterwards become full of repentance for what you have done'.[32] In the Arab secular traditions, the word of mouth was not automatically taken for true. A person's tongue was viewed as a source of evil if not properly shackled. If the person was not able to produce a good conversation, silence was seen as the best alternative 'and was equated with gold if speech was made of silver' (Ba'alabki, 1980: 78).

III.6.3. Intuitive-Rational

Revelation is the most primary knowledge source for Muslims because it is through revelation that man is enabled to attain belief in Allah. Revelation-based belief requires that a Muslim submits to the message of Allah by a trust in a Power Transcendental through Whom everything has become possible. To relate to Allah Almighty, a believer would have to invoke a complete set of intuitive assumptions and values that conjure up images of hope and fear, reward and punishment, Paradise and Hell, good and evil, or this life and the life thereafter. The heart is the chief 'thinking' apparatus. The individual accepts everything revealed from Allah as true and is not supposed to question its validity. An absolute trust in Allah, as a pre-destinator of the course of life, seems to steer the thinking of the believer.

The rise of Arab-Islamic philosophy marked an expansion of the dominantly heart-based thinking process to embrace the intellect. The major task of most Arab-Islamic philosophers, as noted earlier, was to harmonize revelation and

---

[32] Qur'an (33:6)

reason or religion and philosophy. In some cases, reason was given precedence over revelation to produce a rational set of cause-effect relationships. But in the majority of cases, reason and revelation were viewed as sharing full convergence on all issues of intellectual interest. Both were presented as complementing one another in the endless human search for truth. Heart-rooted thought processes are likely to produce an impulsive and ritualistic communication that thrives more on sharing than on a rational exchange of messages. Indulgence in a communication experience is not a pre-meditated act, but is rather a ritual or a habit that confers legitimacy on the living experience. Whether it is part of the devotional rituals or the social interactions, communication is not meant to influence, but to assert common values held by members of the community. In most cases, the outward flows of communication would look spontaneous and grounded in common base of knowledge (revelation). Real communication in Islam takes place only among believers who are rendered equal by virtue of their submission to Allah: 'When thou dost recite the *Qur'an*, we put between thee and those believe not a veil invisible'.[33]

On the other hand, Arab communication has a significant rational ingredient which was behind the various Arab intellectual and scientific contributions to human civilization. The intellect *aql*, as noted earlier was viewed as a blessing from Allah through which Man is elevated to a higher status in the hierarchy of creation. As such, a reason-based thought process often produces communication that is rational, calculated, and influence-oriented. This communication pattern, of course, cannot be fully associated with secular Arab culture, simply because the concept of dignity, on which secular components of the Arab-Islamic world view are based, lends itself much to a good deal of irrationality. In light of the deep permeation of the Islamic faith into the Muslims' life on micro and macro levels, it would be safe to assume that rationality is often subordinated to spontaneity and impulsiveness as a dominant feature of Arab communication.

Although heart-based communication is an important component of interpersonal social interactions in the Arab-Islamic culture, its intra-personal manifestations are immense. One of the outstanding features of Arab-Islamic communication is that it is inwardly-oriented before it takes on more pervasive outward configurations. Inwardly-oriented communication is evident in spiritual contemplation *tasbih*: 'Behold! in the creation of the heavens and the earth; in the alternation of the Night and the Day; In the sailing of the ships through the ocean for the profit of mankind; in the rain which Allah sends down from the skies, and the life which He gives therewith, to an earth that is dead; In the beasts of all kinds that He scatters through the earth; in the change of the winds, and the clouds which they trail like their slaves between the sky and the earth (Here in-

---

[33] Qur'an (17:45)

deed are Signs for a people that are wise'.[34] The authenticity of heart-based belief cannot be ascertained solely by outwardly-oriented expressions: 'Say: Whether ye hide what is in your hearts or reveal it, Allah knows it all: He knows what is in the heavens, and what is on earth. And Allah has power over all things'.[35]

Debates on the notions of faith and reason spawned diverse orientations in Arab-Islamic intellectual traditions. One of them is *al-Ash'aria* which laid the foundation of an orthodox Islamic theology or orthodox *Kalam*, as opposed to the rationalist *Kalam* of the *Mu'tazilites*. In opposition to the extreme orthodox class, *al-Ash'aria* made use of the dialectical method for the defense of the authority of Divine revelation as applied to theological subjects (Valiuddin, 2001). *Al-Ash'ari* maintaines an intermediary position between the two diametrically opposed schools of thought prevailing at the time. At the one extreme end was the *Mu'tazilites* who made reason in preference to revelation the sole criterion of truth and reality and, thus, passed slowly into comparatively innocuous heretics. At the other extreme were the orthodox groups, particularly the *Zahirites*, the *Mujassimites* (anthropomorphists), the *Muhaddithin* (Traditionists), and the Jurists, all of whom were wholly opposed to the use of reason defending or explaining religious dogmas, and condemned any discussion about them as innovation (Valiuddin, 2001). Another dissident group, *Ikhwan al-Safa* formed by a group of libres penseum who cultivated science and philosophy not for the sake of science and philosophy, but in the hope of forming a kind of an ethico spiritual community in which the elites of the heterogeneous Muslim Empire could find a refuge from the struggle that was raging among religious congregations, national societies, and Muslim sects themselves.

III.6.4. Egalitarian-Hierarchical

The egalitarian message of Islam was well-noted earlier in the chapter. All Muslims are equal before Allah, and the most favorite to Allah is the most pious. Sovereignty belonged exclusively to Allah while social power is bestowed on institutions through a process of popular delegation. The Islamic *Wali al-Amr* (leader in charge of) who is the ruler in a generic sense owes the community the establishment of justice in exchange for obedience by community members. Males are granted *quwama* or responsibility over females. Parents in Islamic communities are also provided with a high status within the family. In Arab secular traditions, authority is vested in individuals like the father, the tribal chief or leader, the elderly, the male child, and the rich. Power hierarchies at macro and micro levels have produced highly asymmetrical relationships among

---

[34] Qur'an (2:164)
[35] Qur'an (3:29)

individuals in society. Power holders in Arab culture find a good amount of ego realization through what has been termed 'the politics of charity', that is the extension of benefits to community members not as legal rights, but as charity in exchange for political favors. This benevolent orientation also reflects highly paternalistic attitudes.

Asymmetrical power structures have produced an Arab-Islamic communication that is paternalistic, reflecting centralized control over what is to be communicated and how. Paternalism is rationalized on the basis of the need to maintain and reinforce the collective interests of the population rather than on furthering individual objectives of patriarchy. A poem on behalf of a tribal chief excommunicating a member of the tribe for bringing shame to the family was rationalized by concern for tribal honor. An angry father justifies his fierce and humiliating language as he rebukes a disobedient child by citing his concern for his child's welfare and that of the family. An implicit assumption in this paternalistic orientation is a patriarch's possession (whether he is a father, a brother, a mosque imam, a tribal chief, or a national leader) of a superior vision of what and how ideas should be communicated. While paternalistic communication assumes the superiority of a source's discretion in determining message content and form, it also presupposes receivers' inability to make enlightened decisions on the basis of available information choices. A father, a teacher, or a tribal chief often assume their intellectual superiority by virtue of their more substantive experiences in their respective fields. Yet, in many cases such sense of superiority derives from a socialization process in which the power they hold over their subordinates produces tacit obedience rather than dissent. A child is socialized into accepting his father's harsh rebukes or his teacher's stern corrections because he or she does not view them as adversaries to be reckoned with, but as figures of guidance whose outbursts of anger are meant 'to place him on the right track of life'.

The concept of paternalistic authority has led to viewing Arab-Islamic communication as power. Clan dignitaries used to act as mediators in conflicts in the community more or less by virtue of their communication capabilities. Tribal poets were viewed as part of the political propaganda machine operating in times of crisis, and as symbols of sociopolitical status in times of peace. Like today's TV personalities, tribal chiefs and state leaders who could count on them to defend their tribal and national interest against rival forces held them in high esteem. During the Islamic period, communication was also perceived as a powerful tool for both propagating the faith and maintaining the community *Umma*. But with the establishment of the *Ummayyad* reign (661-750) along tribal lines (the *Ummayyad* clan was dominant), Caliphs began to pay attention to the patronage not only of poets and storytellers, but also of *ulama* (religious scholars) to promote their political line of thinking. The same trend was repeated on a larger scale during the *Abbasid* Caliphate in Baghdad (750-1258) (which belonged to the competing *Hashimite* clan) where more heated theological and intellectual debates took place. Famed poets like Abu Tammam (d. 845), al-Buhturi (d. 897) and al-Mutanabbi (d. 965) were just a few of many literary figures who won Caliphs' attention and support during the Abbasid regime.

III.7. Summary & Conclusions

The main theme of this chapter is that to understand current public sphere realities in the Arab World, we need to gain an insight into the classical genesis of Arab-Islamic moral values and traditions as embedded in the *Qur'an* and *Sunna* as well as tribal traditions. Pre-Islamic Arabian traditions dew on distinctive moral values like lineage, eloquence, paternalism, and honor. Due to Islam's assimilative capacity, these values did exist alongside emerging Islamic traditions. For Arabs, Islam has been the soul that brought life into their bodies, provided them with a human identity, and positioned them as world leaders and innovators in different fields of life. By virtue of its ethical principles and moral values, Islam brought order on the *Umma's* social and cultural life, an order based on justice, equality, freedom, responsibility and submission to Allah. In the political sphere, Islam has embraced a wide range of values and practices that drew on *Shura* (consultation), accountability, community unity, and justice. According to the classical Islamic political theory, leaders are chosen by a select group of knowledgeable and experienced individuals to serve as trustees of religious and temporal interests. Leaders could not be despotic or unjust; they are liable to be sacked if found to be of the true track of justice. The community is not made of submissive subjects, but of vigilant members who share responsibility in running public affairs and ensuring adherence to the values of justice, equality, and unity.

Though Arabs are credited with the spread of the Islamic message into other lands in Persia and Byzantium, their immersion in the spirit of Islam was always shaped by their tribal features. Secular Arab traditions of lineage, eloquence, paternalism and honor continued to define their worldview as they sought to reconcile some of their good pre-Islamic traditions with the spiritual values of Islam that included monotheism, divinity, message, *Khilafa*, justice, community, knowledge, equality, responsibility, and *Shura*. Tribal communication values were also combined with Islamic communication norms like respect, piety, honesty, brotherhood, justice, responsibility, mercy, and freedom. The resulting discourse has been somehow flawed because of the tensions between the two sets of moral values embedded in secular-tribal and religious-Islamic traditions. Features of the classical discourse included dichotomies like: individual-conformist, transcendental-existential, egalitarian-hierarchal and intuitive-rational. The author argues that such tensions have been carried on to contemporary Arab discourse which has apparently failed to reconcile the traditional and modern ingredients of thought processes and argumentation.

IV
THE MODERN ARAB PUBLIC SPHERE

> *For more than a century, mass media in the Middle East have been considered phenomena from the West- products, so to speak, of the impact of the West upon the Middle East. However, the mass media have been used as tools of nationalism or Islamic universalism throughout the recent history of the Middle Eastern societies. In most countries of the Middle East, the spirit of independence at times became fully articulated through the combination of journalism and literature. Therefore, as the waves of anti-colonialism and anti-imperialism broke upon the Middle East, journalism, literature, and politics became identified with one another. Indeed, a common characteristic noted in all the Middle East countries is the historically close relationship between the mass media and political reforms.*
> *(Kamalipour and Mowlana, 1994).*

To understand the dynamics of the emerging Arab public sphere of the early 21st century, it is not enough to grasp the basic intellectual premises and moral values embedded in classical Arab-Islamic traditions. Significant features of the new Arab political communication arena lend themselves to the modern Arab public sphere that had emerged from 1798 (when Napoleon's expeditionary troops landed on Alexandria beaches) to the late 1980s (when the end of the Cold War heralded a new age of globalization in contemporary human history). The writer argues that this period had witnessed the rise and fall of the modern Arab public sphere which, for two centuries, had remained captive to historical trans-fixation and political authoritarianism. A wide range of political and media features, established in this 200-year period, were inherited from the classical traditions noted in Chapter III, and they continue to bear on Arab political communication realities in the age of globalization as we will see in Chapters V & VI. Because of its intermediary historical location between classical and globalization eras, this period has generated pioneering intellectual debates as Arabs and the West experienced their first-hand encounters in the contexts of both domination and modernization. During this modern period, Arab media did not evolve within indigenous and contemporary political traditions, but rather within two broad historical contexts: foreign domination (Ottoman and colonial European) and Cold War politics. In the first context, media served as forums for national liberation and cultural assertion. In the post-colonial context, nation-building efforts were shrouded in modernization and political independence discourse. Across these two historical contexts, the central question of *Nahda* (Renaissance) remained an outstanding issue on political and cultural agendas as Arab societies continued a long-time search for identity, carrying this quest forward into the post-modern era of globalization. In colonial and post-colonial contexts, the democratic discourse was missing as Arabs grappled with national liberation, pan-Arab unity, and national development challenges. The absence of participatory political arrangements in the majority of Arab societies during Ottoman, colonial, and independence phases of their modern history degenerated by the mid 1980s into a mass-mediated public sphere handicapped by paternalism, political authoritarianism, and ideological and cultural disorientation.

This chapter surveys the historical development of the Arab mass-mediated public sphere since Napoleon's expedition to Egypt in 1798 with a prime focus on the media landscape in the post-colonial Cold War era extending into the mid 1980s. As noted earlier, this period was significant for modern Arab development as it embraced the most influential political and intellectual ferment in contemporary Arab history. In this era, new political orientations were established with respect to the tradition-modernity nexus which formed the ideological backbone for contemporary Arab World political and cultural debates. The writer argues here that Napoleon's expedition to Egypt in 1798 sent out shockwaves throughout the Arab World mainly because it marked Arabs' first-hand exposure to a European power in modern history both as an invader and as a carrier of modernity. In significant ways, Napoleon's expedition initiated a new phase of Arab World history characterized by a transition into a more intense intellectual ferment centering on defining the parameters and substance of Arab identity in the midst of growing foreign and cultural rivalry. For 200 years, debates over Arab identity and development vis-à-vis Western models shaped the Arab public sphere during Ottoman, colonial, and independence periods. Public discussions of how to achieve the promised *Nahda* (Renaissance) in modern Arab societies spawned a wide range of ideological and political orientations drawing on Islamic and secular perspectives of society and the state. Mass media, especially newspapers, were key channels for communicating those views. The writer argues that the modern Arab public sphere failed primarily because Arabs could not conceive and apply sound governance practices drawing on a synthesis of classical and contemporary political traditions.

IV.1. The Arab World Media Scene: 1798-1990

When Napoleon carried out his historic expeditionary mission in Egypt in 1798, he was able to gain a direct view of a traditional Arab social and political system marked by strong religious affiliation, intense family and tribal solidarity, and widespread allegiance to the Ottoman Caliph, symbol of the Muslim *Umma*. Community members subscribed to a central Islamic ethos that permeated political, legal, and cultural institutions and shaped social relations in Egypt's consensus-oriented conservative communities. An enduring question contemplated by Napoleon's men as well as by Egyptian intellectual and political communities at the time related to the potential for Egypt's transition from 'tradition' into modernity. Ever since, Western intellectual approaches to the Arab World, either through Orientalism or other frameworks, have centered on the tradition-modernity nexus as composed of two-mutually-exclusive human conditions. Such idea established the genesis for what later came to be known as the 'modernization paradigm' that defined national development approaches in Third World, including Arab societies, in the 20th century. But when dominant imperial Ottoman and nationalist Arab tendencies came to a point of collision at the end of the 19th century, the question of *Nahda* (Renaissance) and Arabs' cultural assertiveness vis-à-vis both the Turks and the Europeans began to dominate intellectual discourse.

A specific perennial outcome of Napoleon's expedition to Egypt in 1798 was the introduction of the printing press that laid the ground for launching the first newspaper in the Arab World. In different parts of Turkish-dominated Arab countries, newspapers were established both as official government mouthpieces and outlets of nationalist ambitions. The same dual functions of the press were noted during the colonial period. In both cases, the press was serving as a public arena for contesting views on issues pertaining to identity, pan-Arab unity, Islamic revivalism, freedom, justice and independence (Abd al-Rahman, 1995). In the post-colonial period, however, the emergence of independent Arab states with generally authoritarian political orientations produced a media sphere characterized as exclusivist, monologist, and formalistic (al-Karni, 1994). The decline of civil society institutions, coupled with the establishment of centralized state-controlled press and broadcast systems in Arab countries turned the public sphere into a public arena for promoting government perspectives as the only viable choices for social development. Al-Jaberi (1982) remarks that upon their awakening on the eve of the 19th century, Arabs found themselves grappling with two cultural models: the European model which presented them with cultural and military challenges, prodding them to address the issue of 'renaissance'. The second model is that of the Arab-Islamic culture which formed a backup frame of reference needed for dealing with the first challenge. Since the European model simultaneously carried with it 'freedom' and repression (Liberal ideology and colonial intervention), and since the Arab-Islamic model presented itself through a long and broad pile of stagnation and 'collapse', Arabs' choices were bound to reflect a state of ambivalence in which feelings of both love and hatred were exhibited towards the same subject. What follows is an overview of the development of Arab media in the context of both foreign domination and national independence.

IV.1.1. The Foreign Domination Context

This includes over 100 years of Turkish rule and over a century of European colonial domination of Arabian lands. This context was instrumental in defining press discourse and shaping its institutional character. Al-Jaberi (1982) notes that Arabs, in seeking to achieve renaissance, were required to deal with the European model while keeping silent on its colonial aspects, something that was not possible simply because European colonialism impeded Arabs' progress and threatened their existence. 'Hence, it has to be opposed, exposed, and resisted.' On the other hand, dealing with the Arab-Islamic model also required keeping silent on long centuries of 'decadence', and such silence seemed not possible because those 'centuries of decadence' were part of this very model and were strongly visible in its discourse. Tensions inherent in those debates, as noted by al-Jaberi, centered on the question of Arab identity in the midst of rising foreign power domination of their lands. The media were integral players in those discussions both as mouthpieces of dominant foreign powers and voices of indigenous orientations.

IV.1.1.1. The Ottoman Era

By the end of the 18th century, the Turkish Empire was already showing signs of disintegration as European winds of change began to blow on an area extending from the eastern coast of the Atlantic Ocean in the West to the Arabian Gulf in the East. As Europeans started their colonial expansion in the southern Mediterranean region in Africa and the Middle East, their confrontation with the five-century Ottoman domination of the region seemed highly unavoidable. Equipped with more advanced military and economic resources and capabilities as well as with liberal social and political values and practices, European powers found in the Turkish-dominated region a convenient and attractive prey as the old empire was turning more and more into 'the ill man'. At a certain point, the Ottomans found themselves fighting on two fronts: the external front brought about by growing European threats to Turkish interests as manifested in the war with Russia in 1877, and the internal front created by increasing religious and nationalist tensions emanating from what were perceived as European-induced nationalist sentiments in different parts of the Ottoman Empire, including the Arab World. For four centuries, the Ottoman Empire had controlled huge areas of the Arab World, safeguarding them against European domination; yet contributing to keeping them transfixed in classical history.

The dramatic landing of French troops on Alexandria in the scorching summer of 1798 and the swift conquest of Egypt that followed had an impact on the Egyptians more dramatic than that which the gradual exposure to Europe had had on the Ottomans during the preceding century. Among other things, the presence of French troops alongside scholars and scientists in Egypt created a shock among the country's leadership and population at large. The trauma of the encounter with the might of modern Europe, Muhammad Ali's ambitious outlook, and Egypt's convenient socio-political cohesion, all combined to put the country on a course of change more rapid than in any other part of the Ottoman Empire, including its Turkish-speaking center. Ayalon (1995: 12) notes that this sweeping transformation was evident in myriad ways, not least in the development of modern communications: Egypt had an official printed bulletin several years before the Ottoman capital did, despite Istanbul's earlier awareness of that potentially powerful medium. The first periodical to appear in an Arabic-speaking land was in French: *Le Courier de L'Egypte*, published by Napoleon's administration in August 1798. Later, the French initiated a newsletter of daily work accounts entitled *al-Hawadith al-Yawmiya* (Daily Events) which was translated into French for circulation among expeditionary personnel. According to Muruwa (1961), *al-Hawadith al-Yawmiya* was the mother of all Arab newspapers. The implications of Napoleon's modern, skillfully-directed propaganda machine bore fruit when Muhammad Ali, the Ottoman officer of Albanian origin who became Egypt's ruler for four decades (1805-1848), demonstrated affection to the French printing press. He launched the first Arabic printing press (*Bulaq* Press) in Egypt in 1819 and made serious efforts to establish sustainable press operations in the country by dispatching Egyptian students to learn modern printing techniques in Europe and setting up local paper mills (Muruwa, 1961).

For Muhammad Ali, the printing press carried promising opportunities for his administration to promote its views and policies and to enhance work efficiency in government departments. Muhammad Ali tried to stimulate the modernization of agriculture as well as industrialization in Egypt, taking Europe as his model. Some Egyptian historians viewed him as the father of modern Egypt and the broader Arab world, the precursor of Arab reformism, nationalism and *Nahda* (Renaissance) (Ayalon, 1995). By the end of his reign, the state-monopolized printing presses produced not only books, mostly translations of European texts, but also original works. In addition, Muhammad Ali also carried out a major restructuring of written communications by issuing a bilingual Arabic-Turkish register to be printed in 1828 under the title *Jurnal al-Kihdiwi*, as the first printed Arabic periodical intended for official usage. Like its predecessor, the paper carried official notices, reports on developments in the capital and in the provinces, as well as stories from the *Thousand and One Nights* (Ayalon, 1995: 14). In 1828 *Jurnal al-Kihdiwi* was succeeded by another publication named *al Waqai' al-Misriya* (Egyptian Events) which served as an effective communication outlet in the country's governmental administration as it was used as an information tool catering to the small circle of high executives and army officers, in addition to local notables, senior *Ulama* (clerics), school teachers, and students. Muhammad Ali's visionary leadership foresaw a central role for such elite audience in the future nation-building projects he was pursuing; hoping to integrate all of them into his ambitious development plans. To this end, *al-Waqai' al-Misriya* carried news of different projects carried out by Muhammad Ali's administration, in addition to instructions and official notices regarding the functions of different departments (Dabbous, 1994).

While the press in its formative period developed in Egypt as part of Muhammad Ali's visionary renaissance projects, the story of its initial development in French-dominated North African countries and Turkish-controlled Arab East was fairly different. Arab newspapers developed under Turkish rule both as outlets for nationalist orientations as well as tools of Ottoman domination of Arabian societies in an era marked by growing colonial rivalry. Reflecting evolving varied nationalist social and intellectual orientations at the time, newspapers appearing in the 19th century provided forums for debates on a wide range of issues relating to *Nahda* discourse. In 1855, Rizqallah Hasoun was the first Arab to publish a newspaper in Constantinople named *Miraat al-Ahwal Arabiya*, followed by Khalil Khouri's *'Hadiqat al-Akhbar'* published in 1858 in Beirut (Muruwa, 1961: 144). In French-colonized North Africa, Kirat (1993: 18) observes that the French introduced the press in Algeria to establish communication networks between the metropolis and the new colony; to inform the settlers and to diffuse their ideology among the Algerian notables and masses. In 1860, *'al-Raid al-Tunisi'* was published in Tunis; *'Tarablus al-Gharb'* Tripoli in 1866, and *al-Maghrib* in Morocco in 1889.

By the end of the 19th century, the Arab press terrain was dotted with scores of new publications with missionary, intellectual and most importantly political orientations. Egypt witnessed the birth of newspapers like *Wadi Nil* (1866), *Nuzhat al-Afkar* (1869) *al-Ahram* (1876); *al-Mahrusa* (1880), *al-Muqattam* (1889), *al-Muayid* (1889), and *al-Liwa* (1900). In Algeria, *al-Mubashir* was published in French in 1847, followed by the Arabic *al-Nasih* in 1899. Azzi (1998), however, notes that the first paper to appear in the Arab North African region was Africa Liberal, a Spanish paper published in Sebta, Morocco in 1820. In Lebanon, as noted earlier, *Hadiqat al-Akhbar* was published in 1858, followed by *Nafir Suriya* (1860), and *al-Bashir* (1870). In neighboring Syria, *Suriya* was published in 1865, followed by *Ghadir al-Furat* (1867), *Shahbaa* (1877), and *Miraat al-Akhlaq* (1886). In Iraq, the first Arabic paper was *al-Zawra* published in 1869, followed by several publications carrying the names of *al-Mosul* (1885), *al-Basra* (1895), and *Baghdad* (1897). In Yemen, the only newspaper published in the 19th century was *Sana'a* (1879) which was a mouthpiece for Ottoman authorities. Palestine and Jordan had no publications in the 19th century (Muruwa, 1961).

Newspapers appearing in Arab countries until the demise of the Turkish Empire were either published by private persons or groups or by government organs to serve as tools of public communication or political indoctrination. It is interesting to note that the Arab press, in its formative phase of development, was credited to Christian Arabs, especially Lebanese, who were attracted to this emerging journalism field as a venue for new interactions with the West. Most of the newspapers carried news of Turkish *Walis* (governors) and glorified the Turkish positions as defenders of Islam against Western onslaughts. It was clear that the discourse carried by the pro-Turkish press was drawing on invoking religious emotions on the part of Muslim populations to stand up to European threats. The pro-Turkish press, especially that sponsored by local Ottoman *Walis*, utilized emotional religious appeals to appease Muslim populations in the Arab world through community leaders like mosque *Imams* and local dignitaries as well as tribal chiefs (Askar, 1982). Those leaders often had a great deal of social and moral credibility and enjoyed high levels of trust among segments of the population with some elementary language and religious education. On the other hand, official Turkish publications were also targeting nationalist Arab movements for what was perceived as their role in promoting the disintegration of the Turkish Empire. Limited literacy rates among Arab populations during the Turkish rule inhibited the widespread circulation of publications, thus rendering most of them virtually ineffective. Only the few who could afford to read in Arabic had access to those publications which were circulated in government departments. The Turks, to some extent, were counting heavily on community leaders to orally communicate press messages to the illiterate masses, especially in remote non-urban centers (Ayalon, 1995).

On the other hand, as the Turkish Empire was experiencing tense political and social strife caused by domestic nationalistic insurgencies and foreign threats, the press was an important player in those developments. Colored with mostly Western liberal orientations, local publications were glorifying Arab nationalism as distinct from Turkish nationalism, often calling for Arab independence from Ottoman domination. Harsh Turkish policies contributed to the rise of pan-Arab movements, calling for the end to Turkish domination of Arab lands with inspiration from liberal European traditions. That movement also received support from European colonial powers like the French in North Africa, Lebanon and Syria, and the British in Jordan, Palestine, Iraq and Yemen. Because of their nationalist orientations, some local Arab newspapers went underground to avoid Turkish reprisals. Clandestine Arab publications were circulated in major urban centers like Baghdad, Damascus, Beirut and Cairo with calls for revolt against the Turkish rule. *Al-Mushir*, which was launched in 1894 by Lebanese Salim Sarkis, adopted hostile positions towards Turkish rule in the Arab World. Lebanese Shakib Arsalan published a poem in the paper echoing nationalist Arab and anti-Turkish sentiments (Muruwa, 1961: 198):

> I have found an Arab Nation of whom Turks see Negroes as more noble.
> They have harbored hatred for Arabs because the Noblest Creature (Prophet Muhammad) was not a Non-Arab.

The growth of the press during the Turkish reign came as Arab societies were engaging in major (elitist) debates over issues of political identity, independence, modernization and Islamic revival. In specific terms, discussions centered on how Islamic enlightenment could be achieved by synthesizing Western social and material frames of reference with Islamic norms and values. Early leaders, such as Muhammad Ali (1805-1809), adopted an eclectic approach to Western civilization, importing military technology, without disturbing indigenous social and cultural equilibrium. The initial process of transformation, therefore, drew on a narrow borrowing of new military organization and technology; but it turned out later that other social and economic institutions could not escape the effects of such reforms. That situation prompted many at the time to call for a comprehensive social, political and cultural disengagement from traditional systems. On the other hand, another stream of thought argued for a more conservative formula for change by developing an original Islamic system that preserves the social and cultural identity of Islamic communities (Abd al-Rahman, 1995).

The most outstanding figures in that debate were Rifa'a Tahtawi (1801-1873), Khairuddin al-Tunisi (1810-99), Jamaluddin al-Afghani (1838-97), Mohammad Abdu (1849-1905) and Abd al-Rahman al-Kawakbi (1849-1903). Rifaat al-Tahtawi, widely viewed as the father of modern Egyptian democracy, was an outspoken advocate of transferring Western enlightenment orientations into the Arab world. In his book *Takhlis al-Ibriz Ila Talkhis Bariz*, (1834), Tahtawi, who lived in Paris as part of an Egyptian team of students and scholars dispatched by Muhammad Ali to France, provided detailed descriptions of French social customs and values which he praised as conducive to democracy and development (Tamimi, 1997). He observed that the French concept of democracy was compatible with the law and spirit of Islam as evident in the concept of justice. He compared political pluralism to forms of ideological and jurisprudential pluralism that existed in the Islamic experience: Religious freedom is the freedom of belief, of opinion and of sect, provided it does not contradict the fundamentals of religion. His revivalist perspectives were featured in newspapers such as *al-Waqai' al-Misriya*. Another important figure in that era was Khairuddin at-Tunisi (1810-99), leader of the 19th-century reform movement in Tunisia, who, in 1867, formulated a general plan for reform in a book entitled *Aqwam al-Masalik Fi Taqwim al-Mamalik* (The Straight Path to Reforming Governments). In his book he appealed to politicians and scholars of his time to seek all possible means to improve the status of the *Umma*. He warned the general Muslim public against shunning the experiences of other nations on the basis of misconceptions that all the writings, inventions, experiences or attitudes of non-Muslims should be rejected or disregarded (Tamimi, 1997).

To some extent, the press, despite its growing political polarization in the late 19th century, was an open arena for public discussions on Islamic revival and modernization initiated by the aforementioned thinkers. In that period, three prominent Muslim revivalist thinkers: Jamaluddin al-Afghani and Muhammad Abdu (in Egypt) and Abd al-Rahman al-Kawakbi (in Syria) were central contributors to the intellectual debates which were also featured in the press. Al-Afghani argued that it was due to the absence of *Adl* (justice) and *Shura* (consultation) and non-adherence by the government to the constitution that Muslim societies were living in backward conditions. He called for empowering people to participate in governing through *Shura* and elections. In an article entitled 'The Despotic Government', published in *Misr* newspaper on 14 February 1879, al-Afghani attributed Muslims' backwardness to despotism which inhibited the enlightenment of the public about the nature and virtues of the 'republican government', noting that 'those governed by a republican form of government alone deserve to be called human; for a true human being is only subdued by a true law that is based on the foundations of justice and that is designed to govern man's moves, actions, transactions and relations with others in a manner that elevates him to the pinnacle of true happiness' (Tamimi, 1997). Abdu, a companion of al-Afghani, believed that Islam's relationship with the modern age was the most crucial issue that Islamic communities needed to address. In an attempt to reconcile Islamic ideas with Western ones, he suggested that *Maslaha* (interest) in Islamic thought corresponded to *Manfa'a* (utility) in Western thought. Similarly, he equated *Shura* with democracy and *Ijma'* with consensus. Addressing the question of authority, Abdu denied the existence of a theocracy in Islam and insisted that the authority of the Hakim (governor) or that of the Qadi (judge) or that of the Mufti was civil. He strongly believed that *Ijtihad* should be revived because ' ...emerging priorities and problems, which are new to the Islamic thought, need to be addressed'. He was a strong advocate of the parliamentary system and defended pluralism, refuting claims that it would undermine the unity of *Umma*. Al-Kawakbi was the first Syrian to establish *al-Shahba* newspaper (1877) in partnership with Hashim al-Attar before he left to launch *al-Itidal* (Moderation) in 1879. In his book 'Features of Despotism (*Tabai al-Istibdad*), al-Kawakbi attributed the backwardness of the *Umma* to the absence of justice and the entrenchment of despotism in Muslim societies (Nooh, 2003).

In addition to engaging in that intellectual discourse, the Arab press in the late 19th century was also fighting on the nationalist front as Arab lands were gradually coming under European domination. The deteriorating situation in Egypt marked by the ouster of Kidivi Ismael in 1778 and the rise of British influence in the country prompted fierce reactions from the local intelligentsia and the press. Abd al-Rahman (1985: 25) notes that growing tensions among major players in the Egyptian arena were accompanied by significant political polarization in the press. In response to the defeat of Ahmad Urabi at the hands of British occupation troops in 1882, writers waged a battle for reform; their publications were considered as weapons, the best the country could produce at the time. Many of their periodicals carried titles like 'Young Egypt', 'Homeland', or 'Egypt'. They lashed out at Ismael, expressing the discontent of the small educated class with his autocracy and inadequate performance and helping create the atmosphere that, along with other factors, brought about his dethronement in June 1879 (Ayalon, 1995). *Al-Ahram*, which was established by the Taqla brothers from Lebanon in 1875, opened its columns to the leader of the anti-British nationalist movement, Mustafa Kemal. The British responded by suspending the paper for a month in 1884, a move that drew strong French protest as *al-Ahram* was believed to be a French mouthpiece. *Al-Mutative*, on the other hand, was a pro-British paper that was succeeded by *al-Muqattam* on Feb. 14, 1889, as a weekly that became a daily within six weeks. In mid 1889, the situation of two leading newspapers in Egypt (*al-Ahram* and *al-Muqattam*) owned by Christian immigrants and backed by two major colonial powers was both alarming and distressing for the local Egyptian intelligentsia (Saleh, 1995). At the end of the year, a new daily appeared in Cairo, *al-Mu'ayyad*, the first powerful voice of anti-British protest, was initiated by Ali Yosuf (1863-1913), an acetic Muslim from a humble family in upper Egypt with some experience in journalism (Yunis, 2003).

An important feature of the Arab press under Ottoman rule was its development in a context of high political patriarchy, thus precluding the rise of solid traditions of media independence. Rugh (1979: 6) notes that Arab information media have always been closely tied to government organs, serving as official mouthpieces for state interests. Muruwa (1961: 143) remarked that the *Courier de l'Egypte*, the first newspaper printed in Egypt on Napoleon's own press in 1798 was intended to inform and instruct French expeditionary forces and improve their morale as they handled different challenges in the country. When Muhammad Ali decided to integrate printing into his nascent modern administration, he ordered the publication of *Jurnal al-Khidivi* in 1827 which was changed into al *Waqa'i al-Misriya* in 1828 to serve as a conduit for official government views and instructions. A host of government-sponsored publications surfaced in the 19th century, underscoring official recognition of the centrality of print media in shaping political developments. Ayalon (1995: 11) noted that as with so many modern innovations in the Middle East, launching newspapers was, at first, the exclusive prerogative of government. In the Ottoman capital, in Egypt, and in several other provinces, official bulletins were the only indigenous periodical for several decades. Aziz (1968: 12) noted that the Egyptian press was born in the patronage of rulers, and initially survived on their subsidies; grew up with their authority; was subjected to their directives; and had no other viable choices in the first half of the 19th century.

Another important aspect of the press development in the Ottoman era was the limited margin of freedom accorded to different publications. Since its formative years, the Arab press was subjected to inhibitive legal provisions that undermined its ability to create a genuine public sphere. Ayalon (1995: 111) notes that when exposure to Western culture generated a demand for newspapers, governments responded by introducing restrictive legislation and by setting up specialized bodies to enforce it. Suppression was one aspect of the response. Another was manipulation and co-option through selective subsidization. The Ottoman Law of 1857 was the earliest legislation bearing on the press as it required anyone wishing to start a publication to obtain permission from two separate authorities: the Council of Education, and the Ministry of Police. Among other things, the legislation required submission of text intended for publication for prior approval by the Council. In the following year, a Penal Code fixed punishments of closure and fines for printing unapproved matter or any 'material harmful to the Sultanate, its government, and its subject peoples' (Cioeta, 1979: 86). Local authorities in some parts of the Ottoman Empire were also able to issue regulations concerning all publications. In Egypt, one rule applied to anyone wishing to publish journals, gazettes, and notices, pledging to prevent the production of 'books and messages offensive to the faith, politics, cultural values, and ethics' (Saleh, 1995). Yet, the first Ottoman law expressly dealing with the press was the 'Law of Journalistic Publications' of 1865 which prescribed additional penalties for offenders. The law remained in effect throughout the Empire until the Young Turk revolution against Sultan Abdul Hamid in 1909.

In French-dominated North Africa, the presence of the colonial press induced local populations to give serious attention to the role such publications could play in fostering people's attachment to their culture and heritage (Azzi, 1998). The press law of 1881 considered Arabic language as a foreign language in the French colonies in Morocco, Algeria and Tunisia. Printing in Arabic and the importation of Arabic papers and documents were considered serious violations of the law, and thus could not be permitted. This law also postulated that only those enjoying civil rights were permitted to issue a publication (Azzi, 1998). The local populations were apparently required to seek French nationality and adopt French language and culture to possibly acquire such rights. This undertaking was rejected by the majority of the people who actually sought to use the press to preserve their Islamic identity and affinity with the Muslim *Umma*. Algerian Ben Badis' statement: 'People of Algeria are Muslims and to the Arab Nation they belong' was characteristic of the prevailing popular sentiment affirming the cultural identity of Algerians at the time.

IV.1.1.2. European Colonial Era

World War I was viewed by many historians as the final battle in a five-century European-Ottoman confrontation. The war ended in the defeat of Turkey and its allies, thus enabling colonial powers, namely Britain and France to extend their domination into the rest of the former Turkish-controlled territories. At the conclusion of the war, North Africa was already controlled by the French and so was Egypt by the British. Libya became an Italian colony and so did Syria and Lebanon (French colonies) and Palestine, Trans-Jordan and Iraq (British colonies). The end of the war was accompanied by rising expectations on the part of Arabs for freedom. But when colonial British and French powers reneged on their promises for granting independence to Arab countries, the region, extending from Morocco to the Arabian Gulf, turned into a bastion of revolt against European colonialism. During the interwar period (1918-1945) dynamic developments in the region produced a politically zealous press and provided a powerful incentive for its growth by enhancing public interest in news and opinion. The press was an integral part of anti-colonial struggle for independence and served as a voice for nationalist leaders as they called for an end to foreign domination of Arab lands.

Striking variations are noted among European colonial attitudes towards the press. In Egypt, hundreds of publications representing government, partisan and private interests were emerging as influential voices in debates over independence and freedom. The press role in nationalist movements was evident in *al-Ahram* which turned anti-British, followed by *al-Akhbar* which appeared in 1920 as the organ of the Nationalist Party. While Egypt enjoyed broader democratic privileges under British rule, Syria, Lebanon, Algeria, Tunisia and Morocco were subjected to repressive French practices. The French colonial policy of suffocating local voices pre-empted the emergence of a vigorous press in Syria, Lebanon, Algeria, Tunisia and Morocco. In the immediate post-World War I period, Egypt had formally gained independence in February 1922; had its own king in March 1923; and at the end of the year had a new constitution that permitted the election of a parliament (Ayalon, 1995: 75). The replacement of autocracy by constitutional monarchy, along with the British presence in the country created tensions that led to the evolution of a dynamic political press representing diverse orientations. Egyptian nationalists led by Saad Zaghloul espoused the cause of independence through the indigenous press (Saleh, 1995).

Ayalon (1995: 78) notes that the political writers of this period were preoccupied with four separate issues: ideological and political conflicts within and among political parties; the confrontation with the foreign-installed governments and their supporters, primarily over the question of press freedom; the battles against the foreign presence; and the long-standing but still intense debate over the desired cultural identity of the new community. Kings Fuad and Faruq came under fire for yielding to the British, for poor performance in domestic matters, and above all for their autocratic style and their encroachment upon freedom of expression (Abd al-Rahman, 1985). In Syria, Ayalon (1995: 85) notes that the first paper appeared in the colonial era in 1918 under title *al-Istiqlal al-Arabi*. In the 22 months until the arrival of French troops, a total of 42 newspapers and 13 periodicals were circulated. The French tried to keep the press under control through manipulation and, when needed, through punishment. They resorted to licensing, suspension, imprisonment. The Ottoman press law was nullified in April 1924 and immediately replaced by an equally rigorous law. The inter-war period was also marked by a struggle for independence against foreign domination and many newspapers were established to undertake that struggle. The *Kutla al-Wataniya* was established and several newspapers voiced its nationalist views and anti-French positions. Between 1918 and 1939, no less than 250 new Arabic journals appeared in Lebanon. But Lebanon's political and communal mosaic precluded the emergence of a broadly-based leadership that could articulate a national program and attract widespread popular recognition. *Beirut* was published as a pan-Arabism paper in 1936, while a Phalange paper *al-Anal* (Action) was launched in 1938. Four years later, *al-Nadia* Muslim group published *al-Hadaf.* In the 1930s, the suspension of the constitution and the formation of Bishara al-Khouri's anti-French bloc increased tensions between French authorities and local segments and leaderships with the press serving as an arena for that conflict (Muruwa, 1961).

While the rise of the Arab press under Turkish rule was accompanied by vigorous intellectual debates on the question of *Nahda* (Renaissance) as led by Tahtawi, Abdu, al-Kawakbi, al-Afghani, the interwar period was also marked by an equally forceful political and ideological advocacy defining Islamic and nationalist orientations. Rashid Rida, Abdu's disciple, published *al-Manar* Journal which attracted a readership of Islamic intellectuals who shared Rida's specific additions to the thoughts of his mentors al-Afghani and Abdu, namely the condemnation of innovations in doctrine and worship and the acceptance of the rights of reason and public welfare in matters of social morality. Hassan al-Banna, who frequented Rida's circle, and who founded the Muslim Brotherhood in 1928, was critical of the evolving concept of the nation state as an alternative to the defunct Ottoman Caliphate. From that moment on, the Muslim Brotherhood launched the struggle for the return of the Islamic Caliphate as a unified state embracing Muslims around the world. Al-Banna noted that in light of their colonial hegemony, the Europeans ceased to be a model for Muslims as they were blamed for the ills of the *Umma*. Noting the mission of the Muslim Brotherhood as one of re-awakening and deliverance, al-Banna called for freeing the Islamic homeland from all foreign power and for establishing an Islamic state within this homeland, which acts according to the precepts of Islam, applies its social regulations, advocates its sound principles; and transmits its mission to all mankind. Leaders of the Muslim Brotherhood took a special interest in stressing that their movement was established in response to the downfall of the Ottoman Caliphate whose restoration was conceived as a religious duty incumbent upon every single Muslim man and woman (Qutb, 1966). Al-Banna called for the re-establishment of Islamic system on three foundations: the ruler's accountability to Allah and to the public, the unity of the *Umma* within a framework of brotherhood, and respect for the will of the *Umma* and its right to check its rulers who are obliged to respect its will and opinions.

Sayyid Qutb (1906-66), a disciple of Hassan al-Banna became the leading ideologue of the Muslim Brotherhood from the mid-fifties. His book *Maalim fi Tariq* (Milestones), which was written in response to Nasser's persecution of the Muslim Brotherhood, acquired wide acclaim. He advanced the thesis of *jahiliya* (ignorance, barbarity or idolatry), from which Islam came to deliver the world. Qutb divided social systems into two categories: the order of Islam and the order of *jahiliya*, which was decadent and ignorant, the type which had existed in Arabia before the Prophet Muhammad received the Word of Allah, when men revered not Allah but other men disguised as deities (Qutb, 1966). Drawing from the theory of al-Maududi (2004) that as Islam had reverted to a state of *Jahiliya*, 'true Muslims find themselves in a state of war against the apostates', Qutb concluded that true Muslims, the *Tali'a* (vanguards), are and must be set apart within the ambient infidel society as a sort of 'counter-society' (Qutb, 1966). However, as far as democracy is concerned, Qutb went much farther than al-Maududi, rejecting the concept altogether, denouncing it as alien, incompatible, and *jahili*. The term *hakimiya* (sovereignty), which Qutb constantly referred to while arguing against man-made political systems (*Wade*), was originally coined by al-Mawdudi, who used it to distinguish between Islamic and *jahili* societies.

In the Arab *Maghrib* (North Africa) region, a different school of thought was developing, largely inspired by the 19th-century reform movement of Khairuddin at-Tunisi and the ideas of Abdul, Bin Badis, al-Tha'alibi, al-Taher al-Haddad, 'Allal al-Fasi and others. Algerian thinker of French culture, Malik Bennabi, however, is credited with having laid the foundations of this modern Maghreb school of thought. Bennabi (1905-73) believed that the advent of European colonialism to Muslim land had enabled Muslims to escape from their decadence as caused by the emergence of a type of mind incapable of thought and afflicted with moral paralysis, by breaking up their rigid social order and freeing them from belief in occult forces and fantasies (Tamimi, 1997). For over three decades, Bennabi generated a huge intellectual output on what he called as 'grand issues' like Islam and democracy and socio-economic development. In addressing those 'grand issues', Bennabi pointed out that defining the concepts of 'Islam' and 'democracy' in a conventional manner would lead to the conclusion that, with respect to time and location, the connection between the two is non-existent. He suggested that deconstructing the concepts in isolation from their historical connotations and re-defining democracy in its broadest terms without linguistic derivatives and free from any ideological implications, would lead to a different conclusion. 'Democracy', he said, 'ought to be looked at from three angles: democracy as a sentiment toward the ego, democracy as a sentiment toward the other, and democracy as the combination of the socio-political conditions necessary for the formation and development of such sentiments in the individual' (Tamimi, 1997).

In the meantime, a secular movement based more on Arab nationalism than on Islamic *Aqida* (Ideology) was taking shape in the region during the colonial era. Arab nationalism refers to a common nationalist ideology in the wider Arab world defining a claim to common heritage – that all Arabs are united by a shared history, culture, and language. In the immediate pre-First World War period, before the end of the Ottoman Empire, Arab nationalism was not yet a prominent political force primarily because Arabs conceived of Islam as the strongest social and political adhesive bond for the *Umma*. The ideologies of Ottomanism and Pan-Islamism were stronger than Arab nationalism. Arab nationalist thought was confined to a few intellectual personalities and circles located mostly in Beirut and Cairo. But as the Ottoman Empire turned more aggressively nationalistic than Islamic, consciousness of Arab identity began to evolve into well-defined political and ideological orientations. The rise of the Young Turks and CUP alienated many of the Ottoman Empire's supporters in the Arab lands. The powerful Arab families and clans, excluded by the new governments in Istanbul, turned towards Arabism as an alternative political choice, playing upon the ethnic divisions between Arabs and Turks, especially as the CUP government was also accused of trying to 'Turkify' the empire. This new spirit became manifest in the Arab Revolt in Mecca during the First World War. Kramer (2003) notes that Arabism first arose in the nineteenth century not as a direct reaction to Western rule, but as a critique of the state of the Ottoman Empire, whose reach had extended over most of the Arabic-speaking peoples since the early sixteenth century. During the war, the British had been a major sponsor of Arab nationalist thought and ideology, mainly to counter Ottoman Empire. In the interwar years and the British-French mandate period, Arab nationalism became an important anti-colonial opposition movement against British and French colonial rule. Dawisha (2003) identifies Sati' al-Husri as a seminal Arab intellectual who truly introduced nationalism to the Arab world. Other important Arab nationalist thinkers include Michel Aflaq and Antun Sa'adah. Ideas promoted by these nationalist intellectual leaders formed the basis for pan-Arab political systems in Egypt (during Nasser), Syria, Libya, Yemen, and Iraq.

As in the previous Ottoman era, the press in the interwar period was marked by colonial and partisan patronage that shaped its handling of political issues and events. During the colonial era, media began to take on partisan features as new political affiliations emerged in different parts of the Arab region. Ayalon (1995: 73) noted that the period from 1918-1945 was marked by an impressive growth of publications and by the rise of a politically-zealous press that enhanced public interest in news and opinion. A 1937 survey in Egypt identified over 250 Arabic and 65 English-language papers, 200 of those published in Arabic were circulated in Cairo, the hub of anti-British and inter-party contention and the center of cultural ferment. In other parts of the Arab world, partisan patronage of newspapers was a common practice in the colonial era. A year after the end of the World War I and the French takeover of the area, an official biweekly *al-Asima* was published in Damascus featuring official announcements alongside calls for an independent government in Syria. Most newspapers established in the formative years of the Hashemite Kingdom in Syria were supportive of nationalist Arab orientations despite the fact that they were not formally connected with King Faisal's government. These papers included *Suriya al-Jadida, al-Fajr, al-Nahda, al-Raya* and *al-Watan* (Ayalon, 1995: 83). When King Faisal-led Syrian nationalist forces were defeated by French army at *Asylum* on July 24, 1920, most of the newspapers disappeared under tight French regulations. As Syrian struggle for independence gained further momentum, newly-formed political groups and parties seemed keener on publishing their own newspapers. The leading political grouping during most of the mandate *al-Kutla al-Wataniya* had its views propagated through several newspapers; the most famous were *al-Muqtabas*, *al-Qabas*, and *al-Ayyam*.

In Lebanon, the Maronite Phalange party published a weekly newspaper named *al-Amal* (Action) in 1938 while the *Najda* Muslim party published *al-Hadaf* (Target) in 1942. In Iraq, anti-British groups and alliances had their own publications like *al-Furat*, *al-Najaf* and *al-Istiqlal* in the 1920s. In 1930, Iraqi *al-Hizb al-Watani* published *Sada al-Istiqlal* while *Hizb al-Sha'ab* published *Hizb al-Sha'ab* newspaper. In 1924, Iraq's *al-Hizb al-Taqaddumi* published *al-Taqaddum* newspaper. In Palestine, *al-Jami'a al-Arabiya* (Arab Union) was published as the organ of the Supreme Muslim Council. In Trans-Jordan, *Al-Haq Yalou*, a handwritten sheet, was the first official newspaper to be published by King Abdalla who in 1923 also ordered the publication of *al-Sharq al-Arabi*. In Yemen, the *Zaydi* Imam Yahya launched a monthly organ, *al-Iman*, turning it later into a weekly publication. In French-colonized areas, Azzi (1998) notes that press partisanships were derived from the launch of newspapers by Muslims' political parties demanding independence from colonial rule. Examples included *al-Alam* paper (1944) by Moroccan *al-Istiqlal* Party; *al-Haq* and *al-Muntaqid* (1925) by Ben Badis, and *l'Action Tunisienne* by Bourguiba (1932).

It should be noted that the colonial era also witnessed the launch of radio broadcasting in the Arab World as part of British, French or Italian efforts to win the hearts and minds of Arab people. Boyd (1999: 16) notes that radio broadcasting began haphazardly in Egypt in the 1920s with over 100 amateur wireless stations operating during that period, mostly in the Cairo area. During the formative years of Egyptian radio, the service attracted many talented announcers, actors, musicians, and journalists from the nascent theatre, film, music and print media sectors of Cairo (Boyd, 1999: 17). In other Arab countries, radio was introduced at different stages mainly to facilitate colonial communications with European and local populations in the area. For example, in Lebanon, the first radio station was constructed in 1937 by the French government partly to counter Arabic-language radio propaganda of the Italians and the Germans. In Syria, radio broadcasting appeared in 1946 when the Syrian Broadcasting Organization was founded. Jordanian radio transmissions are traced back to the Palestinian Broadcasting Service which was established on March 30, 1936 by the British government under mandate authority. Radio broadcasting started in Algeria in 1937 as a service to the one million French colonists and was called 'French Cinq'. Most of the programs were relayed from Paris as production facilities in Algeria were very limited (Boyd, 1999: 205). In Morocco, radio transmissions began in February 1928 from Rabat with a 2-kilowatt medium wave transmitter. Amateur radio was launched from Tunisia in 1924 catering to French colonists in and around Tunis (Boyd, 1999: 263). The BBC Arabic Service was launched in January 1938 to counter German and Italian political propaganda directed at the Arab region (Ayish, 1991).

IV.1.1.3. The Cold War Politics Context of the Independence Era

Arab countries gained their independence as nation-states in the 1950s and 1960s in a heightened Cold War milieu. While some Arab governments were handed over their national powers from former colonial states as in Jordan, and the Gulf countries, other governments took over through military coups that brought military leaders on top of countries' decision making structures as in Egypt, Yemen, Libya, Syria, Iraq, Somalia, and Sudan. Only Algeria, Morocco, and Tunisia had governments deriving from the legitimacy of national struggles with colonial powers. To a great extent, the overwhelming majority of emerging Arab states followed authoritarian political and social systems predicated on the former Soviet experience, while a few maintained some form of free-market economies, yet with strict political systems as in Jordan, the Gulf States, and Morocco. For quite a long time, Lebanon, due to its special communal and political structure, remained the most liberal, but not necessarily the most democratic Arab country. The dominant belief in the early years of independence was that democracy was either luxury Arab societies could not afford in their formative phases of development or a Western practice associated with world capitalism, and thus would not fit into the evolving socialist-oriented political systems in the region. Both Arab Islamists and nationalists showed hostile attitudes towards democracy as a defining feature of their envisioned societies. The result of this orientation was reflected in the illegalization of partisan pluralism, the obliteration of civil society institutions, and the consolidation of authoritarian practices in individual Arab states. Nawar (2000) notes that in the first half of the twentieth century, two developments came to shape attitudes of the major powers towards freedom in the Arab region: the discovery of oil and the establishment of the state of Israel. The existence of large reserves of oil in the region and its dominant role in Western economies made continued supplies at reasonable prices the chief concern of global powers. Additionally, as vested interests in Israel grew, international powers, especially the United States, increasingly took any Arab country's attitude toward Israel and its practices as a major criteria for dealing with that country. Consequently, human rights violations in many Arab states were glossed over by Western powers in return for securing long-term strategic interests.

IV.1.1.3.1. Political Landscape

An overview of the post-colonial political landscape in the Arab World shows the dominance of single-party systems over public life either through constitutional provisions, emergency martial laws, or revolutionary 'decisions' with no democratic constitutional foundations. In Egypt, the 1952 Revolution led by President Nasser and the Free Officers diffused pan-Arabist sentiments and fostered hopes for progressive political and social achievements. In Syria and Iraq, successive military coups were seen as symptoms of yet an instable regional environment. Inter-Arab conflicts began to surface in Yemen and Algeria which in 1962 tasted freedom for the first time in 131 years. Yet, an outstanding challenge facing the Arab World in the colonial period was the declaration of the state of Israel and the expulsion of Palestinians from their lands. Hence, the liberation of Palestine came to occupy a central place in post-independence political discourse in different public spheres. On the other hand, an equally formidable challenge in the post-colonial era was not related to colonialism, feudalism, or Palestine, but to the nature of social and political systems arising in individual states. Apparently in a backlash reaction to the bitter colonial experience, many Arab countries opted for socialist systems that had put them at a head-on collision with former colonial powers in addition to the United States. Even in countries that adopted monarchical capitalism, the question of popular participation and democratization was never elevated to public standing. Two reasons were cited for that situation: First, democracy was viewed as luxury Arab societies could not afford as they struggled to 'fend off imperialist and Zionist threats'. Second, democracy was apparently swapped for more social and cultural development that would enhance material conditions of the population who were perceived not ready yet to democratize. Nabulsi (2001) notes in his study of modern Arab thought that Arabs lost in the second half of the 20th century more than what they did in the first as they sought to grapple with multiple challenges in political, social, and economic spheres. He noted a deep stagnation in Arab World political life induced by built-in tensions between the imperatives of national assertiveness and modern political realities.

The most formidable challenge facing emerging Arab societies in the post-colonial era, however, was that of legitimacy. Theories of political legitimacy in the Arab World in the Cold War era drew either on some self-serving interpretations of religious scriptures, on mass popular support, or on military revolutionary perpetuation of a status quo. More than two centuries of debates over contemporary forms of indigenous Arab-Islamic political systems failed to materialize, giving way to authoritarian singly-party domination, oligarchic control or semi-democratic systems. The notion of creating a convergence between Islamism and modernism in the political arena was already put to death in Egypt with the execution of Sayyed Qutb in the mid 1960s and in Syria with the mass bombing of the city of Hama in the early 1980s where Muslim Brotherhood members were entrenched. In most of the 1960s and 1970s in Iraq, Libya, Sudan, former South Yemen, Algeria and Tunisia, Islamic groups were banned by law. It was only in Jordan and the Gulf States that some form of Islamic organization, though mostly for charitable and humanitarian purposes, was condoned.

But all in all, the same repressive trend was also applied to more secularist democratic voices demanding the institution of participatory structures. In all political schemes offered in the independence era, legitimacy was rarely based on democratic practices and norms, with both the authoritarian political establishment and Islamic streams showing some disenchantment with democracy as a viable political option for Arab societies.

Historical studies on Arab political structures in the independence era identified two categories of Arab political systems. Hudson (2003) notes that one group of Arab states embarked upon a nationalist-reformist project, led mainly by military officers and a professional, reform-minded middle-class stratum. The authoritarian-populist regimes in these states framed public priorities in terms of economic development through import-substitution-industrialization; egalitarianism through land reform, and emasculation of the very wealthy; and mobilization to unify the Arab nation; redress the grievous *Nakba* (catastrophe) of Palestine and prevent 'Western neo-imperialist designs' on the Arab region. Egypt, Algeria, Tunisia, Libya, Syria, Iraq and North and South Yemen pursued this course in numerous ways. Bishara (1998: 11) observed that radical Arab nationalist discourses did not adequately address the functioning of civil society since the discourses' definitions of the 'nation' tied organically the individual, the society, and the state, thus negating the principle of separation between civil society and the state. The second category, while passively accepting much of the nationalist project, including the leading role of the state, possessed regimes with an avowedly 'traditional' and 'patriarchal' outlook. These included Saudi Arabia, the smaller states of the Arabian Peninsula, and Jordan, Lebanon and Morocco. Unlike the 'nationalists', most of these regimes celebrated their Islamic authenticity rather than relegating it to a lower priority. Many were rentier-states with their affluent classes co-opted, rather than suppressed, and harnessed to non-'socialist' development plan. However, according to Hudson (2003), both groups of states practiced, to varying degrees, a monolithic populist mobilization strategy. Political liberalization, let alone pluralistic democracy, was not on the agendas.

The absence of genuine political and social choices drawing on both historical traditions and contemporary practices proved short-lived by the mid 1980s with the outbreak of the Iranian Revolution, and the Islamic World-wide drive against Soviet communist occupation of Afghanistan. The Iranian Revolution of 1979 instilled a new sense of Islamic revivalism across the Muslim World drawing on indigenous cultural imperatives to shape the future of Islamic societies in the latter part of the 20th century. An important outcome of this sweeping ethos was the rise of what was termed 'political Islam' as a huge intellectual and political force to be reckoned with in contemporary life affairs. Of course, the notion of political Islam goes back to the early years of Muslim Brotherhood's theories of *Jahiliya* and *Hakimiya*, but the actual materialization of that notion into a concrete reality came only in the late 1970s with the installation of the Islamic Republic of Iran. Ever since, political Islam has become the meeting point for growing numbers of young people frustrated by political and economic realities of their societies and disenchanted by the potential secular capitalist and socialist systems' failure to deliver on their transformational promises. The rise of political Islam was perceived to have serious potential challenges for both authoritarian governments and democratic political forces alike. As Islamic sentiments against Western support for Israel in general and against Soviet occupation of Afghanistan in particular were building up in the late 1980s, new ideological orientations with violent dimensions were surfacing in the Arab region. The end of the Cold War, coupled with continued U.S. support for radical Israeli policies and the outbreak of the 1991 Gulf War, brought radical Islamic movements into head-on collision with both Western and Arab states positions on major issues facing the area.

IV.1.1.3.2. Media Landscape

As each newly-independent Arab state prescribed a magical role for media in national development, huge investments were diverted to establishing communication infrastructures and media institutions (Kazan, 1993). Rugh (1979) identified three press models in the post-colonial era in the Arab World: the loyalist, the diverse, and the mobilization, with each model mirroring the social and political context in which it evolved. For example, while the diverse press model marked press systems in countries with some form of democratic traditions like Kuwait, Morocco and Lebanon, the mobilization press model was characteristic of media institutions in Naser's Egypt, (former Baathist Iraq) and Syria, *Jamahiriya* system in Libya, and the communist government in South Yemen. The loyalist model defined press systems in Jordan and the Gulf states. Diverse press systems, on the other hand, were dominant in Kuwait, Lebanon, and Morocco. Although Rugh's press system categorization was criticized by some scholars on theoretical and ethnocentric grounds (Azzi, 1989), it remains, along with its updated (2004) version the single most useful framework for understanding contemporary government-press relations in the Arab World.

This section does not offer a detailed account of media development in the Arab World in the post-colonial phase of the modern era, but rather seeks to argue that this period had for the first time witnessed the establishment of modern national media institutions entrusted with huge national development responsibilities. All Arab countries drafted numerous national development plans that incorporated important provisions for media development, especially in light of rising perceptions of an instrumental mass media role in national socio-economic and cultural transformation within what was known as the 'modernization paradigm' (Kazan, 1993). In a political context marked by subdued civil society institutions, political authoritarianism, and limited freedom, Arab media were instituted as tools of national development in the broadest social, economic, and political sense. By virtue of their reach and immediacy, mass media, especially broadcasting, were believed to be key actors facilitating Arab societies' transition from tradition into modernity. Because they have the capacity to communicate with massive audiences across a broad geographical and media landscape, media of communication were entrusted with instrumental roles in political mobilization, diffusion of innovations, and education. But as the 1970s came to a close, historically-prescribed media roles in national development proved to be rather illusive as social and political structures remained off limits for reform in the region.

Available data on the Arab press during four decades of Cold War politics (1950-1990) show that the Arab World had witnessed substantive expansion and development in its media infrastructures as evident in the spiraling number of publications. A comprehensive documentation of Arab press development from 1950-1988 shows the Arab media landscape dotted with hundreds of publications with different cultural and intellectual perspectives, yet with limited political orientations (Berjas, 1988). As for broadcasting, Hale (1975) noted that radio broadcasting in particular was an important tool of communication in the post-independence period as new states sought to reach out to audiences in geographically inaccessible areas of their countries. Boyd (1999) observed that radio broadcasting was used as a political mobilization tool by President Nasser of Egypt as well as by leaders of republican governments in Libya, Iraq, Syria and Yemen. As a government institution, radio broadcasting was meant to propagate official government views and news to audiences as part of national development strategies. It was noted that radio broadcasting carried newscasts, cultural programs, family shows, religious content and entertainment to attract audiences and to stave off foreign radio transmissions with counter political and ideological messages (Ayish and Hijab, 1988). Because radio broadcasting was a government monopoly in the Arab World in the post-colonial era, its sphere was dominated by state views and perspectives on evolving political events. However, Ayish (1991) noted that Arab audiences had always had access to international radio transmissions from international broadcasters in Western Europe and North America to verify the accuracy of news carried by state-run radio. The BBC Arab service, launched in January 1938, was an important source of news and information for Arab audiences for almost six decades. With its fairly balanced and objective political programs, the BBC Arabic service provided Arab listeners with a qualitative public sphere through which they got exposed to diverse views and opinions on matters bearing on their lives. The Voice of America, on the other hand, was failing on the Arab World front primarily because audiences were associating its biased broadcasts with hostile U.S. foreign policies in the region (Ayish, 1987).

As for television, Ayish (2003a) has identified two phases of development in the post-colonial period (mid 1950s to the late 1980s):

a) The Formative Phase (1954-1976): Television broadcasting in the Arab world dates back to the mid-1950s, when most Arab countries were either subject to European colonial rule, or were just experiencing their early years of independence (Boyd, 1999). Although Arab governments had long perceived television as an effective tool of national reconciliation and a symbol of cultural identity, pioneering efforts to introduce television broadcasting into some Arab countries like Kuwait, Morocco, Lebanon, Iraq, and Jordan were ironically initiated by private players for purely commercial purposes (Boyd, 1999). The commercial start of television in the Arab world was due to a combination of factors that included low receiver set diffusion, absent national independence, and full pre-occupation with radio as the most powerful medium of communication. This trend appeared in tune with prevalent thinking about television in the United States as 'a vast wasteland'. Low attention to television in the 1950s was also reflecting certain apathy to the medium on the part of colonial powers in some countries in North Africa (France) and other Arab countries (Britain). Hence, it was left to the private sector to handle.

The promise of television as a powerful tool of communication seemed to have motivated Arab governments to step in to keep it as a state-controlled operation. Egyptian President Nasser's effective use of radio to promote pan-Arabist ideology seemed to have been behind flourishing views of television as a potentially indispensable tool of political mobilization (Hale, 1975). The issue of television control by governments was never debated in Egypt at a time when the private sector had limited role in the country's socialist-oriented system. Nasser's revolutionary leadership was highly cognizant of television's role in standing up to Western post-colonial domination. But when the issue of financing a television broadcasting operation came up, the Egyptian government had no choice but to go for Radio Corporation of America (RCA) to carry out the project (Boyd, 1999). In 1961 the Kuwaiti Government took over television broadcasting by subordinating it to the Ministry of Information. In the post independence period, television in Morocco was subordinated to the Postal Ministry and was controlled by the office of the Prime Minister (Boyd, 1999). In 1962, Radiodiffusion-Television Marocaine (RTM) was established as part of the Ministry of Information. Sudan television was started in 1961 as a token of goodwill from the Federal Republic of Germany to Sudan. Jordan Television began its transmissions as a government service in April 1968.

In a few Arab countries, the formative years of television development came late in the 1970s to cope with statehood formation. In the United Arab Emirates, television was established in Abu Dhabi in 1969, in Dubai in 1974 and in Sharjah in 1989. In Bahrain, Qatar, Oman and Yemen, television was introduced in

1975. Following the British public service model of broadcasting, television in the Gulf region was established as a government-run operation, mostly subordinated to ministries of information. Television's stated missions in those countries provided for harnessing the medium to serve national development goals, including the reinforcement of cultural identity. But once those services went on the air by political decrees, they had to face a host of challenges that ranged from staff and program shortages to inadequate production and transmission facilities (Boyd, 1999). With the flow of oil-generated income to their national economies, Arabian Gulf states seemed to have managed to establish some of the most technologically advanced television systems in the Arab region.

The rising popularity of television as a medium of communication, especially its ability to mobilize and educate Arab masses, presented governments in the 1960s and 1970s with the dual dilemma of having to manage a potentially effective broadcasting medium with no adequate human and technical resources. To surrender television to private hands also raised a new set of issues relating to the transmission of politically and culturally sensitive materials to generally conservative communities. While some argued that television was basically an entertaining medium, and was therefore inappropriate for governments to patronize, others highlighted the political and socio-cultural role of television in a manner that warranted its subordination to government controls (Boyd, 1999; Dajani, 2001; Jarrar, 2000). The second argument seemed to have gained the upper hand in the Arab world in the 1960s and 1970s for three reasons. Firstly, post-independence governments in the Arab countries of North Africa and the Middle East found centralized British and French public-service broadcasting systems as convenient models to emulate in their national broadcasting structures. The Arab region was not quite familiar with the commercial American model of broadcasting due to minimal U.S. geopolitical influence in the area in the immediate post World War II period. Secondly, Arab governments in the 1960s and 1970s were sole players in leading national development efforts. The launch of government-controlled television as a tool of national development was highly valued. Thirdly, political ferment in the region in the mid 1950s and in the 1960s created heightened tensions that warranted full government control of television systems to ensure program homogeneity across national broadcasting operations.

b) The National Expansion Phase (1976-1990): In the national expansion phase, Arab governments sought to build up their national broadcasting capabilities through training national staff; increasing local production; pooling inter-Arab state production resources, and extending transmissions to cover national territories. In this phase, the Arab States Broadcasting Union (ASBU), an Arab League organization based in Tunisia, and the Saudi-Arabia-based Gulfvision were instrumental in realizing collaborative efforts. In larger countries like Saudi Arabia, Algeria and Sudan, satellite and microwave links were used to carry terrestrial television signals to remote areas. Arab viewers had access to a range of 1-3 TV channels depending on reception locations. In many cases, the use of home videocassette machines was a major popular response to 'bad government television', (Boyd et al., 1989). Imported materials from countries like the United States, Britain, France, and Egypt dominated programming. Egypt, with a long tradition of cinematic production, often referred to as the 'Hollywood of the Arab World', has been a major source of drama serials for television stations throughout the Middle East and North Africa, where viewers could conveniently handle colloquial Egyptian Arabic.

Television in this phase was barely visible in political and media debates as audiences were drawing more on radio for news and entertainment. Since the late 1930s, international radio broadcasts to the Arab world were widely received by listeners, especially at times of conflict. Tight government controls over national broadcasting systems (including television) seemed to have forced audiences to look for alternative sources of independent news. Hence, foreign radio broadcasters like BBC Arabic Service and Radio Monte Carlo-Middle East seemed to have managed to build up impressive audience loyalty throughout the region despite dominant negative attitudes towards British colonial and post-colonial (Ayish, 1991). By listening to foreign radio services, Arab audiences had access to information not only about international developments, but about events taking place in their own countries. In commenting about the television-broadcasting situation in the second phase, Abu Bakr, Labib and Kandil (1985: 10) noted that:

> One of the problems in communication planning in the Arab world is the imbalance in distribution among countries. Some states have enormous needs but little money; others may have money but lack qualified personnel; still others may have manpower resources but be short of equipment.

The emerging model of television broadcasting in the Arab world in the national expansion phase suggested a perpetuation of structural and editorial television arrangements and practices initiated in the formative phase. Television organizations continued to have no administrative or financial independence with their funding almost exclusively deriving from annual government subsidies and limited advertising revenue. Heads of television services were appointed by their nations' leaderships and were directly accountable to Prime Ministers or Ministers of Information. This situation seemed to have created numerous problems. Firstly, it deprived television organizations of programming and news editorial discretion by setting red lines and self-censorship practices in tune with national media policies. That required top broadcast managers to continuously resort to senior political or information officials to clarify state positions on handling sensitive developments. Secondly, this subordination of television services to ministries of information had also deprived them of opportunities for technical and human development to cope with accelerating changes in the broadcast industry. With limited or non-existent advertising income to supplement government funding, many broadcasters in the Arab world found themselves lagging behind in technical infrastructures or professional staff standards. Thirdly, as part of government information bureaucracy, television broadcasters were steered by official government orientations rather than by viewers' preferences. This trend has not only adversely affected programming content, but it has also damaged television's credibility among national viewers who perceived broadcasting as a mere propaganda machine for the ruling elite.

One exception to the total government monopoly of television broadcasting in the Arab world is found in Lebanon where multi-system broadcasting dominated the national expansion phase. In the pre-civil war period, there were two private television services in the country: Compagnie de Television du Liban and et du Proch-Orient (Tele Orient) which was launched in 1959 by a group of Lebanese businessmen with backing from American Broadcasting Company (ABC) (Dajani, 2001). In 1974, the Lebanese Cabinet approved a new broadcasting agreement seeking to institutionalize and formalize government control over broadcasting. The agreement allowed the Lebanese government to purchase and lease transmission equipment to CLT, have two censors at the station to gate keep programs, have a daily one-hour program show, and levy 6.5% of net advertising revenue. Both companies suffered heavy losses during the civil war (1975-76) and were forced to dissolve under a new cabinet rule that brought about a new company in which the government had a 50% share. In late 1977, a legislative decree legalized the formation of *Tele Liban* 'to manage, organize and utilize the various television transmitting installations and to undertake all commercial and television production tasks (Dajani, 2001). By doing so, Lebanon had joined other Arab states in placing part of its television system under government control.

By the late 1980s, broadcasting in the Arab world continued to be viewed as too powerful and sacred an institution to be left to non-governmental parties. Like the flag and the national anthem, television was perceived as a symbol of national identity that may not be shared with private-sector, profit-making players (Abu Bakr et al., 1985). In Lebanon, however, the resurgence of illegal private broadcasting by rival political and sectarian factions seemed to have conferred uniqueness on the country's broadcasting system. Among the broadcasters were the Lebanese Broadcasting Company (LBC) (1985) and al-Mashrek Television (1989). Chaos in the broadcasting scene led the government to look for a new regulatory framework, something that was finally realized in 1994 when Parliament passed a new audio-visual law that kept TL under full government control and allowed the establishment of private television after obtaining a renewable 16-year license.

IV.1.1.3.3. Features of the Arab Public Sphere in the Independence Era

Based on the above review of the development of Arab media during Ottoman, colonial, and independence periods, it was clear that media evolved in two major contexts: foreign domination of Arab lands (Ottoman and European) and Cold War politics in the post-World War era. In the first context, media were shaped by two streams of discourse: the nationalist liberation discourse and the cultural/Islamic identity discourse. In the second context, the cultural identity discourse continued to define the mass-mediated public sphere while the nationalist anti-colonial discourse gave way to developmental and nation-building orientations within the confines of East-West politics. In both types of contexts, the democratic discourse took a backburner position as Arab societies grappled with more formidable challenges pertaining to nation-building, independence and pan-Arab unity. With absent democratic arrangements in the nation-state-dominated political arena of the late 1980s, media institutions seemed politically deadlocked in view of 50 years of failed national development. The narrow view of national development as drawing on economic change proved disastrous in the Arab World while democracy, presumably a basic engine of economic and cultural change, remained off reach. The following section reviews basic features of the Arab public sphere in the four decades following independence which turned out to be developmentally rather than democratically-oriented, highly paternalistic rather than participatory, political and legally inhibitive rather than free, and migratory rather than home-grown.

IV.1.1.3.3.1. Developmentally-Oriented

Until the end of the 1980s, media in the post-colonial era were operating within the 'modernization paradigm' in different Arab societies regardless of their political and ideological orientations. All Arab governments placed high confidence in media as tools of national development entrusted with bringing about modernization to their national communities (Kazan, 1993). The notion of communication as a potential engine of socio-economic change gained widespread popularity in the immediate post-World War II period in the midst of rising expectations of media role in nation-building. Following the establishment of post-colonial nation states in Africa and Asia, debates arose among Western academics and policy makers on how to bring about equitable socio-economic transformations into those emerging regions. Works by Lerner et al. (1958) and Schramm (1964) focused on how media in the Arab world and elsewhere could alter individual and group attitudes towards modern issues and practices as prerequisites for socio-economic change. It was suggested that traditional values dominant in Developing Countries were major obstacles to political participation and economic prosperity, the two key elements of modernization. Media of communication were viewed as a panacea for socio-economic and political woes. Hence, communication policies emanating from the modernization paradigm provided for media diffusion to manipulate attitudes in a manner conducive to the realization of desired socio-economic transformations. Communication experts identified what were termed as 'media indicators' (minimum number of cinema seats, radio and television receivers, or copies of daily newspapers as a ratio of population necessary for development). By the late 1970s, however, Arab countries were experiencing a revolution of rising frustrations. In numerous writings, the modernization paradigm was criticized for its ethnocentrism, ahistoricity, linearity, and for advancing solutions which actually reinforced dependency on former colonial powers (Pye, 1963; Rogers, 1962; and Frey, 1973).

The exclusive harnessing of the Arab World media to bringing about socio-economic modernization rather than to inducing political democratization was damaging to the region' development. As media served to perpetuate the political status quo, they seemed to lack the basic tools needed for affecting social and economic change: the tools of freedom and accountability. The totalitarian nation-state promoted the idea that its legitimacy could be better derived either from political rhetoric or economic gains for community members. But as the experience of the past five decades showed, democracy and freedom are far more essential for community development than resource-abundance welfare systems. It was believed that development was no more than a euphemism for further consolidation of authoritarian structures in the Arab states. An effective media role in addressing development issues was virtually impossible in an authoritarian context whereby media could play a more critical investigative role in communicating social and cultural issues. As one scholar (Hroub, 2006) noted, for four decades, Arab governments found convenience in the habit of procrastinating solutions by 'keeping problems under the carpet'; by the early 1990s, the carpet was puncturing under pressures from accumulating problems. In an authoritarian state contractual context providing for population loyalty and acquiescence in return for economic prosperity and public security, media roles as central actors in the public sphere were seriously undermined.

IV.1.1.3.3.2. Politically Paternalistic

Political patronage of the media maintained itself during the post-colonial era with state-run newspapers, broadcasting services, and book publishing operations constituting a major portion of the communications landscape. The 1952 Revolution in Egypt adopted a socialist orientation to government and economic policies, with all media outlets placed under direct state control. The country's two national newspapers: *al-Ahram* and *al-Akhbar* became mouthpieces for Nasser's revolutionary government and so did radio and television services. The same state-media relationship was dominant in countries with republican political systems in Syria, Iraq, Yemen, Libya, Algeria and Sudan. In monarchical systems, broadcasting was a state monopoly while print media were indirectly subject to government patronage. Except for Lebanon, the absence of political diversity suggested that the state was the prime force of media patronage and control in the Arab World. The most conspicuous case of state media paternalism was evident in broadcasting, which as noted earlier, was kept as a government monopoly for four decades. Egyptian President Nasser's effective use of radio broadcasting to expand pan-Arab ideology transformed broadcasting into an indispensable tool of political mobilization in the Arab World (Hale, 1975). By the late 1990s, broadcasting in the Arab World continued to be viewed as too powerful and sacred an institution to be left to non-governmental parties. Like the flag and the national anthem, television was perceived as a symbol of national identity that may not be shared with private-sector, profit-making players (Abu Bakr et al., 1985).

The 40-year paternalistic media traditions in the Arab world have produced a communications discourse that is monologist, elitist, domineering, deeply-rooted in traditions, and anti-democratic (al-Karni, 1994). Nowhere was this orientation more evident than in media systems operating within the mobilization model developed by Rugh (1979). The quality of discourse was undermined by centralized one-way flow of information systems evolved through ministries of information or news agencies. Their handling of political and social issues did not develop in the context of participatory interactions, but in contexts of coercion, exclusion, and inhibition. Many media organizations drew on Arab-Islamic traditions to justify their positions; to add an aura of sacredness on their discourse; and perhaps to pre-empt substantive opposition to established political arrangements. The whole communication experience was not based on diversity of views, but on monopoly of knowledge. Such state authoritarianism was rationalized on grounds of national security, social integration, and economic development. These phrases later proved to be no more than euphemisms designed to perpetuate despotic traditions in modern Arab societies.

While mainstream Arab media in the post independence era engaged in state-sponsored national development efforts, many of them were allowed some space to debate the cultural identity of Arab societies, strongly perceived as less of a threat than political identity. The outbreak of the Iranian Revolution in 1979 revived old debates in the region regarding the value of integrating Islam into contemporary social, political and economic life in the region. The Muslim Brotherhood, along with secularist Arab ideological parties, spearheaded discussions on the most appropriate political identity for Arab societies in the context of Cold War politics. Yet, inhibitive legal provisions, coupled with stringent political controls in different stages of Arab media history, generated a discourse that drew on emotional, transcendental, fatalistic, and monolithic premises. Until the mid 1980s, the idea of Western democracy was viewed with deep suspicions in the Arab World as a Western novelty not compatible with the cultural and social features of Arab-Muslim communities. In 1978, Syrian Paris-based scholar Burhan Ghalyoun issued his *Manifesto for Democracy* book in which he advocated the institution of democratic practices in the Arab World. Bel-Qaziz (2006) in his survey of the modern Arab reform movement in the post-colonial era noted that the press, especially in Lebanon, Kuwait and Morocco was serving as voices of democratization and human rights, albeit within more inhibitive conditions.

It was noted that Arab media could not operate outside paternalistic arrangements not only for political reasons, but also for lacking appropriate economic conditions to sustain their operations in the long run. Researchers have found that national Arab markets in the post-colonial era were disintegrated and lacked the potential to provide adequate advertising revenue for national media systems. Because those media catered to national rather than to regional audiences, their potential to expand their financing base was severely curtailed. On the other hand, the press in some Arab countries with what Rugh (1979) called loyalist and diverse systems, enjoyed more autonomy from government controls despite the fact that government subsidies continued to keep many publications afloat. Like countries with mobilization systems, states with diverse and loyalist systems developed media traditions whereby official patronage of media institutions was maintained alongside more independent media operations. In Jordan and the Gulf States, newspapers were operated either as part of government media organizations (Ministries of Information) or were owned and operated by private persons; yet, were still eligible to receive government subsidies.

IV.1.1.3.3.3. Legally Inhibitive

Paternalism in the Arab media context suggested states' tendencies to keep communications under their control. Yet, those tendencies were not reflecting individualistic or altruistic orientations, but rather legal provisions defining rules for media operations. In the post-colonial period, the situation of legal press frameworks varied from one country to another. In theory, all Arab constitutions provide for freedom of expression and of the press and preclude censorship as a control mechanism. In many cases, however, freedom of speech and of the press was subordinated to the principle of 'social order' which was falling within state authority. It was also noted that those who had political power also possessed the discretionary power to interpret legal provisions at their will. A review of press and media laws in the Arab countries since independence years shows that many Arab countries had specific press provisions embedded in their constitutions while others devoted special 'press and publications' laws to regulate the press system (Mesallami, n. d.). The problem with Arab press laws in the post-colonial era was that they looked impressive on paper, but in reality, they fail to produce the rosy picture embedded in the spirit of their text. For example, some laws provide for freedom of expression and of the press, but they also provide for the government's right to block the publication of some information once it is deemed harmful to national security, cultural traditions or 'brotherly and friendly relations' with other countries. Almost all constitutional provisions relating to the press in the Arab World make top leaderships immune against potential criticism. This overwhelming state discretion in matters relating to press performance has played a frustrating role in press attempts to handle public issues with a reasonable degree of impartiality. Kirat (1993: 43) notes that in the immediate post-colonial period in Algeria (1962), the ruling National Liberation Front (NLF) monopolized the majority of the mass media, but was faced with a host of problems such as personnel incompetence, poor technical infrastructures, absence of a journalistic association and low cooperation with media practitioners on the part of government institutions.

When it comes to broadcasting, radio and television services enjoyed no significant editorial autonomy and were run as government organizations. Hence, they were governed by state-drafted bylaws and charters that defined their missions as tools for national development and cultural integration. Because their staff was considered as part of the government bureaucracy, they were by default integral ingredients of official state orientations and were not expected to take up counter roles. Based on this, most broadcasting stations had no fixed charters or byelaws, but operated in tune with the timely outlooks defined for them by government officials, usually ministers of information. Political communication on Arab World television was developed in the shadow of general government discourse or specific state positions on certain issues. Whenever talk shows were initiated on some local and regional issues, the general orientation is flagrantly governmental with no room for rival views, especially on controversial matters. Due to the limited space devoted to political programs on Arab World television, most of the transmission time carried what was termed 'cultural programming', sporting activities and entertainment. To a great extent, television in the mid 1980s was not substantially perceived as a political communication tool simply because of its terrestrial limited reach and tight state control.

IV.1.1.3.3.4. Migratory

While Arab World-based media were subjected to strict state controls in the post-colonial era within Rugh's loyalist and mobilization systems, more independent and free media outlets were established in diaspora. They initially catered to Arabic-speaking minorities in Europe before expanding to embrace audiences inside the Arab World. The migratory feature of the Arab press was noted in the formative years of press evolution when Lebanese journalists escaped Turkish repression and settled in Egypt's more liberal and secure working environment to launch their papers. In the post-colonial era, the same patterns were repeated with the migration of Arab newspapers to European capitals like London to carry out their journalistic operations away form Arab government censorship. Ermes (2004) noted that media based outside the Arab World were better-positioned to create and contribute to the development of a critical public sphere than their local counterparts. They were free from the conventional state censorship that circumvented public criticism of official policies and leaders. They also had at their disposal huge technical and intellectual resources. Badrkhan (2004) notes the migratory Arab press phenomenon was a result of rising levels of authoritarianism in the Arab World whereby dissidents were subjected to imprisonment or even physical liquidation, and had no choice but to relocate abroad. Restrictive policies adopted by former Egyptian President Anwar Sadat; the civil war in Lebanon; and the repression of press freedom in several countries prompted the migration of the press to Europe. The first Arabic newspaper to appear in London in 1977 was *al-Arab* followed in 1978 by *Asharq al-Awsat*, then *al-Manar* in the same year. By the early 1980s, over 100 publications were produced in London; many of them were sponsored by rival Arab regimes as part of existing political rivalry in the region. In 1988, *al-Hayat* newspaper was published in London with new technological features. Badrkhan (2004) noted that while the Iraq-Iran war induced prosperity in migratory Arab media, the Iraqi invasion of Kuwait marked the demise of this phenomenon. This decline in migratory press significance has also been noted in conjunction with the rise of satellite television as the prime source of news and other information. Middle East Broadcasting Center (MBC) was launched in London in 1991 followed by Orbit Television and Radio Network and ART from Italy in 1994.

IV.2. Summary and Conclusion

The modern Arab public sphere, extending from Napoleon's expedition to Egypt in 1798 to the end of the 1980s, emerged in the most tumultuous phase of modern Arab history as marked by foreign domination, national struggle, cultural assertiveness, and nation-state authoritarianism. For almost 200 years, Arabs found themselves grappling with a wide range of challenges emanating from their quest for *Nahda* (Renaissance) in the contexts of foreign domination and East-West rivalry. The challenges of preserving and reviving cultural heritage and reconciling it with accelerating social and technological developments have been quite immense. Failure to generate workable cultural and political schemes that draw on both tradition and modernity has spilled over to all aspects of Arab World life, including the public sphere. For two centuries, the public sphere has never realized its full identify with well-defined Arab-Islamic and modern boundaries. It has actually been disoriented, fragmented, suppressed, vulgarized, and abused by actors ranging from colonial powers, to authoritarian states, to militant groups, to Cold War politics rivals. As much as the Arab World could not deliver on its political, economic and cultural promises, it also failed to realize progressive political and social values of freedom, justice and equality. The public sphere has been the main casualty of this deterioration as it turned at different times more into a buffer zone in which free and critical exchanges are blocked in favor of more restrictive and rigid views and interpretations. While the colonial era in some Arab countries witnessed a surge in freedom of expression, the main trend across the Arab World in the independence period was of a public sphere marked by state paternalism, political authoritarianism, and cultural ambivalence. These limitations, to some extent, reflected some historical continuity in communication and political traditions that were bound to bear on the evolving Arab public sphere in the age of globalization.

V
THE ARAB WORLD IN THE AGE OF GLOBALIZATION

> *Every single empire in its official discourse has said that it is not like all the others, that its circumstances are special, that it has a mission to enlighten, civilize, bring order and democracy, and that it uses force only as a last resort. And, sadder still, there always is a chorus of willing intellectuals to say calming words about benign or altruistic empires*
> *(Said, E., 2003)*

The end of the Cold War seemed to have demystified the Arab political system which for decades had derived its legitimacy largely from anti-imperialist/anti-Zionist ideology, skewed interpretations of traditional heritage, and a corrupt welfare economy. In most Arab countries, absence of participatory arrangements seemed to have exposed the post-colonial state system to domestic as well as to global scrutiny in the midst of accelerating drives for Western-style democratic reforms. With the demise of the former Soviet Union in 1991, many Arab countries were clamoring for a political and ideological shelter in the face of a sweeping globalization that had initially hit Arabian frontiers in the form of a 30-nation alliance against the Iraqi invasion of Kuwait. With the slogan of pan-Arab unity proving to be a hoax 50 years after the establishment of the Arab League; with the diminution of the struggle against Israel as a bargaining chip for further authoritarianism in Arab societies; with deepening social and economic woes, leading to the obliteration of the middle class; with rising extremist interpretations of Islamic teachings as a serious anti-Western ideology to be reckoned with; and with the virtual absence of genuine democratic arrangements, Arab countries at official and popular levels found themselves seriously vulnerable to the winds of change induced by political globalization. As former U.S. President George Bush announced his New International Order on the eve of the expulsion of Iraqi forces from Kuwait, Arabs, more than ever before, were convinced that the whole region was bound for a new destination with unpredictable outcomes. Such convictions were further boosted by the introduction of new communications technologies represented by satellite television and the World Wide Web. A conspicuous aspect of Arabs' responses to such developments has been a gradual, yet uncertain, opening up of their closed communities to accommodate more diversity and participation in national and domestic political processes, albeit on a limited and ambivalent scale.

This chapter surveys the main features of political developments in the Arab region since the 1991 declaration of Bush's New World Order and the ensuing U.S.-driven democratic reforms in the region that seemed to have reached a dead end in a deepening Middle Eastern quagmire. As the writer argues, the substance and parameters of both locally and externally-induced political reforms in the Arab World have yet to be defined by indigenous political and cultural forces before they could generate a viable public sphere in the region.

V.1. The Arab World in the Eye of the Globalization Storm: Emerging Political Contexts

From a political point of view, globalization has been defined as 'a process by which the capitalist world system spreads across the actual globe' (Wallerstein, 1998). Contemporary globalization is associated with a transformation of state power as the roles and functions of states are re-articulated, reconstituted and re-embedded at the intersection of globalizing and regionalizing networks and systems. Closely relevant to the spread of political globalization is the concept of governance as based on democratic representation and 'free marketplace of ideas'. The break-up of the former Soviet Union and the end of the Cold War did not only cast suspicion on the viability of totalitarian schemes of government, but also unleashed a global search for alternative power-sharing arrangements. In its basic configuration, globalization denotes a multi-faceted process in which the world is being rapidly molded into a shared social space by economic and technological forces. The concept also suggests that developments in one region of the world can have profound consequences for the life chances of individuals and communities in the other side of the globe (Held et al., 1999). Globalization researchers note that among other things, this phenomenon has eroded national sovereignty; boosted the role of transnational corporate and non-governmental organizations; and enhanced the practice of political unilateralism in the conduct of foreign policy. Although globalization embraces a range of political, cultural, economic, and technological facets, it is the political facet that will be addressed in this section as it bears on the formation of the Arab public sphere in the 1990s and beyond.

Globalization, as an evolving process, has been around for the past two decades; yet, there is no consensus among researchers about its peculiar features. Held et al. (1999) identify three broad views of the nature and meaning of globalization. First, the hyper-globalists view, which argues that we live in an increasingly globalized world in which states are being subjected to massive economic and political change. In these conditions, states are increasingly becoming 'decision-takers' and NOT 'decision makers'. Secondly, the skeptics' view that sees contemporary global circumstances as having historical continuity. According to this view, the search for global dominance has been a centuries-old concern, and what we see now is a mere intensification of international and social activity. Tehranian (1999) sees globalization as a process that has been going on for the past 5000 years, but has significantly accelerated. Elements of globalization include massive trans-border flows of capital, labor, management, news, images, and data. Leading the process of globalization are transnational corporations (TNCs), transnational media organizations (TMCs), intergovernmental organizations (IGOs), non-governmental organizations (NGOs), and alternative government organizations (AGOs). Third, the transformationalist view, which argues that globalization, is creating new economic, political and social circumstances which, however unevenly, are serving to transform state powers and the context in which states operate. States, according to this view, have lost their grip on many domains, including economic and political sectors.

Robertson (1992: 8) conceives of globalization as 'the compression of the world and the intensification of consciousness of the world as a whole'. In this sense, globalization involves the crystallization of four main components of the 'global human circumstance': societies (or nation states), the system of societies, individuals (selves), and humankind. This, according to Robertson (1992: 27), takes the form of processes of socialization, internationalization, individuation, and generalization of consciousness about humankind respectively. Unlike Tehranian's reference to globalization as a multitude of historical processes (Tehranian, 1999), Robertson's view captures 'the form in terms of which the world has moved toward unicity' (1992: 175). Robertson's notion of 'glocalization' has been used in reference to the fact that universal ideas and processes involved in globalization necessarily are interpreted and absorbed differently according to the vantage point and history of particular local groups. Giddens (1999) firmly situates globalization as a consequence of modernity, whose dynamics radically transform social relations across time and space. He argues that globalization occurs in four key domains: the extension of the nation-state system; the global reach of the capitalist economy coupled with the international division of labor; and a global system of military alliances.

Like other world regions, Arab societies have witnessed extensive debates on globalization, generating wide-ranging perspectives on the nature of this phenomenon and its implications for the region. Ismael and Ismael (1999) noted that globalization, with its Western standardized recipes for political reform, was bound to foster Islamist opposition. Ali (2003) observes that the Arab World has experienced deepening economic inequality in the age of globalization, leading to further social disintegration. Al-Hamad (2003) argues that globalization has presented the Arab World with three challenges in three basic domains: liberalization, modernization, and integration into the world economy. In 2002, the Mediterranean Development Forum noted that the Arab World civil society institutions have failed to articulate clear and active positions towards globalization (World Bank Group, 2002). It reported that the posture taken by Arab civil societies proved to be increasingly untenable, and indeed quite damaging to social and economic rights of Arab citizens. In surveying Arab intellectual reactions to globalization, Sowwani (2004) noted that Arab thinkers have addressed globalization in the same manner used in handling renaissance at the turn of the 20th century. In a range of conferences convened throughout the Arab World over the past 15 years, it was noted that globalization was bound to have adverse effects on Arab societies which possess no tangible mechanisms for addressing its challenges (ECSSR, 2002; Arab Unity Studies Center, 1998). Nawar (2003) notes that in the context of globalization, the Arab state has lost part of its sovereignty to international actors like trans-national corporations and international organizations, notably in the areas of economic activity. It has thus become critical to strengthen global governance, as embodied in the United Nations. However, this has yet to come about as the advent of a uni-polar world has resulted at times in weakening and marginalizing the world organization and in stifling freedom of expression.

The major part of Arab World debates on globalization have represented this phenomenon in negative terms, mainly as a form of conspiracy that seeks to obliterate Arab-Islamic culture and facilitate U.S. domination of the region. Tarabishi (2004) noted that most of what is being said today about globalization comes close to a repetition of what was said earlier about 'cultural invasion', 'imperialism', 'subordination' or even about 'modernity' as an 'alien' or 'invading' concept. He observed that several Arab scholarly publications have devoted special issues to the analysis of globalization with a skeptical view that demonizes it as an evil wave of transformations. An examination of Arab World writings on globalization show cases of what Tarabishi described as 'neurotic ideologies' dominated by the logic of conspiracy theories. He cited writings by Bel-Qaziz (1998) defining globalization as an 'act of cultural rape and symbolic aggression on other cultures; by Safadi (1999) who likened globalization to the 'imperialism of the absolute'; by Ghalyoun (1998) who described globalization as 'the nom De guerre of Americanization'; by Amin (1997) who referred to globalization as 'the newest and most intelligent stage of this eternal conspiracy'; and by al-Jaberi (1997) who examined globalization as 'a radical negation of the whole nationalist existence, by destroying the three basic categories of this existence: the state, the nation, and the homeland'. Tarabishi concluded that the most dangerous result of this macabre response to globalization may be a downward spiral where the rejection of globalization turns into 'a rejection of modernity and defaming globalization suggests a defamation of modernity.'

If Napoleon's expedition to Egypt in summer 1798 marked Arabs' first-hand modern encounter with a European power, both as a carrier of modernization and as an invader, the 1991 War on Iraq also signified the first massive face-to-face contact with an American power, both as a preacher of universal democracy and a force of political and economic globalization. Both cases carry striking similarities in the sense that they brought forth a host of political, social and cultural challenges Arabs needed to grapple with in two eras a couple of centuries apart. Questions of cultural identity and socio-political renaissance in a fast-changing world have remained enduring issues in modern and post-modern Arab societies. Yet, while the 'Napoleon shock' sparked off a new period of awakening in an Arab world long-dominated by Ottoman rule, the American war on Iraq and its subsequent occupation signaled the flagrant failure of two centuries of Arab aspirations for cultural identification, liberation, and geo-political unity. As the 1798 French landing on Alexandria foreshadowed the rising power of colonial Europe and the gradual suffocation of the Ottoman empire, the Second Gulf War 1991 marked the end of the Cold War, the rise of the United States as the sole global superpower, and the degeneration of Arab states into more helpless entities with a disoriented cultural and political outlook. The re-positioning of the Arab World on top of the U.S. foreign policy agenda in the post-9/11 era has opened a Pandora box of profound transformations embracing social, cultural, political, and economic aspects of contemporary Arab life.

By the end of the 1980s, it was clear that the Arab World was drifting into a new phase of its contemporary history in response to global political, economic and technological transformations. Hudson (2003) noted that Arab states that seemed to dominate their societies began to falter, unable to continue delivering on the socio-economic promises that had tacitly fostered political passivity. A long period of promised economic growth came to an end with the collapse of oil prices in the middle of the 1990s. While oil-rich rentier societies experienced huge revenue declines, nationalist-progressive ideological formulas of other countries began to lose their glamour. The diminution of the middle class as the backbone of social and economic change has been a major outcome of this transition. At the global level, the bipolar political order came to an end with the eclipse and demise of the Soviet Union, leaving the United States the prime force in an increasingly integrated global economy and financial system informed by an ascendant ideology of economic and political liberalism (Hudson, 2003). The rise of global financial institutions like the World Bank and the International Monetary Fund as part of the U.S. foreign policy orientations complicated the situation for most Arab countries which had to grapple with the challenge of securing funding for their development projects without putting their political orientations at risk (UNDP, 2004). As Ali (2003) noted, globalization has deepened social and economic divisions within Arab societies beyond any repair with the disappearance of the middle class, and the rise of unemployment, social inequities and political repression.

By the late 1980s also, most Arab states were convinced that the global system was in transition and they were bound to be part of that transition. Eight years of a bloody Iraqi-Iranian conflict contributed to a revolution of rising frustrations in Arab countries, especially in the Gulf region, which took the major brunt of that conflict, at least in financial terms. Iraq emerged out of that war seriously embattled, but resolved to pursue its disastrous policy of military adventurism by invading the State of Kuwait. Aware of the receding shadow of Cold War politics that had helped them in the past to 'stay in the dark to keep their houses in order their own way', some Arab countries began to find some shelter in some regional bodies like the Gulf Cooperation Council, composed of the six Gulf states (1980), the Arab Cooperation Council, comprising Jordan, Iraq, Yemen and Egypt (1988), and the Magharibi Council, comprising Morocco, Algeria, Libya and Tunisia (1987). Except for the GCC Council, the two other regional bodies were doomed both by domestic failures and global transitions. Faced by transformations in global relations and rising domestic frustrations induced by deteriorating economic conditions, Arab governments never contemplated democratic reforms as a solution to their dilemmas. For most of them, political stability as perceived in mostly security terms was sought in external rather than domestic arenas. Following Iraq's invasion of Kuwait, Arab regimes were experiencing their most dramatic moments in modern history as they found themselves totally exposed to the winds of globalization with its scorching political, social, and economic heat.

V.2. U.S. Spearheading Reform

On March 6, 1991, former U.S. President George Bush delivered a historic speech on the aftermath of Iraqi troop expulsion from Kuwait that was always construed as the principal American policy statement on the then-evolving political order in the Middle East. In the 1990s, Bush's speech outlined four components of his Mideast strategy: creating shared security arrangements in the region; controlling the proliferation of weapons of mass destruction; creating new opportunities for peace and stability in the Middle East; and fostering economic development for the sake of peace and progress (al-Bab (2005). Ever since, the United States has embarked on a strategy of containing and invading Iraq; waging a global war on what it termed as 'Islamic terror'; and supporting the extremist policies of Israeli Likud (and later Kadima) leaders that put an end to the relatively even-handed Clinton-sponsored Palestinian-Israeli peace process. The tragic September 11 events furnished further ammunition for Bush's neo-conservative arsenal, sparking off further interventions in Arab societies and creating an atmosphere of mistrust under the pretext of combating terrorism. In 2002, President George W. Bush announced the Middle East Partnership Initiative (MEPI) structured in the areas of political, economic and educational development as well as women empowerment (U.S. Department of State (2005). The U.S. National Security Strategy document of September 2002 also elucidated a refined conception of security that emphasizes the consequences of internal conditions of other states – particularly the lack of democracy. President G. W. Bush's 'Freedom Agenda' can be considered a U.S. 'grand strategy' in the Global War on Terrorism. In a November 2003 speech before the National Endowment for Democracy, President Bush reiterated his commitment to promoting democracy in Iraq and in the Middle East and likened his 'forward strategy of freedom in the Middle East' to earlier U.S. commitments to see democracy spread throughout Eastern Europe. At the June 8-10, 2004 G8 summit meeting in Sea Island, Georgia, President Bush also called on G8 members to provide technical assistance to monitor elections; sponsor training programs for independent journalists; increase funding for non-governmental organizations; establish a Middle East development bank; and provide training to women interested in running for public offices in countries with upcoming parliamentary elections (Sharp, 2004). By mid 2007, appalling conditions in Iraq seemed to have bought about a major switch in the Bush Middle East democratic-reform-based strategy by forcing recourse to crude security considerations as the foundations for American relations with the region.

The underlying premises of the Bush administration's reformist drive in the Arab World in the immediate September 11 period lend themselves to deep beliefs within ruling neo-conservative circles in Washington, D. C. that political authoritarianism, coupled with militant religious beliefs permeating Arab social life, were the prime causes of the 9/11 terrorist attacks. Terror, according to this view, could not be exterminated only by chasing down *al-Qaida* Network, 'but by hitting deep at the very cultural and religious bases of Arab societies'. A whole array of intellectual ferment on Islam as an 'ideology of hate', 'terror', and 'death' came to define the emerging public discourse. Lynch (2003a) lists assumptions that underlie US policies towards Arabs, one of them is that 'Arabs respect power, and that the way to implement US policies is to cow them into submission'. Another assumption is that in reality, Arab public opinion does not matter, because co-opted authoritarian states that maintain the status quo can control or ignore any discontent. A third assumption is that anger is intrinsic to Islamic or Arab culture, and represents the envy of these weak and failed states, or otherwise is simply cooked up by unpopular leaders to deflect attention from their shortcomings. A final, increasingly popular notion is that anti-Americanism in the Middle East is the result of misunderstanding US policies. In 2007, Rand Corporation issued a report on building moderate Muslim networks. Rabasa, Benard, Schwartz and Sicklein (2007) suggested that the United States should use 'moderate' Muslim intellectuals and community leaders to build extensive networks to counter what it termed as 'radical and dogmatic' interpretations of Islam.

The writer argues that it is within these divergent contexts that the U.S. drive for reform has to be comprehended, spawning wide-spread skepticism within the Muslim World about the real U.S. intentions in the region. Official and popular misgivings in the Arab World about American policies in the region have received renewed boosts with the U.S. invasion of Iraq and the failure to establish connections between its former regime and *al-Qaida* Network, and to prove Iraq's possession of weapons of mass destruction. The humiliating torture of Iraqi prisoners at Abu Gharib and of Arab and Muslim detainees in Guantanamo unveiled the dark side of U.S.-sponsored reformist drives. The very U.S. approach to democracy has also been criticized as bordering on hypocrisy and self-interest. Hostile U.S. policies towards countries with democratically-elected leaders like Colombia, Iran and Palestine have testified to a flagrantly flawed approach. As the United States was reeling under the 9/11 terrorist shock, Stephen Zunes (2001) wrote on September 12, 2001 that Washington has used the threat of Islamic fundamentalism as a justification for keeping a high military, economic and political profile in the Middle East. Yet it has often supported Muslim hardliners when they were perceived to enhance U.S. interests, as they did in Afghanistan, Pakistan, and Saudi Arabia

Criticisms of U.S.-sponsored reformist drives in the Arab World seem to be underlied by cynicism about the real intentions of democratizing the region which had for a long time suffered from systematic American support for state authoritarianism. Inner circles within the Bush administration admit that democratization is used as a euphemism for pre-empting indigenous Islamist initiatives perceived to carry a long-term threat to U.S. global interests. As one writer (Clarke et al., 2004) proposes:

> To defeat the international *jihadist* movement, the United States must promote discussion in the Islamic world of values such as democracy, civil liberties, non-violence, and protection of non-combatants. Traditional propaganda mechanisms and mediums, such as television and radio programs, will only constitute a small part of the solution. In fact, public diplomacy efforts spearheaded by the U.S. government will most likely be looked on with skepticism in the Islamic world. The most effective public diplomacy initiatives will be those led by nongovernmental organizations, governments other than that of the United States, and leaders in the Islamic world.

Traditionally, the United Nations has also been a strong supporter of the global drive for democratization, billing it the best model to ensure a framework of liberties for lasting solutions to political, economic, and social problems facing our societies. Former UN Secretary General Boutros Ghali described democratization as a process leading to a more open, more participatory, and less authoritarian society (Ghali, 1999). He notes that 'democratization has had a marked impact on the United Nations'. Just as newly independent states turned to the United Nations for support during the era of de-colonization, 'so today, following another wave of accession to statehood and political independence, member states are turning to the United Nations for support in democratization'. The notion of democratization has also been taken up by numerous non-governmental organizations (NGOs) around the world. In 2006, the United Nations Development Program (UNDP) launched the Partnership for Democratic Governance to promote democratic values and practices around the world. UNDP has published a series of books addressing different aspects of democratic governance as part of the United Nations political strategy.[36] Amnesty International, Article 19, and

---

[36] Examples include: Sources for Democratic Governance Indicators, Democracy in Latin America, UNDP's Engagement with Political Parties, A Handbook on Working With Political Parties, Governance for the Future: Democracy and Development in the Least Developed Countries, Engaging Parliaments in the Millennium Development Goals: a key part of National MDG strategies, Fast Facts on Parliamentary Development - How UNDP Supports Parliaments, Concept Paper on 'Legislatures and Good Governance', UNDP and

Freedom House are just two examples of those organizations that have placed democratization on top of their global agendas. Such democratization drive has created tensions in NGOs' relations with local political and cultural players in Third World countries, including those in the Middle East. The arrest and imprisonment of Egyptian sociologist Saadiddin Ibrahim on charges of receiving foreign funds to promote democratic and human rights practices was a case in point.

V.3. Arab Responses

The 1990s were a decade of unprecedented political transformations in Arab societies in the aftermath of the Gulf conflict and the emergence of political liberalism as the defining concept of world and national politics. Over the past two decades, 'Democracy is a solution' was a slogan raised in all election campaigns in many Arab countries that experienced a range of varying democratic shifts. Hawthorne (2004) notes that Arab governments and publics have reacted to the democratization drive on two levels. On one level, they have exhibited hostility and defensiveness. They have reacted with particular scorn to Washington's attempt to recast itself as a champion of democracy and as the friend of all Arab reformers. Such hostility is hardly a surprise given the unfriendliness of the environment into which the Bush administration was attempting to project its message. Long-standing Arab suspicion of U.S. motives in the region was only exacerbated by the administration's unconditional support for former Israeli Prime Minister Ariel Sharon. On a second deeper level, despite mistrust of the U.S. mediation, many government officials and other members of the elite have basically accepted the message that it was high time that Arab societies need to experience some political, economic, and social transitions. Thus, as U.S. rhetoric on democracy became more strident in 2003 and 2004, domestic opponents of Arab regimes carried on their criticisms of U.S. policy while calling for reforms in their communities. Some Arabs who had privately supported democratic reform, but had hesitated to voice their opinions publicly, were also emboldened to make their voices more heard. For their part, Arab rulers, suddenly no longer able to depend on the protection offered by U.S. silence about their poor governance and human rights violations, found it difficult to stand up in the face of this sweeping discontent

A major problem with the U.S.-sponsored reform drive in the Arab World has been taken to task for viewing the whole region as a wasteland that needs to be re-constructed from scratch to produce more viable American-style political systems. But as some Arab scholars have noted, the idea of democratic reform in the Arab World is not new; it rather lends itself to the early periods of the region's modern history as noted in the previous chapter. Because it was perceived to contravene mainstream political and cultural views and because it was not substantiated by fair and eve-handed approaches to the region's problems, the U.S. 'reformist drive' was bound to induce an outcry in Arab societies at elitist and grassroots levels. Local voices opposing U.S.-sponsored reform based their positions on concerns about potential threats to Arab cultural and political identity. Zebian (2004) noted that not surprisingly, the American initiative comes saturated with the political hallmarks of that administration, which is perhaps best described as completely self-centered with no regard for Arab and/or Muslim societies that are 'led on by promises of reform while at the same time being existentially threatened'. He notes that economic, social or administrative reform initiatives proposed for any country or region, have always gone hand in hand with political agendas. However, what is striking about the much needed and awaited US initiative was that it was based primarily on political goals. On the other hand, some Muslim scholars like Sheikh Yusuf al-Qaradawi, head of the International Muslim Scholars Association, noted that from an Islamic point of view, reform is provided for in the *Qur'an* as fighting vice and rectifying corrupted situations or behaviors and 'Muslims should undertake to do their own reform rather than to have others do it for them'. 'U.S.-prescribed reform', according to Qaradawi (2004) would guarantee Muslims 'a role in the back of the caravan to always trail behind as a nation that is weak, ignorant and fragmented'.

The Arab World's response to U.S.-driven democratization has been evident in a series of conferences and declarations supporting political reform in the region, yet stopping short of defining the nature, extent, and direction of that reform. At the official level, the May 2004 Arab summit in Tunisia embraced political reform as a long-term Arab strategy, yet on terms indigenously defined by Arab societies rather than being imposed on them. Its 'Declaration on the Process of Reform and Modernization' called for the continuation and intensification of political, economic, social and educational change initiatives that reflect the will and aspirations of Arabs. The Declaration specifically called for action 'to deepen the foundations of democracy and consultation, and to broaden participation in political life and decision-making in tandem with the rule of law, equality among citizens, respect for human rights, freedom of expression and safeguards for the independence of the judiciary'. At the non-governmental level, two documents drafted at the Library of Alexandria in Egypt, and at the Arab National Conference in Beirut in early 2004 agreed that the goal of political reform should be the establishment of democratic regimes in the region. The measures necessary to realize such reform, according to Arab intellectuals, include constitutional and legislative amendments, enhancement of political structures and institutions, ending government control over the press and other media, and lifting restrictions on the establishment of civil society organizations. The Alexandria document called for the peaceful transfer of power, but left this to the specific conditions of each Arab country. It also demanded lifting restrictions on the formation of political parties, but insisted that such formation should be within the laws and regulations of each country. The Beirut declaration cast suspicion on U.S.-sponsored reforms, calling for Arab indigenous democratic solutions to political reform demands on the basis of justice, freedom, and equality.

Another significant indictor of Arabs' struggle with the question of reform has been evident in the annual publication of the *Arab Human Development Report* (AHDR) by the UN Development Program. An enduring feature of official Arab reactions to U.S.-driven reforms is that while governments have been cognizant of the need to affect democratic changes in their societies, they seem to be ambivalent about their substance and parameters. For many, democracy could be confined to electoral processes without having to be accompanied by constitutional transitions. The 2004 AHDR report identified three deficiencies in the Arab World: lack of freedom, knowledge, and women's rights that hold the Arabs back from greater development and from reaching their full potential in comparison with more advanced nations. It noted that 'this freedom deficit undermines human development and is one of the most painful manifestations of lagging political development'. The report went on to say that the global wave of democracy has barely reached the Arab states. In many Arab countries, poverty and illiteracy have reached staggering levels; health care has deteriorated significantly in some countries; human rights abuses are widespread; jails swarm with 'prisoners of conscience'; and freedom of expression is confined to empty promises. When positive change takes place, it is slow and insufficient (UNDP, 2004).

Other reformist initiatives included the 'First International Conference of the Arab Human Rights Movement: Prospects for the Future' held in Casablanca from 23 to 25 April, 1999; Arab Charter on Human Rights, adopted by the Arab Standing Committee for Human Rights (5-14 January 2004); and the 'Sana'a Declaration', emerging from the *Regional Conference on Democracy, Human Rights and the Role of the International Criminal Court* (Sana'a, January 2004). Independent political and civil forces in the Arab world also stepped up their struggle for political reform, resulting in some notable successes. For example, in Morocco, human rights and political organizations persuaded the government to acknowledge earlier violations, in particular relating to the disappearances of political opponents, and to begin to address the issue on a more serious and systematic basis. In Jordan, the Arab Organization for Human Rights (AOHR) in mid 2007 accused the government of human rights violations ranging between encroachment on public freedoms and the extradition of a Jordanian citizen to the United States without prior judicial decision. In Syria, civil society organizations asked for the state of emergency to be lifted and freedoms expanded. In Egypt, the Muslim Brotherhood announced an initiative for general reform. At the beginning of 2004, Saudi Arabia witnessed an unprecedented number of civil initiatives calling for national dialogue and for further integration of women into the workforce. In Palestine, civil society organizations were active in many areas, from resisting occupation and defending human rights to assisting in relief and humanitarian aid operations; to calling for social and political reform. Hamas movement won the 2006 Palestinian parliamentary elections on a change reform and platform.[37]

Writers with Western perspectives, on the other hand, also seem to see the notion of forcing political reforms on the Arab World as inconceivable, at least in the short run. Hamzawi (2005a, 2005b), notes that the Arab World is changing: popular protest movements, parliamentary and municipal elections, and successive concessions by the ruling elites, are creating a momentum for political transformation in countries as different as Lebanon and Palestine, Egypt and Saudi Arabia. However, he notes that it is difficult to foresee what the outcome of the long-anticipated 'Arab democratization wave' is likely to be. The dream of pluralist polities and open public spheres goes hand in hand with the risk of what he calls authoritarian backlashes and radical Islamist insurgencies. Hamzawi (2005a) concludes that the path to Arab democracy continues to be problematic. Reading the contemporary regional political scene, legitimate doubts emerge at three central levels: the degree of commitment to reform by governments, the limits of internal democratization pressures, and the plausibility of effective democracy promotion strategies implemented by the United States (Hamzawi, 2005a). Hamzawi's observations that democratic reforms in authoritarian polities never happen out of impulsive noble motivations of auto-

---

[37] Civil society organizations across the Arab World with active contributions to the pursuit of human rights legislations and policies include: the Arab Standing Committee for Human Rights, the Arab Organization for Human Rights, the Algerian League for the Defense of Human Rights, Human Rights Information Network in Algeria, Bahrain Association for Human Rights, Bahrain Center for Human Rights, Bahrain Human Rights Watch Society, Al- Nadim Center for Treatment and Rehabilitation for the Victims of Violence, Association of Legal Assistance on Human Rights, Center for Egyptian Women's Legal Assistance Foundation, Egyptian Association against Torture, Egyptian Initiative for Personal Rights, Egyptian Organization for Human Rights, Association Of Human Rights in Babil, Human rights in Iraq & Kurdistan, Iraqi Human Rights Group, Al-Urdun Al-Jadid Research Center, Human Rights Program, Amman Human Rights Studies Center, Association for Victims of Torture and Arbitrary Detention, Human Rights Information Network in Kuwait, Human Rights Information Network in Libya, Libya Watch For Human Rights, Libyan Union for Human Rights Defenders, Magreb Human Rights, Moroccan Association for Human Rights, Association of Early Intervention for Children with Special Needs (Oman), Al Mezan Center for Human Rights, Al-Dameer Association for Human Rights, Human Rights Information Network in Qatar, Committee for defense of human rights in Arabian Peninsula, Saudi Human Rights Center, Sudan Human Rights Organization, Arab Organization for Human Rights in Syria, Human Rights Association In Syria, Human Rights Information Network in Tunisia, National Council For Freedom in Tunisia, UAE Human Rights Association, National Organization for Defending Rights and Freedoms – Hood.

cratic rulers seems insightful. Khouri (2005) observes, however, that political reform in the Arab World was underlied by three key factors: homegrown demands for dignity and better governance by the citizens of the Middle East; increasingly vulnerable and more thinly legitimate Arab regimes that find it difficult to maintain the existing political and economic order; and external pressures to reform and modernize (mainly from the U.S., but also from Europe and other industrialized nations).

V.4. The Unfolding Political Scene

Despite the potential paradoxes involved in the democratization of non-Western societies, the Arab world has shown sluggish receptivity to global calls for democratic reforms. Moore (1994) notes that in the Arab context, external pressures have played a key role in setting and altering the domestic political environment (both positively and negatively) in the struggle for democratization. On the other hand, the state has remained resilient in its opposition to genuine democratization mainly out of what are perceived as serious security concerns emanating from an overall restless regional situation marked by multiple wars, civil strife and ambivalent global attitudes (Hawthorne, 2004). As the U.S. democratization drive was losing its momentum in the region, prospects for reform continue to be rather dim despite the numerous achievements over the past two decades which may be summarized as follows:

- Restoration of democratic practices that had been confiscated by governments in the late 1970s and during the 1980s. This was the case of elections held in Jordan (1989), Bahrain (2001), Yemen (1993), Sudan (2000), and Egypt, 2001 and 2005), Algeria (2005), and Kuwait (2005), the UAE (2006), Morocco and Mauritania (2007).

- Initiation of constitutional amendments pertaining to freedom of speech and of the press as in Jordan, the UAE, Kuwait, Morocco, Yemen and Egypt.

- Formation of power-sharing arrangements as represented by parliamentary and consultative bodies in the conservative states of the Gulf region (Saudi Arabia, 1993 and the UAE, 2006).

- Legalization of politically and ethnically diverse groups and parties as in Algeria, Lebanon, Bahrain, Morocco, and Palestine. Algeria and Morocco switched to multi-party systems in 1988 and 1989 respectively in the aftermath of popular revolts that were triggered by harsh economic measures.

- Providing more political and civil rights to women both as voters and candidates for public offices in Oman, Jordan, Qatar, the UAE, Palestine, Egypt, and Bahrain.

Although documentation of political and social reform in the Arab World has been produced by a wide range of local civil society organizations and international NGOs, the most comprehensive account of political participation and civil liberties in the region has been made available through the UN Development Program Human Rights Index (UNDP, 2006). In Algeria, the report noted that Algeria promulgated on March 16, 2005 a law that enables the children of Algerian women married to non-Algerians to acquire their mother's citizenship, and since November 2005, the government has launched a program for combating corruption in the judicial system. In Bahrain, the UNDP document reported the promulgation of a new constitution on February 14, 2002 that includes many guarantees of human rights and public freedoms. The constitution adopted a two-chamber legislative system, approved women's right to vote and run in public elections, and stipulated the establishment of a supreme constitutional court to monitor the constitutionality of the law. The UNDP Report noted that Egypt carried out legal reforms in 2006 that included amending the criminal procedures law; amending the penal code on crimes of expression; passing a law establishing the 'national commission for quality of education' and a law for consumer protection. In Jordan, the government in 2006 published 5 international agreements on human rights in the official gazette making them part of the Jordanian legal system and promulgated the law of the National Centre for Human Rights (Law no. 51/2006) through the two chambers of parliament. In Kuwait, parliamentary elections were held at the end of June 2006 and witnessed a high participation rate marked by women's first time ever participation. The parliament amended on May 16, 2005 the first article of the elections law which restricted the right of voting and running in elections to Kuwaiti males, thereby extending that right to Kuwaiti women. Qatar also carried out significant reforms when in April 2003; the country's first constitution was approved in a national referendum. Saudi Arabia, according to the report, has also witnessed developments relating to holding the first municipal election in the country's history in 2005, establishing a journalists association, and Establishing 'King Abdul Aziz Centre for National Dialogue'. The UNDP document noted that the United Arab Emirates has a good record in the field of human development scoring more than 5 points on the Corruption Perceptions Index of Transparency International in 2005 (more than 159 countries scored less than 5 points). The UAE also held its first legislative elections in December 2006.

With regard to human rights reforms, many Arab governments have taken steps that signaled a growing acceptance of human rights as a legitimate public policy issue. Morocco, which has shown the greatest inclination of any Arab country to improve its human rights record, took another step by forming the Equity and Reconciliation Commission in January 2004, an institution unique in the region

(Nawar, 2003). Its mandate was to produce a public report on state repression from 1956 to 1999 and to compensate the families of Moroccans who 'disappeared' during these years. The Arab League at its May 2004 summit in Tunis approved revisions to the 1994 Arab Human Rights Charter that strengthen the rights to fair trial and political asylum, affirm prohibitions on torture, and endorse gender equality. Jordan, Egypt, Saudi Arabia and the UAE set up national human rights councils or committees in 2002 and 2003, 2004, and 2006 respectively. The purpose of these bodies is to expand public awareness of human rights and to increase government compliance with international human rights conventions. In 2003 the Egyptian government also allowed the Egyptian Organization for Human Rights to register as a nongovernmental organization. In 2004, Kuwait issued an operating license to a human rights organization for the first time. Saudi Arabia has made significant gestures toward human rights, allowing Human Rights Watch and Amnesty International to visit the country for the first time in 2003 and establishing a quasigovernmental human rights group in 2004. In 2006, the United Arab Emirates had its national human rights committee[38].

In outlining prospects for the future, Arab responses to the global reform drives have generated some visions. The 2004 Arab Human Development Report noted the need for change according to three scenarios defining developments in Arab societies in the first two decades of the 21st century. The first is called 'The Impending Disaster Scenario' in which conditions in the Arab World would stay unaltered as inaction will lead to intensified societal conflict. The second alternative scenario drawing on a process of peaceful negotiation on the redistribution of power in Arab countries represents 'the optimum approach for a transitional phase towards good governance', characterized by safeguarding freedom for all; effective political participation; inclusion of all political and religious groups, which respect the rights and freedoms of others; efficient institutions, which are transparent and accountable; and an independent judiciary—all of which ensure a smooth and uninterrupted alternation of power. The third alternative promotes gradual and moderate reform by Arab countries. This alternative, while not ideal, draws on a pragmatic attempt to make the best of regional and international initiatives, from the standpoint of it being a partnership of equals, and taking into consideration respect for Arab ownership and leadership of these processes; adherence to international human rights laws; inclusion of all societal forces; and respect for outcomes freely chosen by the people.

But despite aforementioned advances in political reform, the Arab World, according to regional and international reports, has yet to come a long way in real-

---

[38] Available early 2006 data show that the number of human rights organizations in the Arab World jumped to 75, most of them operate as civil society organizations concerned with broad human rights issues (Awadh, 2006).

izing expected transformations as the extent, nature, and direction of these changes remains enigmatic to political analysts and commentators. International human rights organizations have published scores of reports denouncing state violations of individual and community rights to free speech, assembly and political participation. More reports have been addressing rising levels of corruption as noted by the 2007 *Transparency International* report in which several Arab countries were topping the list of world corrupt entities. Strangely enough, some thinkers seem to frame the U.S. reformist drive in the Arab World as part of a broader battle between U.S.-tailored democratization and *al-Qaida*-inspired strategies to dominate the Arab World. Should any one of the two visions prevail, centrist Arab-Islamic views would be the prime losers. If both visions share one common feature, it is their obfuscation and abuse of the cherished centrist Arab-Islamic heritage. While President G. W. Bush has ruled out any room for Islamic variables in the evolving Arab World political experience, *al-Qaida* harnesses a myopic view of those same variables as the sole social option for the *Umma* in the 21st century and beyond. The writer argues that a new political vision drawing on the synthesis of Islamic morality and contemporary practices within the concept of 'Islamocracy' offers the Arab nation a third choice that safeguards its cherished traditions without being alienated from contemporary global realities.

The following section surveys key features of developments in the region since the early 1990s as manifestations of the slow political transformations evolving in the Arab World in the age of globalization. As the author notes, most of these changes, though carrying promising signs, are problematic and could not be viewed as credible foundations for making conclusions about future situations. There are at least three reasons for this argument. First, these changes, preached by the U.S., are mainly exogenously-motivated, initiated namely by the United States as part of a backlash strategy in the post-9/11 era. Hence, they would not necessarily echo real Arab concerns and interests at elite and popular levels. Second, the Arab authoritarian state is still well-entrenched in the age of globalization and has always been able to perpetuate its survival or to postpone its demise at the least costly compromises. Hence, serious efforts to bring about substantive structural changes in the Arab political system are likely to come into collision with the steel-wall resilience of the authoritarian state. Third, the widely-popularized 'Arab Street' remains in a prolonged state of stagnation and inactivity following decades of domestication and pre-emption by the authoritarian state. Hence, the popular variable often accounted for in social and political change is hardly visible in the Arab World, at least in the short run.

V.4.1. Civil Society Institutions

An important feature of political changes in the Arab World in the 1990s often invoked by reform researchers has been the re-invigoration of civil society structures and practices in varying degrees across the region. Ismael and Ismael (1997) noted that the retreat of the authoritarian state created 'a free space' for the emergence of voluntary organizations or civil society. However, the retreat was not without a cultural toll that afflicted the character and outlook of individuals and groups. By 1995, the number of civil society organizations in the Arab World was estimated at 70,000; about 20,000 of them were in Egypt. On the other hand, Yom (2005) notes that during this period, civil society grew not because the state retreated, but because authoritarian incumbents deployed a new tactic of control – they could reassert power and slake dissension by granting concessions too mild to produce systemic change, but hefty enough to merit symbolic applause at home and abroad. In this situation, while Arab states demonstrated tolerance for the establishment of 'competing' civil society institutions, they have also endeavored to reduce them into hollow structures with no real decision-making powers. Yom (2005) identifies three components underlying this ecology of civil society control by the state, the most obvious of them is blatant repression; when the demands of civil society violate the state's threshold of comfort, the regime clamps down with targeted arrests, harassment, and other forms of legal coercion against opposition groups. Second, Arab autocracies utilize systematic policies of legal constriction that defuse civic activism long before it becomes threatening. Third, co-optation, which dilutes opposition forces and drives the civic sector towards dependency on the state. Hudson (2003) suggests two international factors have intervened to strengthen state will and capacity to co-opt and stifle civil society orientations. First, the external strategic demands of Western allies endured well after the Cold War ended. Thus, the unrelenting refusal of Arab leaders to heed democratic demands and instead repress or co-opt civil society failed to trigger deep international consequences from global powers, which reinforced their coercive will. Second, while traditional rents like oil revenues did diminish in the 1980s, Arab regimes found new fiscal resources to underwrite their coercive capacity. Rent-seeking behavior became institutionalized on the international level, with Arab autocrats perennially searching for new external patrons and sources of monies.

V.4.2 Islamic Resurgence

With rising state repression of mushrooming Islamic orientations in Egypt, Jordan, Syria, Iraq, Tunisia, Morocco, Algeria and Libya, radical Islam, drawing on a fundamentalist interpretation of Scriptures was taking shape, especially on the wake of the establishment of the Taliban government in Afghanistan. On the other hand, a moderate stream of Islam that renounces violence as a means of achieving political goals and also accepts integration into democratic processes was also taking shape in the region. Moderate Islamic thinkers believe that Islam is compatible with electoral democracy that empowers the best and the brightest members of the community to be in decision-making positions. If the majority of those elected believe in Islam as a basis for government, then they would put their vision into effect in their capacities as members of law-making bodies. The rise of this orientation suggests clear transformations in the attitudes of mainstream Islamic movements towards democracy as the defining feature of political processes in the Arab World. In the 1950s, Sayyed Qutb was highly critical of democracy as a Western novelty that contravenes the fundamental foundations of Islamic political theory. According to this view, sovereignty in Islam belongs solely to Allah, while in a democratic system it belongs to the people. Thus, by the mid 1980s Arab World debates on democracy came to center not on its compatibility with Islam, but rather on how to harness it to promote Islamic interests.

Wright (1992) notes that thirteen years after the Iranian Revolution wrought the world's first modern Islamic republic, Islam is once again emerging as a powerful political idiom. Not only in the Middle East, but from North and West Africa to the former Asian republics of the Soviet Union, from India to Western China, Islam has become increasingly a defining force in evolving political agendas. The new burst of Islamic activism has reached high proportions that, with the demise of communism, Islam have been erroneously perceived as one of the future ideological rivals to the West. Esposito and Voll (1996) observed that throughout much of the Muslim World, the 1990s witnessed the impact and interaction of the forces of resurgent Islam and democratization. Issues of religious and cultural identity, authenticity, and legitimacy have been intertwined with those of political participation, empowerment, and civil society. The post-independence drift along a more Western secular path of development has been challenged if not rejected. Both governments and civil society movements have often re-appropriated religious symbols and vocabulary; they have used and abused implemented and manipulated religion in politics and society.

Muslim experiences in reformist transitions, however, have not occurred in isolation. Esposito and Voll (1996) see a global movement of religious and communal (ethnic, linguistic, and cultural) resurgence and democratization. The global tendency toward de-secularization has challenged the presuppositions of modernization, the progressive Westernization and secularization of societies which had often been articulated as inevitable evolutionary principles of development. Nations and religious traditions, political and religious leaders, have had to contend with religious and ethnic/nationalist forces that reassert their identity and seek empowerment. The many forms of this post-modern transformation can be seen not only in Muslim societies, but also in the disintegration of the former Soviet Union and of Yugoslavia, communal confrontations between

Hindus and Muslims in India, and the revolt of Sikh nationalists in the Punjab, Muslims in Kashmir, Tamils in Sri Lanka, and confrontations between militant Jewish religious groups and their more secular counterparts in Israel. For some observers, the reassertion of age-old religious and ethnic identities has led to the thesis of a clash of civilizations, of a post-Cold War period or New World Order in which the threat of global confrontation will no longer be between superpowers or nation-states but civilizations.

On the ground, as noted earlier, debate about centrist Islam (*Islam Wasati*) has come to focus no longer on the relevance of democracy for Islam, but rather on how Islamic groups could maximize their gains from involvement in democratic processes. Despite Islamic groups' misgivings about Western calls for political reforms, the interaction of Islamic movements with democratic politics in the Arab World has been evident in countries like Bahrain, Egypt (2005) Muslim Brotherhood's rise in national elections), Algeria, Morocco, Lebanon, Sudan, Kuwait, and Palestine (Hamas 2006 rise to power) and post-Saddam Iraq. Such involvement in democratic practices has prompted Western thinkers and politicians to speak of 'moderate Islam' as an evolving political phenomenon that stands in stark contrast with 'fundamentalist Islam', which looks down on Western democratic systems as lacking any affinity to Islamic teachings, and thus should be rejected. The January 2006 speech by *al-Qaida* second man Ayman al-Zawahri on *al-Jazeera* Satellite Channel in which he deplored Muslim Brotherhood's participation in Egypt's November 2005 parliamentary elections and his February 2007 criticism of Hamas' consent to set up a national unity government in Palestine induced fiery responses that seemed to underscore growing diverse views about the institution of democratic practices in Arab societies. For Muslim thinkers with moderate orientations, the introduction of democratic elections into Arab societies does not contravene Islam as it provides community members as equal citizens with appropriate mechanisms for addressing their political affairs in tune with Islamic moral values and at the same time within contemporary frameworks (Tamimi, 1997).

V.4.3. Women in Politics

A third feature of the developing political landscape is the rise of women as a political force to reckon with in the Arab region. Most Arab states have been signatories to major international conventions relating to women rights including the Convention on the Elimination of All Forms of Discrimination Against Women that commits states to eliminate discrimination against women through integrating the principle of gender equality in their national constitutions and legislation, and guaranteeing the realization of this principle through amending or abolishing laws that discriminate against women. Some writers argue that despite advances achieved in the past two decades to enhance women access to political and economic life and the labor market, the role of women in the Arab World region is still strongly limited to the domestic sphere, assuming their traditional roles within family confines. The United Nations Development Fund for Women's (UNIFEM, 2004) Report on 'Progress of Arab Women 2004' stated that the number of Arab women involved in politics was still far from representative of their population in society. For the authors of the report, the obstacles are related to lack of support and guidance necessary for women to reach decision-making positions and lack of knowledge and understanding of political rights and responsibilities. At the same time, an extensive report by Freedom House on 17 Arab countries in the Middle East and North Africa stated in May 2005 that the region was marked by an extreme lack of women's rights. According to this report, only Tunisia, Morocco, and Algeria have developed women's rights in some areas (Freedom House, 2005). The Millennium Development Goal of Gender Equality and Empowerment of Women developed by the United Nations shows that women in MENA countries have the smallest share of seats in national parliaments, a minimum percentage of six percent. However, since 1987, the number of countries with parliamentarian females has risen from three to 11 in 2003. Some feminists have called for a deeper understanding of women conditions in Arab societies by reconsidering the traditional Western-biased conceptual percepts that view traditions as a hindrances to women visibility in the public sphere vis-à-vis her conventional private sphere context (Asfaruddin, 1999).

A second reform trend evident since 2001 is the empowerment of women to bolster and expand their positions in government organizations. Many governments have enacted progressive 'personal status' legislation – new laws pertaining to marriage and divorce, child custody, and inheritance that decrease traditional discrimination against women. Morocco has seen the most extensive change in this regard with the passing of a new family law based on equality between men and women with regard to caring for the family, marriage age, equality between boys and girls in terms of custody, and made guardianship in marriage a right exercised by adult females according to their choosing and interest. In Bahrain, Parliament enhanced the principle of equality between men and women through granting political rights to women, appointing six women to the consultative council, facilitating women's right to occupy high-level public positions. Egypt has introduced more modest reforms pertaining to women's rights. In a 2002 landmark decision, the judiciary ruled that women could travel abroad without the permission of their husbands or fathers. In 2004, parliament passed legislation granting citizenship to children born to Egyptian mothers and foreign fathers. In March 2007, women were appointed as judges in Egypt despite opposition from conservative groups. The Jordanian government has also tried to enact legislation to increase penalties for household violence against women; curtail 'honor killings; and expand women's divorce and inheritance rights, but conservative members of the lower house of parliament have repeatedly blocked such reforms. Algeria, Jordan, and Morocco introduced electoral quotas to increase the number of women in parliament. In Oman, the first full-suffrage elections took place in October 2003, a vote that was the culmination of a process begun in 1991 of gradually expanding enfranchisement to all Omani adults. In the United Arab Emirates, women have been able to take up parliamentary and cabinet positions.

V.5. Implications for the Public Sphere

It has become clear that despite two decades of externally-induced democratic reforms in the Arab World, the region remains resilient in its resistance to substantive political changes despite sporadic breakthroughs. In the absence of effective civil society institutions; in the face of waning U.S. enthusiasm for real democratic change; and with the consolidation of brutal state authoritarianism, political reform remains an illusive goal. Even in countries which have introduced some reforms, the change has been confined at its best to electoral democracy, always taken as a procedural matter enabling the free election of candidates to parliamentary bodies while legal and authoritarian constitutional settings remain intact. A significant ingredient of the problem derives not only from the aforementioned factors, but from varying definitions of reform as espoused by parties with divergent political and ideological orientations. While the Bush administration pushed for a liberal Western-style reform, Arab intellectuals and civil society groups promoted a more localized formula drawing on exterminating corruption; introducing more participatory political arrangements; and far more important, harnessing the universal values of Islamic political traditions in the context of global realism. The failure of such democratic reforms to materialize across the region could also be rooted in the fact that we are talking about 22 Arab states with varying socio-political and economic conditions. This suggests that even in the Arab region, it is not plausible to apply a standardized formula for political reform. As noted earlier, the modern Arab state, with its executive powerful security apparatus, converts its surrounding social environment into 'a setting in which nothing moves and from which nothing escapes'. This increasing centralization of the executive is embossed in constitutional texts which vest wide-ranging powers in the head of state.

The uncertainty of political reforms in the Arab World is bound to adversely bear on the development of the public sphere in the region for decades to come. The 2004 Arab Human Development Report (UNDP, 2004) notes that the failure of democracy in several Arab countries is not cultural in origin, but is rather a function of the convergence of political, social and economic structures that have suppressed or eliminated organized social and political actors capable of turning the crisis of authoritarian and totalitarian regimes to their advantage. The elimination of such forces has sapped the democratic movement of any real forward momentum. This fragmentation of political entities has been instrumental in assisting states to stifle real political change as the Arab World continues to be viewed as a pool of political islands independently surviving on their own self-perceived agendas. If the public sphere is the political space embracing diverse actors seeking to reach a consensus on different issues, then one expects to see the existence of solid political institutions to undertake this discursive function. This aspect, unfortunately, continues to be missing in the region.

V.6. Summary and Conclusion

Although the public sphere is considered a central component of participatory politics, it could not exist outside a system of democratic values and practices. A public sphere arising in an undemocratic setting is mostly likely to turn into an arena for subjugation and manipulation. This has exactly been the case in the Arab World since the early 1990s. Political reform has been a buzz phrase that dominated scores of conferences and research reports; yet its concrete manifestations on the ground have been rather limited. Several advancements have been noted with respect to the institution of electoral processes, civil society sectors, and women rights. However, the degree to which this has yet to be realized seems highly contingent on the evolution of a viable synthetic option that draws on Islamic morality and contemporary political practices within the notion of 'Islamocracy'. The author argues that by mid 2007, political reform in the Arab World had failed not only because of authoritarian state resistance, but also because of the failure of Arab intellectual community to define a third scenario for change, a scenario that synthesizes basic Islamic moral values and traditions with contemporary political practices into a new political vision deeply rooted in Islamic heritage; yet closely reflective of contemporary political patterns. The writer concludes that this intellectual deficiency has turned the Arab political landscape into a murky arena of ceaseless political ferment that could never lead to the institution of a genuine public sphere in the region.

VI
THE EMERGING ARAB PUBLIC SPHERE

> The mass media in the Arab World and the Middle East have undergone profound changes since the beginning of the 1990s. The introduction and spread of new technologies such as satellite television and the Internet have extended media spaces beyond the local, national, and regional realm. Trans-border flows of communication have enabled some consumers- those with access to the new technologies- to interact with a global discourse and bypass the limits of authoritarian information control........ The question remains, however, whether new access to external media and the widening of media horizons is sufficient to generate political and social changes in the Arab World and the Middle East.
> (Hafez, 2001)

In November 2004, the Middle East Broadcasting Center (MBC) stopped airing a nightly television series entitled *The Road to Kabul*, a drama work depicting the evolution of *Jihadist* sentiments among Arabs volunteering to fight against Soviet occupation of Afghanistan in the 1980s. Although the real reason for MBC's decision to discontinue showing the program was not made public, it was circulated at the time that the television broadcaster received threats from *al-Qaida* Group which protested the way the *Mujahiddin* were represented in the show[39]. One year later, the London *Daily Mirror* reported that U.S. President G. W. Bush told British Prime Minister Tony Blair in April 2005 that he planned a military strike on the Qatar-based *al-Jazeera Satellite Channel* (JSC) to avenge the pan-Arab television service's critical coverage of the war in Iraq. If both stories suggest anything significant, it is obviously how media in the Arab World are increasingly coming not only under traditional authoritarian state pressures, but also under trans-national influences as well. It also underscores the changing realities of the Arab media landscape in the 1990s and beyond where the communications scene has turned more trans-nationalized, engaging multiple players in public debates about the current and future realities of the region. The concept of the public sphere is used in this book to described mass-mediated space associated with conventional and new media institutions. The use of the phrase is never meant to suggest any value judgment relating to the confluence of technological and political developments in the region, although the author argues that

---

[39] Another show that came under external pressures was *Al Hoor Al Ain* which focused on a number of families from across the Arab world who the audience knew would fall victim to the attacks by the end of the series. The show juxtaposed detailed accounts of these families' lives, relationships and troubles with sequences from camps in which rigid fundamentalists indoctrinated the young terrorists who later carried out the attacks. The show provoked controversy in Saudi Arabia, where it was attacked in the press and especially on Islamist Web sites. Because of the controversy, the Saudi satellite channel MBC, which aired the show, ended up releasing a statement, reading in part: 'Our choice of this title from the Koran in no way aims to ridicule the Maidens of Paradise but rather to show how religion is diverted from its initial mission and [to show] that the attacks committed in its name are nothing other than acts of terrorism, which are prejudicial to it [religion]' (Lindsey, 2006).

political and communications developments have fallen short of producing solid public sphere to be reckoned with.

Since 1991, the Arab pubic sphere has shifted towards further expansion and more inclusiveness, with more actors being featured in public discussions and more taboo issues being openly addressed for the first time in the region's history. The Arab public sphere has become no longer confined to its national or local boundaries; it has meshed well with the global public sphere, the Middle East increasingly turns into a top priority region on successive U.S. administrations' foreign policy agendas, especially in the post- 9/11 era. Likewise, as much as the region has become a battleground for the U.S.-led global war on terror, its media sphere has also turned into a fighting arena among players with divergent political orientations to win Arabs' hearts and minds.

VI.1. Defining the Arab Public Sphere

The unprecedented explosion of communication channels in the Arab region since the early 1990s coincided with the region's political ferment as represented by Arab World's debates on political reform. The national media expansion per se does not seem to wholly reflect a genuine public sphere as most media outlets remained constrained by heavy-handed state policies; yet, the writer argues that only few media services could be classified as active components of the emerging public sphere by virtue of their pan-Arab and global reach, their critical discourse, and their diverse output. Hence, some researchers speak of the emerging institutions of the Arab public sphere in its ideal type form as embracing few media outlets that are either editorially or financially independent; or are part of the evolving open Web-based communications arena. On the other hand, other researchers refer to the Arab public sphere in mere physical terms, incorporating a wide range of media outlets regardless of their institutional affiliation or editorial orientations. This conception of the Arab pubic sphere is rather flawed because it describes mass-mediated public arenas that have evolved either in response to global political and technological forces or have existed as part of state media systems. But as Lynch (2006: 29) notes, the new Arab public sphere should be understood in terms of the public arguments enacted by self-defined Arabs within widely-accessible new media. He argues (2006: 31) that despite skepticisms, the public sphere has been increasingly central to the analysis of Arab and Islamic politics. In both cases, however, the missing feature of the public sphere as evolving out of genuine indigenous socio-political processes remains a central issue to be addressed.

The argument offered here is that due to its global induction, the Arab public sphere carries little affinity to domestic political developments, though it has some impact in shaping them in the long run. A major implication of this situation is that the emerging public sphere, by virtue of its global and state domination, is turning into a buffer zone inhibiting the advancement of a genuine political and cultural discourse. The author defines a genuine Arab public sphere as the public arena to which local and global state and non-state actors are given free access to debate issues of concern to the local citizenry. Lynch (2006: 32) defines the public sphere in terms of active arguments before an audience about issues of shared concern. He notes that the mobilization media characteristic of authoritarian Arab states can be seen as the antithesis of the public sphere, with a single voice driving out all dissent, questioning, and critical reason. The two definitions suggest a dichotomous nature of the new public sphere in which global and state forces compete for space in the public arena while indigenous non-state actors are excluded. As noted in the previous chapter, the failure of civil society institutions to materialize in many parts of the Arab World in the 1990s and beyond has stifled genuine public sphere debates that came to be dominated by state and global discourse. In this case, if the existing mass-mediated public sphere in the Arab World lacks the indigenous features vital for its balanced ideological representation, then we are talking about an emerging political space that reproduces itself in tune with the perpetuation of global and national power structures. Global and state hegemony of public life in the Arab World has pre-empted the emergence of any significant community input into policy-making, thus creating a revolution of rising frustrations in the region. As noted in Chapter II, the emerging Arab public sphere is problematic because it is intellectually Western-oriented; globally-located; economically-unviable; and politically-authoritarian. In the following section, the writer analyzes the Arab public sphere in terms of four components: players, institutions, discourse, and effects.

VI.2. Components of the Arab Public Sphere

To shed light on the dynamics of the emerging Arab public sphere, the following section describes major players, media institutions, discourse types, and potential effects on national and global politics. The basic assumption here is that the public sphere in the Arab World serves more as an instrument for bolstering authoritarian state entrenchment and global power consolidation than as an expression of alternative indigenous concerns and visions.

VI.2.1. Players

The emerging Arab public sphere has come to embrace new players not accounted for in the former modern public sphere of the 1960s and 1970s when government views and policies dominantly defined public discussions. Players in the new public sphere range from preachers of unorthodox ideas to those with extra-conservative perspectives, and from state mainstream voices to global proponents of new political reforms. The diffusion of novel views concerning religion, politics and taboo-related issues has always prompted public outcries against channels like *al-Jazeera, al-Arabiya, New TV*, and *al-Hurra* and Internet outlets like *Elaf, al-Jazeera.net* and *Arab Times*. In the meantime, thousands of highly-provocative exchanges posted as part of free Weblog outlets or other interactive forums go without public reactions due to their limited ubiquity and diffusion (Za'atreh, 2006). Yet, one should not perceive the evolving public sphere as a totally-free space accessible to all actors in the Arab World political terrain as it continues to be subjected to exclusion, omission, and manipulation when opportunities arise. Players in the new arena, more or less, represent established political orientations associated with local and global power structures. Without alluding to any conspiratorial analysis, the writer argues that while the Arab public sphere has witnessed greater pluralism in player composition, this diversity should never be construed as an indicator of real institutional democratic transitions. The expansion of the public sphere is no more than a further growth in the number of media outlets drawing on technological advancements and representing already well-established power centers.

Ironically, access to the new public sphere has been offered to individuals and groups with unorthodox ideas that are offensive to Islamic values and traditions, under freedom of expression rubric. An example is the publication of Syrian Mohamed Shahrour's book *al-Kitab wal-Qur'an* (The Book and the Qur'an) (1992), which sold tens of thousands of copies throughout the Arab World in spite of the fact that its circulation was banned or discouraged in many places. Its success could not have been imagined before there were large numbers of people able to read it and understand its advocacy or the need to reinterpret ideas of religious authority and tradition, and apply Islamic precepts to contemporary society. On issues ranging from the role of women in society to rekindling 'creative interactions' with non-Muslim philosophies, Shahrour argues that Muslims should reinterpret sacred texts and apply them to contemporary social and moral issues. Another work is the novel authored by Syrian writer *Walimat Aashab al-Bahr* (Banquet of Sea Weeds) which created a public uproar in 2000 'as an example of blasphemous works'. On television, secularist Sadiq Jalal al-'Azm, debated Sheikh Yussuf al-Qaradawi, an Islamic scholar, on *al-Jazeera* Satellite TV in May 1997 on a range of contemporary issues facing the Arab World on the eve of the 21st century.

On the other hand, the evolving Arab public sphere has embraced two versions of Islam: the centrist (*Wasatiya*) and the fundamentalist (*Asouliya*). The centrists are often described as mirroring the moderate version represented by religious talk shows with evangelical dimensions. Yussuf al-Qaradawi's weekly talk show on *al-Jazeera*[40] and former Egyptian Islamic evangelist Amr Khaled television evangelism offer an intriguing model of social change through mass media. Khaled, who started out in the early 1990s by speaking in country clubs and upper class living rooms of Cairo, became a media sensation due to his clear talk about how Muslims can – and should – sanctify their everyday living experience. An accountant by training, Khaled adopted neither the hectoring tone often associated with clerics, nor the anger of militant Islam; instead, his style is empathetic and almost plaintive. For Khaled's followers, the central organizing principle is bridging the communal and the individual (Lindsey, 2006). In early March 2006, Khaled spearheaded a global effort to reconcile Muslim and Danish communities on the aftermath of the publication of cartoons offensive to the Prophet of Islam in several European newspapers. The centrist view is also visible in a plethora of state-run broadcast programs as well as the press, highlighting the moderate nature of Islam. On the other hand, the fundamentalist version is represented by radical voices of militant groups with outright rejection of emerging Western-style socio-political and cultural arrangements in the Muslim World. On January 6, 2006, *al-Jazeera* Channel aired a video tape showing *al-Qaida* second man Ayman al-Zawahri declaring 'U.S. defeat in Iraq and promising future victories in Afghanistan and Palestine'. In the meantime, the World Wide Web is used as an effective communication outlet for militant groups seeking to build up public support for their causes. Unable to have access to established media outlets, these organizations draw on the Web to propagate their extremist views of Islam and their sweeping campaign against the West and 'its allies' in the Muslim World'. In many cases, those groups use the Web to demonstrate their military accomplishments as represented by attacks on American forces in both Afghanistan and Iraq (Za'atreh, 2006). Eickelman (2002a) comments on their use of new communications technologies as follows:

> Alternating with these scenes of devastation and oppression of Muslims are images of Osama bin Laden: posing in front of bookshelves or seated on the ground like a religious scholar, holding the *Qur'an* in his hand. Bin Laden radiates charismatic authority and control as he narrates the Prophet Muhammad's flight from Mecca to Medina, when the early Islamic movement was threatened by the idolaters, but returned to conquer them. This allusion is repeatedly invoked in the video. Bin Laden also stresses the need for a *jihad*, or struggle for the cause of Islam, against the 'crusaders' and 'Zionists'. Later images show military training in Afghanistan (including target practice at a video of Bill Clinton projected against a wall), and a final sequence – the word 'solution' flashes across the screen – portrays an Israeli soldier in full riot gear retreating from a Palestinian boy throwing stones, and a *Qur'anic* recitation.

---

[40] This program, entitled *'Al-Shari'a wal-Hayat'* (Islamic Law and Life), had systematically featured Sheikh Qaradawi since its launch in 1997, but by early 2005, other religious scholars from around the Arab World were hosted on the show.

State actors are the dominant players in the emerging public arena. By virtue of their ownership and control of media institutions, government officials have convenient access to media space which is originally designed to serve as a launching pad for communicating their views on a range of local, regional and global issues. State actors are featured on newspapers and radio and television shows as they make political statements or as they are involved in different activities, mostly with protocol-oriented nature. State actors receive widespread publicity in state-run media because they engage, from official points of view, in newsworthy events that deserve to be highlighted. When events involve heads of state, they are shown on front pages and prime time TV news shows. If low-ranking officials are the subject of news, they are featured in local news pages and newscasts. The tradition of according outstanding publicity to state actors in national media goes back, as noted in Chapter V, to the immediate post-colonial period to foster their image as symbols of national pride and independence. In all state-owned media, this trend has continued well into the first years of the 21st century, thus substantiating claims about the unchanged role of national as tools of government propaganda and political legitimation.

Global actors are also taking part in the evolving public sphere. American and European officials are highly featured in the Arab press as well as in broadcast news and talk shows. Most Arab media have correspondents stationed in major world capitals like Washington, D. C., London, Paris, Berlin, Tokyo and Moscow. American and European political experts and media commentators are featured on TV shows and newspaper interviews. U.S. officials have access to the evolving public sphere as part of their endeavors have publicity as part of U.S. public diplomacy campaign in the Arab World. U.S. State Department and White House statements are often carried live on Arab World television in addition to U.S. channels like *al-Hurra*. Many Arab television channels normally cut off their regular programming to broadcast live statements and press conferences from world capitals simply because those events are viewed as newsworthy by virtue of their association with a global power like the United States. On many occasions, *al-Jazeera* and *al-Arabiya* satellite channels host by video conferencing numerous Western political figures and experts to comment on emerging developments in the region. At least in the cases of the United States and the United Kingdom, some State Department and Foreign Office spokesman do their broadcast interviews in Arabic despite risks of mis-speaking as was the case with the Alberto Fernandez who told al-Jazeera satellite channel that 'there is a strong possibility history will show the United States displayed 'arrogance' and 'stupidity' in its handling of the Iraq war.'
Another category of actors with increasing access to the emerging public sphere in the region includes members of the nascent civil society sector ranging from women organizations, to political parties, to the intelligentsia, to business interests, to religious and ethnic groupings, to human rights activists. These voices generally project moderate views on social and political issues, framing them

within liberal intellectual perspectives. They seem to reflect rational, yet sometimes critical orientations to political and social issues drawing on peaceful problem-solving mechanisms. These civil society groupings have opted to act within democratic rules as established through constitutional arrangements. Yet, state control remains the most chronic problem plaguing civil society in the Arab World. States' intervention in civil society institutions has ranged from crude repression to manipulation to co-optation, thus rendering democracy a useless pursuit in the majority of Arab societies. In a sense, these frustrating realities were bound to circumvent any potential civil society impact on political processes in the region (UNDP, 2004).

VI.2.2. Institutions

As noted earlier in this chapter, the broad definition of the Arab public sphere incorporates a wide range of media outlets that include state, private, and global foreign media, in addition to the World Wide Web. The institutional diversity of public sphere affiliations seems to reflect the new mosaic of the emerging public arena in the region. Following is an overview of the institutional terrain of the Arab public sphere.

VI.2.2.1. Satellite Television

As the backbone of the evolving public sphere, satellite television has presented itself as the promised arena for public discussions of politics, religion, and other issues. Talk shows like *al-Jazeera's* 'Opposite Direction', 'More Than One Opinion', and 'Without Frontiers' have offered Arab audiences a wide range of unorthodox views and perspectives on issues and events impinging on their life. Other channels like *al-Arabiya, al-Mustakilla, Abu Dhabi, Dubai,* and *New TV* feature daring interviews with controversial personalities and political figures. The rise of some of these channels has been induced by the emergence of some divergent political visions associated with different players. Occasional tensions between Qatar and Saudi Arabia were believed to have induced the launch of *al-Jazeera* in 1996 to counter 'Saudi-affiliated media' (Sakr, 2006). In January 2003, *al-Arabiya* Satellite Television Channel was launched from Dubai Media City to provide Arab viewers with alternative perspectives regarding issues and events relating to the conflict in Iraq, the U.S.-waged global 'war on terror', and political reforms in the region. Television channels were also launched by non-Arab governments as part of ongoing political rivalry in the region. Examples include U.S.-sponsored *al-Hurra* Channel, Iran's *al-Alam* Channel, France 24, Russia Today, and the expected BBC Arabic television channel slated for launch in late 2007.

The proliferation of satellite television in the Arab region has contributed to its gaining largest share of the public sphere. Arab States Broadcasting Union (ASBU) statistics (2005) noted that there were 47 television broadcast organizations in the Arab World that included 20 government and 27 private bodies. They operated 75 variety channels and 65 specialized channels distributed among: children (6); sports (6); news (12); drama (12); music (11); documentaries (5); and cultural (13). Seventy eight channels offer free-to-air programs while 59 channels are based on subscriptions (ASBU, 2005). Eighty one broadcast television channels were in Arabic, while 40 in English, and 11 in French. Imported Arabic programs amount to 70% while foreign programs reach 60%. Local production ranges from 30-100%. By early 2007, there were over 300 satellite television chancels with diverse news and entertainment content accessible to views across the region. The numbers do not seem impressive in an Arab world of 250 million people or more, but they represent a more diverse platform for news and opinion comparable to the traditional print news media. *Al-Jazeera*, with its Western-style news programs, has left a marked effect on other region-wide satellite channels, such as LBC and *al-Mustaqbal* (Future Television) of Lebanon, Abu Dhabi and Dubai channels of the United Arab Emirates, the Saudi-owned MBC (Middle East Broadcasting Center), and Egypt's Nile and ESC (Egyptian Satellite Channel), as well as others (Ayish, 2003a). New satellite channels are also marked by some interactivity with viewers around the Arab World, as evident in audience participation in live television shows. The following section surveys major satellite television broadcasters in the Arab World.

VI.2.2.1.1. State-Run Television

By the mid-1980s, the winds of change were already blowing on the Arab region as a result of global and local developments that included increasing literacy and education rates, urbanization, and privatization. The 1991 Gulf war, credited with the acceleration of those transformations, also served as a catalyst for further political reforms, privatization programs, and communications technology diffusions (al-Umran, 1996). These three factors, growing, more or less, out of broader global trends, seemed to have had an enduring impact on the Arab broadcasting scene. In a way, they seem to have contributed to relaxing government broadcast controls; abolishing some information regulatory bodies; granting more airtime access to diverse political views; enabling communication with international audiences beyond national frontiers; and allowing more advertising on state television. These conditions, more importantly, seemed to have created favorable attitudes on the part of both Arab governments and private businesses for the launch of fully commercial television operations alongside government-controlled services (Ayish, 2000).

Regional and global television expansion has been a major feature of the 1990s in the region. Boukhnoufah (2001) notes that the audio-visual sector in the Arab world has developed outside national boundaries vis-à-vis local arenas because of lacking national audio-visual policies, belated openness to local forces, and absence of centralized regulatory frameworks. The traditional model of a national television system drawing on a government-controlled and operated service began to experience major cracks in the early 1990s in the face of global technological and political pressures. This transformation is marked by the institutionalization of a 'mixed television system' model; the restructuring of television organizations into more financially, editorially and administratively autonomous bodies, and the opening up of airwaves to accommodate a wider spectrum of views. These trends seemed to have flown from wider global developments pertaining to the changing status of public service television around the world. Achilles and Miege (1994) note that since the mid 1980s, public service television in Western Europe has had to confront competition from new commercial, and for the most part, generalist television channels. They noted that the financial crisis flowing from this situation was heightened by the clear failure of states to draw more revenue from heavily- exhausted national budgets. Financial constraints have brought about a strategic reorientation on the part of public channels, leading to a sweeping restructuring of their organizational resources. Karthigesu (1994: 20) notes that changes in the Asia broadcasting scene are driven by an identity crisis in public service television. This crisis seems to be exacerbated by the introduction of new media technologies, the subordination of television to industrial policy considerations; the application to broadcasting of principles of economic and political liberalism; and the rise of production costs beyond the financial capacities of public service broadcasters. Commenting on this grim reality, Willard (1991: 315) notes that:

> Public service broadcasting is a fading star. Its moment has passed and the continuing need for its institutions must be evaluated. New technologies, alternative financing options and changing political attitudes in post-industrial democracies seriously undermine the traditional rationales for state sponsored, public authority broadcasting structures. Public service broadcasting is as vital and as necessary as ever. The forces of contemporary technological and economic change provide only the illusion of program diversity and choice. Progressive societies require positive public policies to guarantee the existence of strong cultural institutions of various sorts, including radio and television that place goals of information and education, as well as entertainment, above the imperatives of the commercial marketplace.

The restructuring of state television organizations in numerous Arab countries in the 1990s has led to the creation of more autonomous entities as evident in Jordan, Bahrain, the United Arab Emirates, Syria, Qatar, Kuwait, and Lebanon. In 1985 Radio Jordan and Jordan Television were merged into a single corporation. In early 2001, three channels in the indebted and overstaffed Jordan Radio and

Television Corporation were combined into a single channel to save on resources (Digital Studio, 2001a: 6). Six months later, Jordan Television reported its super channel proved to be successful in terms of regional television competition (Digital Studio, 2001b: 8). In the United Arab Emirates, Emirates Media Inc. was created in 1999 as an umbrella organization housing numerous broadcast and print media activities including the highly reputed Abu Dhabi Satellite Channel and Emirates Satellite Channel. In 2005, Dubai Media Incorporated was established as part of local media restructuring arrangements. These moves have been initiated primarily to enhance performance and cope with spiraling television production costs.

The introduction of satellite television into the Middle East in the early 1990s has, more than ever before, also presented viewers with diverse television contents. In the pre-1990s period, terrestrial television broadcasting covering national territories and border areas was the main feature of the broadcasting landscape. The diffusion of satellite television reception equipment and cable delivery systems expanded audiences' choices to include program offerings from countries as far as the United States, Western Europe, and Japan. According to 2000 data, Arab viewers were able to receive up to 200 television channels from around the world (Labib, 2000). The launch of regional satellite systems like ARABSAT, NILESAT, HOTBIRD, and THURAYYA provided government and private broadcasters in the region with new outlets to reach audiences around the Arab World. On the other hand, international satellite systems like EUTELSAT, PANAMSAT, and ASIASAT have served as platforms for global television networks targeting the Middle East and North Africa. Arab Radio and Television Network (ART) and ORBIT Television and Radio Network are two examples of global digital broadcasters catering to viewers in the Arab region and around the world with encrypted packages.

The launch of satellite television channels in the Arab world has not led to the diminution of terrestrial channels. Government-controlled television organizations continue to maintain terrestrial transmissions with regular or mostly local programming despite the fact that more viewers are turning to satellite television channels. Terrestrial transmissions continue to constitute a major part of television in large Arab world areas where satellite reception technology is either banned or not available (Ayish, 2003a). Terrestrial television channels are used to relay local programming to audiences with no satellite television reception capabilities. In Arab countries with single-channel services, satellite television had been a replica of terrestrial services, which raises the question of addressing local and regional audiences with the same television messages. On the other hand, the operation of separate terrestrial and satellite television channels seems to have financially overburdened television organizations as they grappled with two sets of programming requirements. One of the potential negative consequences of this practice is to compromise quality in local transmissions in order to compete with other broadcaster in capturing larger regional and international audiences.[41]

VI.2.2.1.2. Private Television

The launch of private television in the Arab World in the early 1990s marked a breakthrough in the Arab world television landscape which had long been monopolized by states. Although Ayish (2003a) notes that Arab television started initially as a private enterprise in the 1950s and 1960s, governments' take over of broadcasting operations signaled an era of exclusive state control of this media sphere. In 1991, the widely-acclaimed CNN coverage of the First Gulf War raised Arabs' awareness of the centrality of diversifying television ownership by allowing private players in the television broadcasting business. The Middle East Broadcasting Center (MBC) was the first private television operation to be launched from studio facilities in London. Although by the end of 2006, more than 200 private television channels were operational, the following section sheds light on selected services with outstanding news and public affairs programming compared with government-controlled or private entertainment-oriented services.

Al-Jazeera Satellite Channel (JSC)

Al-Jazeera Satellite Channel (JSC) was launched in 1997 from Qatar in the aftermath of the discontinuation of a BBC Arabic Satellite Channel's joint venture with Saudi-owned Orbit Television and Radio Network following editorial disagreements over the airing of an interview with a London-based Saudi dissident. Over the past few years, JSC has presented itself as a forum for 'the Opinion and the Other Opinion'. Funded by advertising revenue and subsidies from the Government of Qatar, JSC has marked a major transition in Arab world broadcast media with its critical talk shows and live coverage of regional and global events. The channel's critical reporting of domestic political and religious affairs in several Arab countries has led to a series of diplomatic incidents as well as to the closure of some of its offices abroad (Da Lage, 2005: 56). The channel's bold approach to political issues and developments has also generated misgivings about its journalistic performance, even within the Bush administration which on several occasions asked its staff to shun the channel on the basis of its anti-U.S. reporting of the Iraqi conflict (Hudson, 2006). In April 2005, President G. W. Bush was quoted in a meeting with British Prime Minister Tony Blaire as floating the idea of bombing JSC's headquarters to avenge what he perceived as the channel's pro-terror stands. One of JSC's reporters was shot dead by Ameri-

---

[41] See *Middle East Media Guide* (2007) at:
http://www.middleeastmediaguide.com/television.htm

can forces on the eve of the fall of Baghdad while two of its staff, Tayseer Allouni and Sami al-Hajj were serving prison sentences in Guantanamo and Spain respectively on charges of promoting *al-Qaida* ideology.

But regardless of the debate over the circumstances giving rise to al Jazeera or to conspiratorial thoughts about its connections with global and regional powers and groups, it is inarguable that JSC has brought about a dramatic transformation in the long-stagnant Arab World media sphere. Lynch (2004)) notes that al Jazeera has presented itself as an alternative to state-run television, providing a forum for political views that are not likely to be positively received by government-operated media in the Arab World. He cited the example of the pre-eminent Egyptian journalist Muhammad Hassanayn Haykal who was summarily banned in the spring 2004 from appearing on Egyptian television after he broached the deeply sensitive topic of Gamal Mubarak's aspirations to succeed his father as president. In response to the ban, Haykal signed a blockbuster deal with al-Jazeera, to air a weekly show entitled *'With Haykal: A Life Experience'*, devoting the first episode of the show to exposing the Egyptian government's efforts to silence his dissent. From Lynch's point of view, the experience of the venerable Haykal demonstrates how, by shattering state control over public debate, Arab satellite television 'is building the foundation of a more democratic Arab political culture' (Lynch, 2004).

Al-Jazeera Satellite Channel, as a new media phenomenon in the Arab World, has attracted a wide range of research, seeking to investigate how this pan-Arab television channel contributes to the transformation of the traditionally state-controlled media environment. Miles (2003) notes that as a result of *Al-Jazeera*'s critique of many Arab governments, Arab television has been labeled by some observers as a virtual 'political party'. But he remarks that media can surely not compensate for the lack of civil society organization and the weakness of the existing opposition. Another volume edited by Zayani (2005) took a more critical approach to *Al-Jazeera* while recognizing its impressive contributions to the emerging Arab public sphere in the area. Zayani notes that in spite of its relatively short history, this Qatar-based news network seems to have left an indelible mark in the Arab world that has changed the face of the otherwise parochial Arab media – although in the West, it is largely perceived as a channel that is set on countering Western ideologies. In an earlier book on JSC El-Nawawy and Iskander (2002) also spoke lyrically of the channel's pro-democratization orientations in the Arab region and its role in pre-empting traditional Arab state media censorship by providing alternative perspectives on issues relating to politics, religion, and other sensitive cultural aspects of contemporary Arabian societies. Both authors noted that the Qatar-based television network has been a hugely positive force in the Middle East 'because it has put pressure on authoritarian Arab regimes and helped to promote freedom of expression'. According to the two authors, the network differs from Western news networks because it has an 'Arab perspective', they say, but this does not make it any more biased than American networks that have an 'American perspective'. In late 2006, *al-Jazeera International*, and English language channel was launched to be followed by *al-Jazeera Documentary* in the same year.

The channel's newscasts, political and cultural talk shows and documentaries provide the staple for its daily programming to global audiences inside the Arab World and beyond. There are regular newscasts carried at the top of the hour, in addition to three major news round-up programs in the morning, at noon and at midnight. The channel maintains a huge network of correspondents covering almost all Arab countries and major world capitals. In addition, the channel draws on a wide range of political and cultural talk shows, the most imminent of which are '*Opposite Direction*', a *Cross-Fire* style political show; '*More Than One Opinion*', a live talk program in which studio and remote-site guests are engaged; and '*Without Frontiers*', a *Hard Talk*-style show in which one personality is interviewed with audience call-in feedback. Other programs include '*al-Jazeera Forum*' which discusses an important topic with full audience participation; '*Open Dialogue*' which is town-hall style show on selected topics, and '*Behind the News*' which is a 30-minute nightly discussion of an important issue arising in the context of local, national or international developments. The channel also runs a news text strip carrying the main headlines that are updated when necessary to keep audiences abreast of regional and global news developments.

Al-Arabiya Channel
This is a 24-hour television channel launched in Dubai in January 2003 on the eve of the Anglo-American invasion of Iraq. The channel is backed by MBC, Lebanon's Hariri group and other investors from Saudi Arabia, Kuwait and other Gulf states. As part of what some call the 'Saudi media empire', (Sakr, 2006) *al-Arabiya* has risen to prominence in the past three years in the context of covering the conflict in Iraq, tending mainly to promote the new political developments in the country. On the eve of its establishment, some views circulated that the channel was intended to counterbalance the growing JSC popularity as a critical media outlet with minimum appreciation in Saudi Arabia. During the pilgrimage season in early 2006, *al-Arabiya* was carrying live coverage of Saudi handling of the stampede in which over 300 pilgrims died. JSC, by Saudi law, was banned from covering the pilgrimage for the third year in a row. With no correspondents based in Mecca to report about the tragic incident, JSC used live video from Saudi television accompanied by views and observations of individual pilgrims who witnessed the accident. Satellite and telephone technologies made it impossible for Saudi authorities to circumvent coverage of a pilgrimage disaster by channels banned from operating on Saudi soil. Lynch (2004) noted that *al-Arabiya*, has since its launch in early 2003, offered a platform to

liberal reformers, with a tone tempered by greater restraint and sensitivity to the concerns of major Arab states.

New TV

New TV was launched in Lebanon on October 4, 2001 as a variety channel with a focus on news and current affairs. The channel's slogan is 'respecting the public and being respected by the public'. Since its inception, NTV has been embroiled in successive controversies. In December 2003, channel owner Tahseen Khayyat was arrested by Lebanese authorities on charges of having links with Israel. Earlier, NTV's satellite transmissions were suspended for few days following its airing of a show critical of Saudi Arabia. With Syrian forces out of Lebanon on the aftermath of the assassination of the late Lebanese Prime Minister Rafiq al-Hariri in mid February 2005, NTV's critical tone towards Syria has been on the rise.

Al-Manar TV

This channel was launched in Lebanon in 1999 as a media organ for Lebanese Hizbullah Party. The channel's stated goal is to 'preserve the Islamic values and to enhance the civilized role of the Arab and Islamic community'. The channel also plays a significant role in Hizbullah's struggle against Israel. Its program offerings comprise of news and current affairs, talk shows, cultural and religious segments, and historical drama. *Al-Manar* is distributed also via cable networks in Europe and North America. In March 2006, *al-Manar* was banned from showing on local U.S. cable networks on charges of fomenting anti-Israeli sentiments. During the 2006 Israeli war on Lebanon, *al-Manar* studios were bombed, but transmission continued from underground make-shift facilities.

Future TV

Future Television was launched on February 15, 1993 with eccentric funky-looking, family-oriented programs that drew on a blend of Western and Arabian lifestyle patterns. In 1996, in compliance with the new Lebanese audio-visual law, *Future Television* restructured its ownership to embrace about 90 shareholders in addition to the late Lebanese Prime Minister Rafiq al-Hariri, whose family remains owner of majority shares in this channel. Since Hariri's assassination in February 2005, Future Television has been engaged in a drive to expose the perpetrators with a lot of fiery coverage directed at suspected Syrian involvement in the atrocity.

Al-Mustakilla

This London-based channel was launched from London in 1999. It is owned by Tunisian businessman Mohammed al-Hachemi Hamdi through UK-based Nova TV Company. In June 2005, another channel named 'Democracy Channel' was launched by the same group with most of its programs devoted to discussions of political reform and democratization in the Arab World.

Arab News Network

This all-news channel was launched in London in 1997 by Somer Rifaat al-Assad, nephew of the late Syrian President Hafez al-Assad. By 2003, ANN was plagued by financial woes caused by diminishing advertising dollars, forcing it to close down some of its foreign news bureaus. The channel resumed its transmissions later with mostly political talk shows and documentaries, primarily addressing the situation in Syria. The channel turned more critical of the ruling regime in Syria in the aftermath of Hariri' assassination and mounting international pressures on Syria to cooperate with the U.N.-sponsored investigation of the case.

Khalifa TV

This 12-hour broadcaster is owned by Algerian businessman Abdul Muneim Khalifa who is reportedly very committed to secularism and enjoys the confidence of Algeria's military elite. Launched on November 6, 2002, this all-news channel transmits on Nilesat and is expected to expand its broadcasts on an around-the-clock basis.

Murr TV (MTV)

This Christian Lebanese channel was launched in 2000. It is owned by Gabriel al-Murr who also owns Radio Mount Lebanon. In September 2002, Lebanese security forces closed MTV offices after the channel was accused of airing propaganda programs during parliamentary elections. Some of these programs were reportedly critical of Syria. The channel was expected to re-launch its transmissions in mid 2006 following Syria's pull out from Lebanon.

V.2.2.2. The Press

The 1990s witnessed a huge expansion in the number of publications in the Arab World and diaspora, marked by a further rise of partisan press and the diversification of its ownership.[42] The relative opening up of political life in the Arab

---

[42] See *Middle East Media Guide* (2007) at:

world in the 1990s induced the emergence of more diverse publications. Although many newspapers continue to exhibit political and ideological preferences inherited from the pre-1990 era, new publications have emerged with a discourse more oriented to global political trends grounded in democratic politics, pan-Arab solidarity, and Islamic cohesion. Some of the papers continue to survive under government patronage on state subsidies while others maintain some sort of independent partisan affiliation. While some media commentators speak of a decline in the role of the press in the emerging public sphere as they get overshadowed by satellite television and Internet-based communications, it remains evident that the press will continue to play a major role, at least among the Arab elite as print media provide editorial coverage and analysis not matched by other radio and television outlets (Abdallah, 2004). The majority of Arabic newspapers are based inside the Arab World, and hence are subject to press and publications laws as enforced by state authorities. Because of its marked local orientations, the Arab press is expected to be a central player in the emerging public sphere. But as empirical evidence demonstrates, state restrictions on editorial policies continue to inhibit free expression and publishing practices (ECSSR, 2006). International and Arab human rights and journalistic associations have provided appalling accounts of continued punishments of press institutions and of individual journalists ranging from temporary closures to imprisonment to suspension to financial fines.[43] The general trend in the local press is to 'watch out' when addressing local issues and to 'feel free' when dealing with regional or global developments that are not directly bearing on their mother countries. Economic pressures on the press seem to play an inhibitive role in enforcing this conformist journalistic culture in different Arab societies.[44]

When it comes to building up a genuine public sphere in the Arab World, newspapers published in diaspora seem to enjoy more freedom, allowing for airing more critical views. This press category includes newspapers like *Asharq al-Awsat*, *al-Hayat* and *al-Quds al-Arabi*, all are based in London. It should be noted here that even though these papers are physically located apart from Arab World territories, they are still commercially and organizationally part of the Arab media system. For example, *al-Hayat* newspaper, considered one of the finest in the Arab press arena, is owned by Saudi Prince Khaled bin Sultan while *Asharq al-Awsat* is part of the Saudi Company for Publishing and Distribution. These two publications have often been taken to task for promoting Saudi poli-

---

http://www.middleeastmediaguide.com/newspapers.htm

[43] Reports of press freedom violations in the Arab World have been frequently published by a range of human rights organizations, both Arab and Western. These include the World Press Freedom Committee; Arab Press Freedom Watch; Center for Media Freedom; Reporters sans frontières; International Press Freedom Institute; Freedom House; and the Arab Organization for the Defense of Press Freedom and Freedom of Expression.

[44] Total advertising spending in the Arab World in 2005 was put at $4,438 with newspapers constituting 43% of the advertising pie. See PARC (2006).

cies and perspectives, refraining from criticizing Saudi government officials while heaping fiery criticism on the former Iraqi regime and fundamentalist Islamist groups (Boyd, 2001). They are seen as integral ingredients of a regional Saudi media empire taking shape in the Arab World communications terrain, seeking to provide a political discourse that promotes Western liberal views while stopping short of criticizing existing political arrangements in Saudi Arabia (Boyd, 2001). On the other hand, *al-Quds al-Arabi*, founded by Abdul Bari Atwan, a Palestinian journalist with a British citizenship, has provided forum for anti-American and pro-Arabist views, using a mostly sensational approach to issues and developments in the region. *Al-Quds al-Arabi* has been especially critical of Egypt and Saudi Arabia's regional policies and local orientations, always insinuating some Saudi role in realizing an American strategy for the Arab World.

It would be unfair to view the Arab World press in monolithic terms when it comes to their role in the emerging public sphere. In countries with well-established traditions of political diversity like Lebanon, Kuwait and Morocco, the press, defined by Rugh (2004) as transitional, continues to play a significant role. A review of op-pages of newspapers available on the World Wide Web shows that newspapers in these countries are serving as key arenas for critical views of domestic developments.[45] They provide some room for readers' views and opinions and do adopt critical approaches to different regional and global issues and events; yet, when it comes to domestic developments, the vigor of debate common in some satellite television channels does not seem to be matched in the press which gets dampened by potential reprisals. In Morocco, the press has even taken a neutral stand in addressing partisan issues, playing a mediating role between rival parties. Jamai (2004) notes that in June 2002, the independent weekly *Le Journal Hebdomadaire* convened and published the proceedings of a debate between Nadia Yassine, a representative of *al-Adl wal-Ihsan*, one of Morocco's most popular Islamist movements, and Said Saadi, a former minister who had first proposed the reforms. The debate allowed both points of view to be expressed in a peaceful setting, and signaled the possibility of adopting changes without great social cleavage[46].

---

[45] The author has surveyed 20 papers published in 20 Arab countries showing varying degrees of criticism pertaining to national politics if it ever exists in the Western sense of the word. Lebanese and Moroccan papers led this trend while papers in the Gulf region trailed behind.

[46] Data in 2005 show that the Arab press witnessed major expansions in the number of outlets as follows: Bahrain (9); Iraq (45); Jordan (10); Kuwait (11); Lebanon (36); Oman (8); Palestine (23); Qatar (8); Saudi Arabia (30); Syria (11); UAE (12); Yemen (18); Algeria (30); Egypt (30); Libya (9); Mauritania (3); Morocco (29); Sudan (12); Tunisia (5). Source: http://www.onlinenewspapers.com/

V.2.2.3. Radio Broadcasting

Although radio continued to serve as a significant institution of the evolving Arab public sphere, the introduction of satellite television seems to have adversely affected radio popularity as a source of political news and analysis. With news immediacy no longer an exclusive feature of radio, radio broadcasting has been relegated to a secondary position, accessible mainly by motorists in urban centers as well as inhabitants of remote areas with no satellite television access. As part of the modern era media traditions, all Arab states continue to have broadcasting services carrying a wide range of programs (Boyd, 1999). Though radio services continue to transmit on medium wave frequencies, the use of FM method has seen remarkable expansions in light of its high quality and tuning convenience. The conversion of radio transmission into FM technique has also embraced foreign broadcasters like the BBC Arabic service and U.S. Radio *Sawa*. The BBC Arabic Service, initially launched in January 1938 carries its news bulletins and political talk shows via FM transmitters in different Arabic countries. Local Arab state radio broadcasters carry newscasts, music, and talk shows on matters pertaining to politics, culture, religion and community affairs.[47]

But regardless of the recession of its traditionally-dominant role in the Arab mass media scene, the mushrooming of radio services, especially at local levels, has provided new public sphere venues for local communities across the Arab World. Several studies show that local radio markets have been fragmented to meet specialized preferences of different audiences. Arab States Broadcasting Union (ASBU) data show that while local radio has been generally entrusted with a mainly cultural and developmental role, its contribution to political debates has been minimal partly because of lacking democratic structures. Talk shows continue to be the defining features of non-entertainment radio services. But their subjects often pertain to social and cultural issues. When talk shows address political issues, they do that within regional or global contexts, especially when local politics in the pluralistic sense is virtually non-existent.[48]

V.2.2.4. The World Wide Web

An important challenge presented by the global information and communications revolution in the Arab World has been the creation and enhancement of new telecommunications and information technology infrastructures. The Arab region has witnessed the diversion of huge investments, both government and private, into the emerging information technology sector. Available data demonstrate remarkable increases in the number of telephone lines and Internet sub-

---

[47] See *Middle East Media Guide* at: http://www.middleeastmediaguide.com/radio.htm
[48] Source: http://www.onlinenewspapers.com/

scription rates across the Arab World though the Gulf region remains the leading area in this field[49]. Although Arabs have started to go on-line at an impressive pace, with the highest growth rate of 311% in the world between 2000-2005, Internet integration within the population is still miniscule, and the second lowest penetration rate/population (8.11%), in the world after Africa. In Lebanon, Jordan and Syria, integration is 11.2%, 7.9% and 3.3% consecutively.

The entry of the private sector into the long-dominated telecommunications sector has substantially contributed to its development. The proliferation of the World Wide Web across the Arab World has led some researchers to conceive of the emergence of a new public sphere whereby private individuals are no longer constrained by state censorship in expressing and imparting their views. The Internet, as an alternative venue and outlet for expression, has empowered private individuals and underground groups to share and diffuse their views on a wide range of issues, most of them classified as taboos in the traditional Arab media environment. Rinnawi (2002) notes that the Internet has essentially created a new public space – 'cyberspace' – in the Arab World with the formation of news groups and the establishment of Web-based patrols and other outlets. Although some scholars, as noted in Chapter I, tend to discount the Internet as a viable public sphere tool because of its individualized communication patterns,[50] Rinnawi (2002) sees a promising potential for the Web in social and political change in an Arab World still subject to oppressive state authoritarianism. On the other hand, the frustrating realities of state controls over communications remain more concrete than ever before. Arab states continue to practice censorship over Web communications. The Center for Defending Freedom of Journalists, for example, noted that though the Egyptian government had extended support to Internet communications and infrastructures, it has also continued to bloc a significant number of sites like Muslim Brotherhood and Egyptian outlawed Labor Party newspaper *al-Sha'ab* (Arab Media Free Network, 2005).

The use of the Internet as a public sphere in the Arab World has been manifested in two key areas: online journalism and weblogging. By the early years of the 21st century, there was a proliferation of Arab portals; according to Anderson (1995), there were more than 50, with most of them operating in Arabic as well as English. *Al-Jazeera.net*, launched in 2001, receives some 300,000 visits a day, making it one of the Arab world's busiest websites. When it invites its 'community' to participate in online polling on Islam, current affairs, sports, or the like, it usually pulls in 20,000-35,000 'votes'. Other news portals include *al-*

---

[49] There are significant variations among Arab countries in levels of Internet diffusion and usage. While Internet subscription rates are estimated in the UAE at 65%, they stay at a low 5% in Sudan. This lack of accessibility to the Web is bound to limit the impact of the Internet in the evolving public sphere. It is not significant to load the Web sphere with political debates, but rather to empower users to have access to this virtual space.

[50] See Chapter IV.

Jazeera.net, al-Arabiya.net, Emirates Media Incorporated, Elaph, BBCarabic.com; *CNNarabic.com, Islamonline,* and *Arab Media Internet Network* (AMIN)[51]. In 2005, there were over 120 newspapers and magazines with online editions. The interactive behavior of the Web audience significantly contributes to the construction of identity and communal solidarity in the Arab region despite alarming signs of abuses (Za'atreh, 2006).

An important feature of the World Wide Web in the Arab World relates to weblogging or 'blogging' in short used as a venue for political expression in a region long-dominated by state media. A survey by Taki (2005) of Arabic language blogging on the Web in August 2005 identified over 200 blogs in Jordan, Syria and Lebanon. The majority of respondents were of Lebanese origin (47.3%), then Syrian (22%) and Jordanian with 23.1%. In total, the population consisted of 222 bloggers. Syrians accounted for 61 of them, Lebanese for 122 and Jordanians 29. She concluded that Weblogging is still an elitist movement both in the West and even so in Arab countries with '*Mudawanat*' represent a form of free of expression that takes place outside state censorship. The majority of those of Lebanese origin discussed 'politics in country of origin' on their blogs. While in Jordan only 4.8% (N=21) ranked this as their number one most mentioned topic. In Syria this topic scored very low as well with only three out of the 20 respondents (20%) rating it as their most mentioned. On the other hand, 45% scored 'day to day activities' as number one in Syria. Lebanon has been going through huge political changes since March after the assassination of former Prime Minister Rafik Hariri, Syria's withdrawal from Lebanon, the return of previous politicians into the arena and re-elections of the government. These changes together with Lebanon's constant political turmoil, probably explains many bloggers' deep involvement in 'politics in country of origin' in comparison to Syria and Jordan. But perhaps more importantly; Jordanian and Syrian (Taki, 2005). Za'atreh (2006) notes that Arab World Islamic blogs cover many perspectives ranging from the most militant to the moderate; all preaching different versions of Islam in the age of globalization. He notes that this diversity, due to its extremely paradoxical composition, could have a serious backlash effect on the message of Islam as a religion of peace, tolerance and co-existence.

---

[51] These news portals are accessed at the following URLs: al-Jazeera.net (http://www.alJazeera.net/NR/exeres/8FD54E7F-56C5-49A0-B60A-89A67426F3B3.htm); al-Arabiya.net (http://www.alarabiya.net/), EMI (http://www.emi.ae/home.asp), Elaph (http://www.elaph.com/), BBC (http://news.bbc.co.uk/hi/arabic/news/), CNN (http://arabic.cnn.com/), Islamonline (http://www.islamonline.net/english/index.shtml), AMIN (http://www.amin.org/)

VI.2.3. Discourse

The multiplicity of Arab public sphere players and institutions is bound to generate varying types of political discourse. The major implication of this situation is that it is not plausible to speak of a single political discourse dominating public debates in the region, especially in the post 9/11 era. Local and global political, economic and technological developments have created new anchoring points for political actors, both local and global, to address issues of concern to Arab populations, namely political reform and combating terrorism. Yet, generally speaking, one could speak of five categories of discourse played out in the new public sphere: The liberal Western-oriented discourse that carries the vision of the United States as embedded in President Bush's Broader Middle East and North Africa strategy; the mainstream state-sponsored discourse that seeks to come to terms with the U.S. strategy without risking local political and cultural balances; the militant Islamist discourse which views the West and its aligned political structures in the area as illegitimate, anti-Islamic, and seeking to dominate the Muslim World; the secularist nationalist discourse; and the centrist discourse that promotes a synthetic Islamic contemporary vision of society drawing on cherished Islamic morality and contemporary cultural and political practices. In this latter discourse category, Islam and democracy are viewed as fully compatible within the concept of 'Islamocracy', or Islamic democracy as both seek to realize a totality of human political and cultural fulfillment. The five discourse orientations compete to have a niche in the growing mass-mediated public sphere as a means of winning the hearts and minds of 'the Arab street'. Such rivalry among different players seems to underscore their deep realization of the centrality of securing footholds in public arenas to control public opinion in the region. Despite their deep political and ideological variations, the five discourse types share one common concern: all are offering recipes for Arab world salvation from its dire state of defeat and backwardness; in some ways, they are reproducing the 200-year old debate on the question of *Nahda* (Renaissance) that has been debated since Napoleon's expedition to Egypt in 1798.

VI.2.3.1. The Liberal Reform Discourse

This discourse is represented by global, pan-Arab and local actors like the Bush administration, human rights activists, NGO representatives, and individual Arab liberals. It is carried by media institutions like *al-Jazeera* Satellite Channel, *al-Hurra* Channel and some Iraqi and Lebanese stations and media. The basic tenet of this discourse is that Arab World problems are caused by long traditions of despotism and corruption; and liberal democracy, drawing on Western-style politics is the panacea for the region's woes. By juxtaposing the new promised liberal democracy as the antithesis of traditional social and political systems, this discourse has shown little respect for Islamic heritage as embracing the seeds of a viable political option. Whether they are government officials, international human rights activists, or local Arab liberals, proponents of this discourse see the Arab World as a political and cultural wasteland that needs to be brought back to life through liberal democracy. They base their arguments on existing authoritarian state transgressions, human rights violations, rigid educational systems, and fundamentalist interpretations of Islamic scriptures. The main argument offered here is that Arab countries have suffered from decades if not centuries of political despotism, cultural narrow-mindedness, and religious fanaticism, and it is high time for them to consider another more viable and fruitful option 'for building their brighter future, which is democracy'. Proponents of this thesis argue that the fact that all presumed perpetrators of the 9/11 attacks were raised in traditional religious Arab settings proved that the Arab World was a breeding people bent on carrying out acts of terror as the only way to communicate their grievances. This perception of the Arab (and of course the Muslim) World as a breeding ground for terror has focused global attention on the quality of education and culture in the Islamic world as bearing 'seeds of bigotry, hatred and violence'.

VI.2.3.2. The Authoritarian State Discourse

This category is represented by discourse carried in state-sponsored or subsidized media, seeking to establish some balance between externally-induced Western democratic drives and militant Islamist orientations. Media affiliated with this type of discourse are replete with rhetoric about democracy, participation, and transparency while at the same time glorifying aspects of past Arab-Islamic heritage that could carry values and norms incompatible with contemporary universal morality. Reflecting the built-in paradoxes of the authoritarian state as it grapples with local and global challenges, this discourse is full of tensions as it seeks to strike a compromise between the past and the present, the traditional and the modern, the intuitive and the rational, the patriarchal and the free, and the community-oriented and the individual-oriented. Because this compromising discourse represents the mainstream state-controlled public sphere, its contradictory impact has been widely felt in radio and television broadcasts, publications and Web-based communications. Inconsistency is the prime feature of this discourse which has proven its fragility in the face of growing 'democratic' and militant 'Islamist' orientations competing to win the hearts and minds of the 'Arab street'. This discourse is significantly grounded in different legitimacies ranging from developmental achievements, to formalistic electoral politics, to religious and tribal traditions. In most cases, this discourse is monologist and exclusionist on matters relating to domestic politics. It is marked by a mixture of religious, patriotic, and tribal orientations shrouded in yet more paradoxical emotional, rational, and formalistic language structures. This type of discourse is evident in newscasts, print media news, editorials, talk shows, speeches, and religious sermons carried live by state-run television (el-Aswad, 2001).

VI.2.3.3. The Militant Islamist Discourse

This discourse has been associated with militant Islamic groups seeking to assert their fundamentalist interpretations of Scriptures as a basis for facing up to the challenges of globalization. This discourse embraces what has been described as 'Jihadist' visions of society and the state (Yom, 2005). The major thrust of this discourse is that democracy is a corrupt Western concept promoted in the Muslim World to undermine the social and cultural fabric of society; to pre-empt Islamic renaissance; and to usurp Muslim natural resources. Proponents of this discourse draw on past Islamic experiences and normative fundamentalist teachings to prescribe solutions to contemporary world problems facing the Muslim World. Some groups do not seem hesitant to resort to violence as a means of asserting their positions, using traditional Islamic notions of *Jihad* to justify their acts. For them, the ongoing conflict is a struggle between followers of true '*Salafi*' Islam and proponents of '*Satanic*' ideas of Western origin. A conspiratorial sense of historical determinism seems to define these orientations as their advocates believe in the eventual defeat of 'the infidels' and the supremacy of Islam in this everlasting struggle. Interestingly enough, though militant Islamist discourse has not only moved to the vernacular and become accessible to significantly wider publics, it has also become framed in styles of reasoning and forms of argument that draw on wider, less exclusive or erudite bodies of knowledge. 'In an intellectual world of systems and subjects, Islam becomes approachable in different ways as one system in a world of systems' (Eickelman and Anderson 1999: 12). This type of discourse also draws on a solemn traditionalist language that describes current world realities through a fundamentalist prism. Speeches by *al-Qaida* leader Osama bin Laden and his deputy Ayman Zawahiri represent this orientation.

VI.2.3.4. Secularist Arabist Discourse

Although pan-Arabism has been on the decline ever since the Iraqi invasion of Kuwait in 1990, its philosophical premises continue to inform intellectual writings and media contents well into the 21st century. The Pan-Arabist National Congress, launched in 1991, has been the prime platform for secularist nationalist ideas and views in the Arab World. Its advocates recognize the centrality of Islam as an Arab historical experience; yet, they believe that an Arab political system should be based on state-religion separation. They strongly believe in Western liberalism as a basis for World Arab emancipation; yet, their political orientations are not in tune with American policies and strategies in the region.

They take anti-American stands because they believe that Arab World problems are generated by 'imperialist' U.S. policies that seek to dominate the region and exploit its resources. Though this type of discourse is historically rooted in the traditional socialist nation state ideology, it has come since the early 1990s to promote a more liberal democratic view of the state and society.

VI.2.3.5. The Synthetic Arab-Islamic Discourse

This discourse is rooted in both revolutionary Arab World politics as well as in modern Islamic revivalism of the 1950s and 1960s. In its basic configuration, this discourse sees salvation from the current Arab World debacle in the integration of basic Islamic moral traditions and contemporary political practices to generate an Arab World-specific vision. The concept of 'Islamocracy' or Islamic democracy stands out as the best example of this integrationist discourse that sees viable coexistence between Arab-Islamic societies, on the one hand, and other nations with different political and ideological orientations, on the other hand. This centrist discourse views with deep cynicism both American-prescribed political reforms and militant Islamic recipes for an Islamic state. It incorporates the views of the intelligentsia who were disenchanted by American democratization drives; victimized by state repression; frustrated by nationalist secularist orientations; and horrified by militant *al-Qaida*-style rhetoric. Proponents of this discourse, though they have the least access to the public sphere, are normally featured in media institutions ranging from state to private media outlets to provide alternative visions on arising events and issues.

VI.2.4. The Public Sphere Trickle Down Effect?

One researcher noted that had Arab satellite television channels existed during the first Palestinian *Intifada* (Uprising) in 1988, Palestinians would have made more political gains (Ayish, 2004). Thirteen years later, Palestinians in the West Bank and Gaza Strip started their 2nd *Intifada* in the midst of a new Arab World environment bustling with hundreds of satellite television channels and Web-based news portals. They ended up as the biggest losers in a bloody political game witnessed live by millions on television screens, newspaper pages and online outlets. On the eve of the launch of satellite television in the Arab World, an air of optimism dominated the Arab region that political reforms in traditional political systems as recipes for more democratic arrangements marked by free and participatory modes of governance proved to be illusive. Fifteen years later, the Arab World remains, more than ever before, bogged down in its futile search for a way out of religious militancy, state authoritarianism and American imperialism. Following the fall of Baghdad on April 9, 2003, Arab media were accused of fomenting anti-American sentiments in Iraq and sawing seeds of sectarian divisions in the war-wary country. Four years later, Iraq had three 'democratic elections', two governments; but still a murky vision for the future. So, are Arab media having a real effect on political realities or is that effect a figment of some conspiratorial imagination?

Literature on democratic politics suggests a powerful public opinion as a natural outcome of a genuine public sphere is bound to effectively bear on political processes at national and global levels (Ajibola, 1978). If the public sphere fails to generate shared ideas of community, identity, and leadership, then the missing link seems to be rooted in the institutional environment constituting the political, social and intellectual foundations for political communication. Media, though forming the backbone of the public sphere, seem either unable to leave any significant impact on public opinion, or the Arab publics appear to be affected by media discourse, yet are unable to translate such effects into concrete actions. At this point, the chain of effects breaks down either because Arabs are intimidated into a state of coerced acquiescence or they lack the institutional mechanisms to make their voices heard in one way or another. As such, some form of a vicious circle has defined media effects on politics in the region. The media grinding machine is creating a lot of commotion in the evolving public sphere, but little crushed wheat is tricking down. Saudi writer and diplomat Ghazi al-Qussaibi, referring to this enduring feature of the Arab public sphere, describes Arabs as no more than 'a noise phenomenon'; they do a lot of talking but little action. Is this the legacy of the oral heritage of poetry and oration?

It has become clear that while subtle long-term media effects on Arab World politics are hard to account for, the past 15 years have seen occasional 'Arab Street' outbursts in response to dramatic media coverage of events and issues. Examples include the reporting of the suicide bombing attack on civilians in the Iraqi town of *Hilla* by Jordan's *al-Ghad* newspaper. Ridolfo (2005) noted that Iraqis took to the streets in three days of protests against *al-Ghad* 11 March, 2005 article claiming the family of an alleged Jordanian suicide bomber celebrated their son's 'martyrdom' in Iraq. The Live TV showing of protests in Beirut against the assassination of late Lebanese Prime Minister Rafiq al-Hariri was instrumental in mustering up public support for the withdrawal of Syrian troops from Lebanon and spiraling anti-Syrian sentiments in Lebanon. In Beirut, protestors imitated the symbols of Egypt's *Kifaya* movement which mounted massive demonstrations in Cairo and other Egyptian cities demanding political reform. *Al-Arabiya* TV channel's exclusive interview with former Syrian Vice President Abdul Halim Khaddam in Paris prompted heated reactions in Damascus and some Arab countries. Al-Jazeera's airing of a program in which the Shi'a spiritual leader Ayatollah Sistani was criticized also created demonstrations in many parts of Iraq against al-Jazeera which has a record of creating diplomatic incidents in the Arab World. Ridolfo (2005) noted that the Arab media influenced the region's discourse on the war in Iraq by largely framing it in the context of 'invasion' and 'imperialism'.

The failure of the Arab public sphere to generate tangible results on the ground has been addressed by numerous researchers. In identifying the structural factors inhibiting the emergence of a genuine public sphere in the Muslim World (including the Arab region), Hamza and Noor (2005) argued that 'apart from the structural realities of modern authoritarian states, one of the main reasons why a public sphere has not emerged in the Muslim World is the discursive culture and practice of hate-mongering that has become so prevalent in our societies'. Both argue that the march of political religion 'has been in keeping with the development of a hate-machine, culminating in an expansive discourse replete with conspiracy theories, bellicose slogans and the constant baiting of their opponents and enemies'. Alterman (2004) notes that one reason for that gap is that debate in the Arab World is still largely about spectacle and not about participation, and nowhere is this more true than on Arab satellite television. To use the American metaphor, media debates in the Arab World generate far more heat than light. On a mass level, they generate little action other than fingers pressing a television's remote control. Khouri (2001) also astutely observes that:

> Hugely entertaining shows and shouting matches do not have any significant impact on Arab political culture or decision making by the existing Arab elites. This is because the media activities in the region care still totally divorced from the political processes. An Arab viewer who might change his or her mind because of something he or she saw on television has no effective means of translating their views into political action or impact. For the political systems in most Arab countries are pre-configured to maintain a pro-government, centrist majority that allows more and more debate and discussion of important issues, but maintains real decision making in the hands of small elite groups who have managed public affairs and matters of state for some decades now. How many times in recent years, for example, have you seen any discussion of military versus developmental budget expenditures in an Arab country?

Sharabi (2004) identified areas of potential television effects in the Arab World: on the level of awareness, where a new political knowledge or perspective has been acquired, a 'raising' of political consciousness among large segments of the population has definitely taken place; on the level of attitude, a corresponding capacity has been gained for making judgments, and for taking definite political stands; and on the level of potential political practice, commitment and action have become possible on a mass scale never known before.
But regardless of the fluid nature of the public sphere effects, one could identify three areas of potential impact on Arab politics in the age of globalization: consolidating state authoritarianism; promoting U.S. public diplomacy; and diffusing alternative political visions.

VI. 2.4.1. Consolidating State Authoritarianism

The Arab nation state in the age of globalization continues to view communication media as tools for consolidating its control at national and global levels. Since the early 1990s, Arab states have shown profound interest not only in building up their national media capabilities, but in extending their patronage to media services outside their national borders. States' interest in using the media sphere as a source of political legitimization is traced to the early days of independence from colonial rule. This domineering state tendency, however, has gained significance only in recent years when the political and ideological foundations of Arab regimes began to shake under the tremors of globalization. New media empires have been established to ensure greater control over the public sphere (ECSSR, 2006).

The changing global political environment, more than ever before, has made the state's mission in the public sphere more difficult than ever before. Deteriorating domestic economic conditions, spiraling religious militancy; emerging alternative media outlets of anti-state expression and diminishing political democratization, all have contributed to the erosion of state standing. States' input into the public sphere has been generally predicated on maintaining security and social order, national cohesion, development achievements, and cultural identity. States, in unison with global political trends, have drawn on a collective discourse that sets them in tune with international community attitudes pertaining to universal and human prosperity and progress. Hudson (2003) notes that in an era of American hegemony, little meaningful social change could be expected in the region as a whole. There will be no easy way out from the patriarchal and neo-patriarchal systems that have dominated Arab political life over the last half-century. Under American imperial sway, what will be cultivated are not the democratic forces of civil society, but the authoritarian power of 'friendly' patriarchal regimes. In all Arab countries, Hudson (2003) notes, the only refuge for the mass of the populace is not the vague and false promises of democracy, equality and human rights, but the religion of Islam. This reality has been central to the formulation of 'Islamocracy' (Islamic democracy) as the best political formula for the institutions of a viable public sphere in the Arab World.

VI.2.4.2. Promoting U.S. Public Diplomacy

For the United States, as much as the emerging public sphere in the Arab World generates new challenges for the Bush administration's Mideast policy, it also offers ample opportunities for communication with Arab publics within the practice of public diplomacy. In July 2003, the US Congress mandated a bipartisan 13-member Advisory Group on Public Diplomacy for the Arab and Muslim World, chaired by Edward P. Djerejian, former ambassador to Syria and Israel.

The group published a report on October 1, 2003, calling for a new White House office with a cabinet rank, backed by an advisory board of experts, to manage strategic direction and the government-wide coordination of public diplomacy in promoting national interests by informing, engaging and influencing the global community, in particular Arabs and Muslims. The report concludes, 'America can achieve dramatic results with a consistent, strategic, well-managed, and properly funded approach to public diplomacy, one that credibly reflects US values, promotes the positive thrust of US policies, and takes seriously the needs and aspirations of Arabs and Muslims for peace, prosperity, and social justice' (Gregory, 2005).

Revived U.S. interest in public diplomacy in the Arab World was initially induced by growing popular opposition to American policies in the region, especially in the post-9/11 era. A University of Jordan's Center for Strategic Studies (CSS, 2005) survey revealed that Arabs do not 'hate' the US and UK for 'who they are' or for the cultural values they hold. Negative sentiments are being fueled, rather, by 'what they do' – that is, for specific policies and the impact these policies have on the Arab world. Neither a cultural nor a religious gap is found to be the fundamental motivation for tensions between the Arab world and the West. Rather, the study found that the Arab public disagrees profoundly with the foreign policies of the US (and the UK when they are in agreement) and that this disagreement was at the root of anti-American, and, by extension, anti-Western, sentiments which permeated the region. U.S. spending on public diplomacy has risen 9% since the 9/11 attacks, and more than 50% in the Middle East and South Asia. But a comprehensive poll in foreign countries in early 2002 showed that in Muslim nations from Morocco to Indonesia, the United States has fallen far from favor (Stone, 2002).

Ironically, spiraling anti-American sentiments in the Arab World are perceived in Washington, D. C. to be fueled by media with hostile attitudes towards the United States. On many occasions, *al-Jazeera* and *al-Manar* channels were explicitly singled out by U.S. officials as engaging in anti-American propaganda campaigns. Rugh (2005) notes that for starters, the tendency to blame Arab TV for most of America's poor image problems in the Arab World ignores the fact that opinion polls taken in Europe and Asia showed very low respect for America, and people in those areas don't watch Arab TV. Moreover, Zogby polls taken in the Arab World show television viewers who regularly watched Arab satellite channels tended to have a more favorable opinion of America, not less, than those who did not watch it. That probably was due to the fact that those TV channels carried not only political programs that appealed to Arab nationalist and patriotic feelings, but also material from American commercial networks that might, on balance, present aspects of the United States that Arabs liked. The view of Arabs' association of U.S. government media activities with American policies in the Middle East is not new. Ayish (1986) noted that one of the reasons for the failure of the former Voice of America Arabic Service in the region was listeners' perception of its broadcasts as reflecting biased U.S. policies against Arabs in the 1960s and 1970s. New media outlets launched in the 1990s and beyond like *Radio Sawa*, *al-Hurra* Television Channel, and *Hi* magazine have turned out to be less popular primarily because of audience associations between hostile U.S. stands on Arab issues and media content (Melhem, 2005).

U.S. public diplomacy efforts via the Arab public sphere are plagued even with more fundamental problems pertaining to their very intellectual premises and means of implementation. Fakhreddin (2006) notes that the United States' 2002 public diplomacy campaign in the mainstream media of Arab and Muslim countries lacked a coherent message and was a liability rather than an asset. Alterman (1998) also suggests that the U.S. should devote far more attention to monitoring developments in 'mid-tech' Arab media – satellite television, videocassettes, and photocopiers often associated with the 1970s – instead of focusing on 'high-tech' advances such as the Internet. Cull (2006) noted the shift to a public diplomacy in which the Pentagon and its private contractors have become key players has fundamental implications. The Pentagon immediately brings an emphasis on communications as a force multiplier, a means to the end of victory rather than a dimension of international interaction. Furthermore, there is a core difference between a public diplomacy based on in-house capabilities of the sort provided by USIA and an effort drawing on contractors. The basic need to secure and maintain a contract makes the private sector player much less likely to stress the limits on public diplomacy. Unlike a public diplomat, a contractor is not paid to feed back into the policymaking process and question the fundamental premises of their mission or the policy that motivated it (Cull, 2006). In the past, this sort of feedback was rare in US public diplomacy, but given the emerging paradigm of privatization, it promised to be even rarer in the future, and to the detriment of the operation of US public diplomacy.

To rectify this problem, Eickelman (2002b) suggests that Washington policy makers acknowledge a new sense of public in the Muslim majority and Arab worlds even before the September 11, 2001 terrorist attacks. For them, it is called the 'Arab Street', a new phenomenon of public accountability, 'which we have seldom had to factor into our projections of Arab behavior in the past'. Melhem (2005) notes that *al-Hurra* is largely an ineffective initiative and even before it began, there was a negative reaction on the part of many Arabs just because it was financed by the US government. Lynch (2003b) thinks rather than shunning *al-Jazeera* and its counterparts out of pique, the United States should try to change the terms of debate in the Arab world by working through them and opening a genuine discussion. The goal of American policy should be to find ways to engage this kind of opinion and establish itself as an ally of the Arab public in its own demands for liberal reform, rather than making such reform an external imposition.

While some writers argue that the rise of a public opinion in the Arab World hostile to U.S. policies in the region would help shape global attitudes towards Arab countries, others seem to minimize the impact of this variable, at least in the real political context of U.S.-Arab relations. The United States, as a superpower with substantial military, political and economic leverage on Arab countries, enjoys a cutting edge in imposing its political agenda in the region with the minimum losses, at least in the short term. From Washington's imperial perspective, the anti-American hostility of civil society and public opinion in the Arab World counts for little, so there is no reason to return to diplomacy to settle the Palestinian-Israeli conflict before launching the next military campaign in the 'war on terrorism', this time against Iraq (Hudson, 2003). This neo-conservative U.S. stance, as Hudson (2003) sees it, dovetails seamlessly with the agenda of Israel's lobby in the United States and is reflected, as well, in the Republican Party and in the fundamentalist Christian churches. As a result, public opinion throughout the Arab countries now considers the United States an enemy and its 'war on terrorism' a euphemism for war against Islam and the Arabs. Because the more intemperate imperialists in the American political establishment call for 'democracy' in a post-Saddam Hussein Iraq and in other Arab countries, the advocates of genuine democracy in the Arab world have suffered a setback, while those advocating extremist responses to the American presence have gained ground (Hudson, 2003).

VI.2.4.3. Diffusing Alternative Political Visions

Although state and global influences over the public sphere have not receded, the proliferation of new media outlets has presented Arab publics with new political perspectives unaccounted for in the traditional government-controlled media setting. The break-up of traditional state monopoly of the media scene, especially broadcasting, has opened the way for new political expressions reflecting ethnic, communal, religious, secularist and gender-based affiliations. Advocates of competing political visions have offered their interpretations of evolving political developments using a wide range of perspectives, many of them were on a collision course with mainstream state orientations. Those mushrooming perspectives have not been accorded appropriate access to the public sphere; yet, they have found in the new communications outlets promising venues of expression. Hudson (2003) suggests that the ICT revolution in the Arab world seems to be favoring the development of an expanded national and transnational public sphere, as well as civil society NGOs and networks associated with it, at the relative expense of the state and authoritarian regimes. In some way, ICT is loosening the grip of authoritarian states and societies. Even though there is scanty evidence of any significant relaxation of control in the years less than a decade since the rise of satellite television and the internet, Hudson (2003) believes that the proliferation of new electronic voices, which can only be silenced with difficulty, is forcing power-holders to interact with these independent 'centers of influence'. Sadly enough, this optimistic note has proven to be rather illusive as countries like Egypt and Jordan have expanded their press and publications laws to embrace Web-based blogs.

The new public sphere as a discourse arena for new non-state political and cultural voices in the Arab World has received increasing scholarly attention. Al-Jazeera Satellite Channel has served as a platform for numerous unorthodox views ranging from those of *al-Qaida* militants to Islamic moderates, to secular nationalists, to ethnic group leaders, to even Israeli officials. Lynch (2005) notes that talk shows on *al-Jazeera* and other Arab television stations have contributed enormously to building the underpinnings of a more pluralist political culture, one which welcomes and thrives on open and contentious political debate. News coverage of political protests and struggles has opened up the realm of possibility across the Arab world, inspiring political activists and shifting the real balance of power on the ground. Furthermore, the huge expansion of the Arab public sphere as an incubator of alternative political perspectives has prompted some researchers to speak of an impending revolution in 'the Arab Street' as satellite television and the World Wide Web serve to mobilize public opinion in the region. Apart from state-sponsored discourse, this contention is untenable on two grounds. First, it is based on the erroneous assumption that media are really engaged in fomenting revolutionary sentiments when in fact they are hardly in a position to do so. On many occasions, this conception was espoused by the Bush administration and some Arab governments with reference to both *al-Jazeera* and *al-Manar* television channels. Both satellite television services have been criticized for offering homage to anti-U.S. positions. Al-*Jazeera*, in particular, has been accused of sawing seeds of division between Arab governments and their societies through providing a forum to dissident views (Ayish, 2003a). By highlighting demonstrations by *Kifaya* movement against the ruling National Democratic Party in Egypt and by anti-Syrian groups in Lebanon, JSC was presented as a source of instability in the region. From its point of view, *al-Jazeera* has defended its editorial policies by invoking its mission as the channel of 'the opinion and the other opinion', that it would not submit to political pressures, but would adhere to its highest professional standards in broadcast journalism (Zayani, 2005).

The mere presence of multiple political and ideological perspectives in the emerging Arab public sphere seems highly insignificant in the absence of viable civil society structures in the region. The new voices of the Arab public sphere argue their cases in a political and constitutional vacuum, created by entrenched authoritarian state apparatus and by enduring U.S. political double-standardism. Scores of perspectives are carried on airwaves, print media front pages, and Web outlets, but they seem more like lonely voices in the wilderness than politically-effective ideas. For those perspectives to bear on domestic politics, they need first to operate through relevant institutional arrangements conducive to political changes. These arrangements are largely absent, and even when they exist, they are co-opted by influential state mechanisms. The institutional vacuum precluding the efficacy of a significant public sphere in the Arab World has created further interest among researchers seeking to understand relationships between media performance and political practices. Said (A., 2003) notes that satellite channels have broadened the free space available to ordinary Arabs whose feedback had long been stifled by state censorship. Yet their mere appearance on television cannot be taken as a substitute for the creation of the institutions through which policy research and design take place. A 2004 Rand Corporation study concluded that it is unlikely that any country in the Middle East or North Africa will experience a full information revolution during the next decade, as media reform has too many impediments and too few champions, and – in most countries – too few resources (Burchart and Older, 2004). Hafez (2006) argues the idea that Arab satellite broadcasting could compensate for some of the inability of Arab political parties to mobilize links with civil society as media-civil-society-alliance could pave the road to democracy. However, he concludes that after 10 years of Arab transnational news journalism, there has been no significant development for democracy in the Arab world. Although critical elites and NGOs are heard on television, their real political impact remains weak.

It should be noted that the effects of the public sphere cannot be conceived outside existing power structures for the public sphere is always a reflection of power relations at national and global levels. Many actors take up a huge space in the public sphere; yet their impact on political developments on the ground is minimal. The public sphere does not create political change, but rather serves to facilitate its realization by actors who possess appropriate resources. In a world run by crude power diplomacy, rational and critical arguments are rendered useless even when they are advanced in favor of morally and legally-justified causes. This observation, more than anything else, seeks to confer a sense of realism on our expectations of the Arab public sphere. Unless Arabs turn into real players in the power politics game, their bright ideas, moral norms, and just causes would be of no value in this highly-competitive world. On the other hand, sheer political and economic power would also be rendered useless in a moral vacuum. The evolution of the Arab public sphere needs to be founded on sound morality backed up and safeguarded by real power and not vice versa.

VI.3. Summary and Conclusion

It is inarguable that the Arab public sphere has experienced impressive structural transformations since the late 1980s with the advent of globalization as the defining concept of international political, cultural and economic transitions. It is also obvious that the Arab World has been at the center of those global transformations, especially in the post-September 11 era, as marked by the initiation of U.S.-sponsored reforms and the diffusion of new communications technologies. The convergence of the democratization drive and new media outlets has generated unprecedented political ferment in the region. The evolving Arab public sphere, as a result, has seen more diversity in its actors, institutions, discourse orientations, and potential effects. Yet, due to the fact that this public sphere lends itself more to global genesis, Western intellectual roots, economic uncertainty, and authoritarian practices, it is expected to be plagued by a plethora of woes. In this chapter, the author argues that unless the evolving public sphere is based on solid indigenous and contemporary premises, its foundations are likely to remain shaky. A sustainable public sphere could never exist in a political vacuum. In the Arab World, the conduct of politics remains, more than ever before, captive to exogenous variables. The public sphere, therefore, is bound to remain dependent in its substance and parameters on external developments and considerations.

VII
TOWARDS AN ARAB-ISLAMIC PUBLIC SPHERE

> 'We should not forget that we are now in the 14th rather than the 10th Hijri century or earlier times. We have our peculiar needs and problems that had never been addressed before. We are required to come up with new interpretations (Ijtihad) for ourselves rather than to throw this task on people who had lived centuries before us. Had they lived in our contemporary times and suffered what we suffer, they would have retracted many of their views, and changed many of their Scripture interpretations, because (those interpretations) were generated to fit their times not ours. To cope with the development of the age, we may extract from Eastern and Western systems what does not contravene our Aqida and Shari'a and what achieves community interests. We need to confer on it our own coloration and spirit so that it turns into an integral part of our system by losing its original identity, as noted in what Muslims imported from other nations in their golden ages.
> (Qaradawi, 1998)

If the previous chapter has demonstrated serious flaws in the evolving Arab public sphere's contribution to genuine political processes on the ground, it is primarily because such a sphere has either developed outside local political and social structures or has been co-opted by states and harnessed to serve their authoritarian interests. Because political reforms could not deliver on promised democratic practices for reasons cited in Chapter V, it was natural to see the public sphere reaching this impasse, for the public sphere is no more than a legitimate child of a specific political and legal environment that promotes open rational and critical discussions within progressive social and constitutional boundaries; albeit that it turned out later to be one of its sustainers. In one way or another, the author argues that the public sphere in the Arab World has failed not only because of what is described as 'state authoritarianism' or U.S. 'interventionism and double-standardism', but primarily because of the failure of the intellectual political community in the region to provide a workable political choice that combines the best of our cultural traditions with the brightest of contemporary democratic practices.

As long as we continue to view democracy as an exclusive Western commodity, we will remain chronically entangled in the vast wasteland of our intellectual dearth. Democracy needs to be viewed as no more than a mechanism for instituting justice, freedom, equality, and the rule of law for the purpose of advancing the public good (*Maslaha*) or community interest (*Manfa'a*). As one scholar notes, when you are genuinely democratic in today's Islamic world, you are most likely to end up in an anti-American camp simply because American policies in the Arab World have always promoted injustice and oppression, whether through supporting Israeli aggression against the Palestinians, or condoning state authoritarianism in the region (Gause III, 2005). To contribute to the ongoing debate on how to rid the Arab World of its current debacle (which I think is intrinsically cultural in the broadest sense of the word), this chapter offers a theoretical framework for realizing a genuine and sustainable Arab public sphere drawing on cherished Islamic traditions and contemporary political practices.

Though this synthetic framework represents an ideal type vision of how the public sphere needs to be constructed in the Arab World, the way globalization bears on the region's political realities is a central defining concept in this intellectual endeavor. While Chapter III presented a normative classical Arab-Islamic perspective of communication and politics, and while Chapter IV identified modern schools of thinking on the tradition-modernity nexus, this chapter draws on this intellectual heritage to evolve a new vision that derives a major part of its intellectual substance from contemporary Islamic thought. It describes the public sphere as a central component of the contemporary-Islamic democratic system of governance referred to in this book as 'Islamocracy' or Islamic democracy.

The failure of the new Arab public sphere to generate minimal political changes on the ground has elicited unpleasant reactions on the part of media critics and intellectuals at large, inducing some sort of despair over the future of this issue in an Arab World aspiring to survive its woes at local and global fronts. If the notion of the public sphere is viewed according to purely Western benchmarks, then neither the classical, nor the modern, or the globalized Arab public sphere would pass the test. It was noted that the transplantation of Western norms in an Arab culture was bound to create more troubles and complicate an already complex issue that defines how Arabs are supposed to address a plethora of contemporary problems arising in the post September 11 era. Although the concept of the public sphere in its specific boundaries pertains to discursive activities drawing on Western political standards and practices, the concept in fact embraces broader areas relating to current and future identity, cultural values, religious norms, and philosophical worldviews. In light of such overwhelming challenges facing Arabs (those challenges are taking on a more direct style with the forceful diffusion of American norms of democratization and the waging of a global war against what has been termed as 'Islamic terror'), Arab thinkers representing diverse theoretical and political interests, need to mobilize the historical arsenal of norms, ideas, values, orientations, and anecdotes to evolve a public sphere formula that neither compromises our pivotal Islamic values and tenets, nor keeps closed eyes on valid contemporary democratic practices. Within this context, this chapter seeks to outline a framework for an Arab-Islamic public sphere that would serve as a genuine arena of public interactions defined by reverence for religious ideals, the institution of justice, and adherence to 'freesponsibility' as key ethical foundations for the practice of public debates. Since the public sphere is a function of the existing national and social system, this chapter also elaborates a general political perspective drawing on the notion of 'Islamocracy' as a hybrid combination of Islamic and contemporary political norms and practices.

VII.1. Islam and Democracy: The Ongoing Debate

An enduring question permeating intellectual and political debates in the Arab World over the past two centuries relates to the relevance and applicability of Islamic-based political systems in contemporary living contexts. Throughout the past two centuries, a wide range of perspectives have been offered for the integration of Islamic principles into modern political systems. Bel-Qaziz (2002) notes that contemporary Islamic discourse has been shaped by the thesis of Western domination of Muslim nations. He observes that contemporary Islamic perspectives have been overshadowed by political investigations focusing on five generations of thinkers: the first was the reformist generation represented by Rifaat al-Tahtawi, Khaireddin Tunisi, Jamaluddin Afaghani and Mohammad Abdu. The second generation was represented by Abdu Rahman al-Kawakbi, and Rashid Ridha. The third generation was represented by Abdul Hamid bin Badis, Ali Abdul Raziq, Hassan al-Banna, Abu Ala al-Maududi, Abu al-Hassan al-Nadawi, Khomeini, Allal al-Fasi, Mohammad al-Ghazali, Sayyed Qutb, and Hassan al-Hudaibi. The fourth generation is represented by Mohammad Qutb, Yussuf al-Qaradawi, Mustafa Sibaai, and Abdul Salam Yassin. The fifth generation is represented by Abdul Salam Faraj, Rashid al-Ghanoushi, Hassan Turabi, Fahmi Huwaidi and Mohammad Amara. Early reformists were critical of despotism and called for justice and freedom; Tahtawi and Tunisi thought that justice and freedom should be viewed as nation state imperatives. Abdu separated political power from religion, affirming the civil nature of Islam, while Kawakbi stood up to despotism at his time. In the 20th century, the fall of the Ottoman Empire induced calls for reviving the Caliphate as noted in writings by Rashid Ridha whose ideas were inspired from works by classical scholars like al-Mawardi, Ibn Taymiya, and Ibn al-Qayyem.

Contemporary Muslim thinkers have drawn on a special stream of *Fiqh* (Jurisprudence) called *Maqasid Shari'a* (Ends of Islamic Law) to extract current applications of Islamic political practices. Safi (2004) argues that theorizing about Islam in politics is shaped by two variables: *Aqida* and *Umma*. *Aqida* is the base on which *Umma* political unity draws. The concept of *Umma* represents an ideological percept reflecting the convergence of individual and group interactions with general principles transcending variations in ethnicity, color, origin, or language. The *Umma* rather than the ruler is the basis of the Caliphate. What counts is not the act, but the general interactions between action and socio-political contexts. There are five basic *Maqasid* in Islam that need to be safeguarded: religion, individual self, off-spring, reason, and wealth. Mady (2004) notes that *Maqasid al-Shari'a* in Islam, or the ends of Islamic law, seek to fulfill or maintain people's interests: their lives, mentalities, honor, properties and religion. In the political sphere, the purpose of *Shari'a* is to construct human life on the basis of justice (*Adl*) and good virtues (*Marouf*); and to cleanse it of injustice (*Zulum*) and all kinds of evils (*Munkarat*). According to Islamic teachings, the main purpose of Prophetic missions was to establish justice and to exterminate oppression. Al-Qadhi (2005) notes that the moderate- moderationist or Intentionalist (*Wasati* or *Maqasidi*) stream of *Shari'a* seeks to uncover the original intentions of *Shari'a* provisions as noted by Ibn Rushd in *Fasl al-Maqal*:

> Since rationality in physical sciences and philosophical knowledge is based on causality, rationality in *Shari'a* is also based on the intentions of the legislator. Hence, interpretations in religion *(Ijtihad)* should draw on proving the rightness of ideologies as intended by the legislator. Proponents of this stream seek to interact with other cultures as a means of self-consciousness. There is no sense of guilt involved as proponents of this stream view the history as embedding mistakes and its makers are not infallible angels.

Contemporary theorization about Islam and politics has been evolved largely in the context of global realities, taking the Western concept of democracy as a point of both convergence and divergence. Proponents of Islam's compatibility with democracy note that the concept should not be construed as an exclusively Western invention because it represents a universal mechanism for empowering community members to have a say in their affairs. Electoral democracy, based on public election of community representatives and incumbents of public offices within well-defined constitutional provisions, has been taken as harmonious with Islamic political traditions (Tamimi, 1997). Muslim scholars and thinkers note that democracy and Islam share major significant features like rejection of despotism and authoritarianism; institution of power-sharing arrangements; 'freesponsibility', and community role in public affairs. Rashid al-Ghanoushi (Tamimi, 2001), founder of the Tunisian *Nahda* movement notes that the Islamic state is a social and political system whose identity is defined by its adherence to Scriptures as supreme sources of legislation and commitment to *Shura* as a source of legitimacy, thus the *Umma* becomes the source of legitimacy for the ruled and the ruler. *Shura* is conducted within well-defined ethical parameters rather than within narrow parochial interests of ethnic or nationalist groups as in secular societies. There is no room for legislations that contravene religious text as much as there is no room for policies that clash with public opinion in its consensus or majority. This dictates the establishment of mechanisms for empowering the *Shari'a*-committed *Umma* to exercise real power in installing or sacking rulers. Though there are meeting grounds between *Shura* and democracy, the former operates within well-defined ethical values and norms unlike the interest-induced democracy which justifies unethical actions as evident in the U.S. Congress's support for the invasion of Iraq.

Those advocating compatibility between Islam and democracy base their view on both historical traditions as well as on contemporary imperatives. Robin Wright (1992), a well-known American expert on the Middle East and the Muslim World, writes: 'neither Islam nor its culture is the major obstacle to political modernity'. In his magnum opus 'Asian Drama', Nobel Laureate Gunnar Myrdal identified a set of 'modernization ideals' that included democracy. In regard to religion in general and Islam in particular, he noted that 'the basic doctrine of the old religions in the region – Hinduism, Islam and Buddhism – are not necessarily inimical to modernization'. For example, Islamic, and less explicitly, Buddhist doctrines are advanced to support reforms along the lines of modernization ideals'. If democracy is intimately related to egalitarianism, he further comments: 'Islam and Buddhism can provide support for one of the modernization ideals in particular: egalitarian reforms' (Farooq, 2002). In explaining some common western misperception, Fuller (2002) noted that 'most Western observers tend to look at the phenomenon of political Islam as if it were butterfly in a collection box, captured and skewered for eternity, or as a set of texts unbendingly prescribing a single path. This is why some scholars who examine its core writings proclaim Islam to be incompatible with democracy – as if any religion in its origins was about democracy at all'.

On the other hand, some contemporary Muslim thinkers have dismissed the compatibility of Islam with democracy as a secular concept that contravenes Islamic principles, arguing that Islam and secularism are opposite forces; that the rule of Allah is not compatible with rule of Man; and that Muslim culture lacks the liberal social attitudes necessary for free, democratic societies to exist. Early contemporary Islamic thinkers like al-Maududi, Hassan al-Banna and Sayyed Qutb rejected democracy as a novelty in Islamic life. Qutb seems to have been completely opposed to any reconciliation with democracy (Tamimi, 1997). In the beginning, he was opposed to the idea of calling Islam democratic and even campaigned for a just dictatorship that would grant political liberties to the virtuous alone. In his *Tafsir* (interpretation) of *Sura al-Shura* (Chapter 42 of the Qur'an), he said: 'democracy is, as a form of government, already bankrupt in the West; why should it be imported to the Middle East?' (Tessler, 2002). On the other hand, Said Hawwa, of the Syrian Islamic Brotherhood initially wrote that 'democracy is a Greek term which signifies sovereignty of the people; the people being the source of legitimacy'. In other words, 'it is the people who legislate and rule. In Islam the people are governed by a regime and a set of laws imposed by Allah.' Later in his life, however, Hawwa revised his ideas about democracy, noting that 'we see that democracy in the Muslim World will eventually produce victory for Islam. Thus, we warn ourselves and our brothers against fighting practical democracy. In fact, we see that asking for more democracy is the practical way to the success of Islam on Islam's territory' (Tamimi, 1997). He went on to say that 'our enemies have realized this fact, and that is why they have assassinated democracy and established dictatorships and other alternatives' (Hawwa, 1988: 71).

Arguments that dismiss the notion of an Islamic democracy presuppose that democracy is a static system that only embraces a particular type of social and cultural vision. However, as Sultan (2004) argues, democracy, like Islam, is an assimilative system that has the ability to adapt to various societies and cultures because it is built on certain universally-acceptable ideas. Dajani (1984) notes that the concept of democracy has evolved in a range of social, political and cultural contexts that shaped its inception in public consciousness. Algerian thinker Bennabi (1991) warns that the answer to the question of 'Is there democracy within Islam?' is not necessarily pertinent to a *fiqh* (jurisprudence) rule deduced from the *Qur'an* or the *Sunna*, but is one which is related to the essence of Islam as a whole. 'In this sense', he argues, 'Islam should be viewed not as a constitution that proclaims the sovereignty of a given community, or that states the rights or liberties of a certain people, but as a democratic enterprise that is the product of an exercise, through which the position of a Muslim vis-a-vis his or her encompassing society is defined, along the path toward accomplishing democratic values and norms. He stipulates that a Muslim's temporal activity is tied to the general principles 'endorsed by Islam in the form of a seed sown in the Islamic conscience, and in the form of a general sentiment, and of motives, that constitute the Islamic equilibrium within every member of the community' (Tamimi, 1997).

In significant ways, Islam and democracy share important features pertaining to human morality. Lewis (1996) notes that Islamic traditions strongly disapprove of arbitrary rule. The central institution of sovereignty in the traditional Islamic world, the Caliphate, is defined by the *Sunni* jurists to have contractual and consensual features that distinguish Caliphs from despots. The exercise of political power is conceived and presented as a contract, creating bonds of mutual obligation between the ruler and the ruled. Subjects are duty-bound to obey the ruler and carry out his orders, but the ruler also has duties toward the subject, similar to those set forth in most cultures. The contract can be dissolved if the ruler fails to fulfill or ceases to be capable of fulfilling his obligations. On the other hand, there is also an element of consent in the traditional Islamic view of government. Many *hadiths* (Prophet's traditions) prescribe obedience as an obligation of a subject, but some indicate exceptions. One, for example, says, 'Do not obey a creature against his creator' – in other words, do not obey a human command to violate divine law. Another says, similarly, 'There is no duty of obedience in sin'. That is to say, if the sovereign commands something that is sinful, the duty of obedience lapses. Prophetic utterances like these point not merely to a right of disobedience (such as would be familiar from Western political thought), but to a divinely-ordained duty of disobedience. Esposito and Voll (1996) refute the common Western view that political Islam and democracy are antithetical. 'Identifying governments as regimes committed either to implementing religious law or Westernization', they say, 'provides no prediction as to whether or not the regime will be authoritarian or democratic', adding that 'the historic situation of the present cannot be understood in monolithic terms, but must be seen as a complex, multifaceted reality in which both complementarities and contradictions [between Islamism and democracy] can be seen'. If the West fails to perceive the democratic quality of the Islamist movements, the fault, according to Esposito and Voll, 'lies in the ethnocentricity of Western perceptions'. Confronting the view of those who suggest the incompatibility, Voll and Esposito note that the' Islamic heritage, in fact, contains concepts that provide a foundation for contemporary Muslims to develop authentically Islamic programs of democracy'.

If democracy is 'government by the people, exercised either directly or through elected representatives', then, elections that express popular consent, freedom of political and social mobilization, and equality of all citizens under the rule of law are essential components of democracy. Those who argue against the compatibility of Islam and democracy usually claim that democracy gives sovereignty or power of rule to the people, while Islam gives sovereignty or power of rule to Allah, which would not allow for a 'government by the people'. In other words, these skeptics believe that the opposite of democracy in relation to a religious political system must be theocracy, meaning the rule of Allah on earth by a religious authority or class. However, this argument presupposes that there is a single religious authority or class within the Islamic tradition that has special access to Allah's will and therefore has the right and power to impose divine will on the land (Sultan, 2004). This is where the argument fails in relation to Islam, because Islamic teachings, at least in the majority *Sunni* traditions, do not recognize a Pope-like figure, nor do they preach the establishment of a religious class that has special access to Divine Will. In fact, to the contrary, it can be argued that the *Qur'an* warns against the establishment of a religious class. The *Qur'an* says that past religious communities took their religious leaders for their lords beside Allah)[52]. Furthermore, Muslims believe that after Prophet Muhammad, there is no one who has direct access to Allah's will, and therefore no one person or group has the legitimacy or authority to claim a pope- or priesthood-like status in the Muslim community.

To some extent, there seems to be no immediate resolution to the debate among traditionalists, Islamists, and intellectual reformists on Islam and democracy. Abootalebi (1999) notes:

> An 'Islamic' democracy will not embrace all the secular values adopted in the West. However, the initial steps taken toward such an end will need to include a process of institutionalization in Islam. The incorporation of an institutionalized Islam in the process of development will help the cause of democracy should Islamists successfully challenge the hegemony of the traditionalists in both the religious and political arenas. To play the democratic game, religious leaders will have to better organize themselves, to propose alternative plans for socio-economic and political issues facing the country. This in turn can help them maintain legitimacy and popular support, facili-

---

[52] Qur'an (9:31)

tating their struggle for political power. Organization is the key to the success of any group seeking to achieve its goals.

By the mid 1990s, with more centrist-Islamic movements in the Arab World getting involved in national democratic politics, the question of Islam's incompatibility with democracy lost most of its relevance. From Morocco in the West to Iraq in the East, Islamic movements in the Arab World have become increasingly assimilated into democratic processes without relinquishing their declared Islamic platforms. They have become influential players in Arab national politics, operating alongside liberal and national secularists. Hamas' victory in Palestine's national elections of 2006 also demonstrated that democracy could also empower Islamists to lead their people as long as they abide by the rules of the democratic game. Among other things, such developments have induced some thinkers to evolve the concept of 'Islamocracy' to define Islam's compatibility with modern democratic practices. The concept was used by former Iranian President Mohammad Khatami, and later promoted by centrist Muslim thinkers like Ali Mazrui. In one of his insightful articles, Mazrui (2005) believes that democracy is the most humane system of government that the human race has so far invented, noting the 'if Scandinavians can combine liberal democracy with socialist principles, and the English can combine a formal Protestant theocracy with a practical liberal democracy, can Muslims combine liberal democracy with Islamic principles? Can Islamocracy be a new vision of governance?'

Another Muslim thinker, Azzam Tamimi (2001), an advocate of Islamocracy, has worked hard to refute conclusions made by some Muslim political writers that Islam and democracy are incompatible. His writings about Tunisian Islamist Rashid al-Ghannoushi were specifically inspired by the democratic experiment in Jordan, where, despite a fully-fledged Islamist participation in the political process, there was still a debate within Islamic movement circles as to whether democracy did, or did not, contradict Islam. This debate had actually been going on in much of the Arab world since the mid-1980s 'when the breeze of democratization seemed to blow across the region'. The most significant development accompanying this trend had been the emergence within political Islam of groups willing to take part in the democratic process and pledging to respect the results of the elections and to play by the rules of the game. When he referred to the obstacles to the progress of democracy, he suggested going beyond the notions of secularization and modernization, the nation state and the new world order. Tamimi (2001) suggested al-Ghanoushi believes that the opposition to democracy in some factional and academic Islamic quarters represents the most formidable challenge.

Louay Safi, a member of the board of directors of the Washington, D.C.-based Center for the Study of Islam and Democracy (CSID), has spent a lot of time thinking about the pairing of Islam and democratic forms of government. He sees a good fit. Handwerk (2003) quoted Safi as saying that that Islam as a set of norms and ideals that emphasizes the equality of people, the accountability of leaders to community, and the respect of diversity and other faiths, is fully compatible with democracy. He wrote that he does not 'see how it could be compatible with a government that would take away those values'. Safi observes that some of the people who say that democracy has no place in Islam express a sense that the word 'democracy' as presented in international discourse appears to be wholly owned by the West and has, for some, a connotation of cultural imperialism'. Self-government does have some roots in the Islamic world. Safi explains that historic Muslim societies were more representative than their modern counterparts because the central state was not as powerful

In its basic configuration, 'Islamocracy' describes a new perspective that combines fundamental Islamic moral values with modern democratic practices. It postulates a scheme of governance that draws on Islamic morality as its soul and contemporary democratic procedures and instructions as its body. From the beginning it should be clear that Islamocracy is not synonymous with theocracy, but is rather a full-fledged civil state drawing on Islamic moral values and using modern participatory procedures and structures. In Islamocracy, there are written constitutions, representative bodies, and separated powers. As two Danish scholars in the field of Islam and democracy noted, Islamocracy is a hybrid word denoting Islamic (Isla-) and democratic (mo) kind of government (cracy) (Hjroto and Olufsen, 2003). The constitution is viewed as the reference point for the state and society as well as the legal background where the foundations and principles of Islam and democracy are balanced. In no way should this proposed scheme suggest that democratic procedures and structures are mere formalities with no substantive bearing on governance. The constitution, inspired by Islamic morality, is a binding document that delineates rights and duties of the state and community members in their official and private capacities. It embraces explicit provisions for human rights, freedom of religion and expression, accountability, and cultural identity. It details issues pertaining to women and minority rights, communication rights, political participation, power mandates and other matters. Representative bodies are chosen freely by community members according to diverse political and cultural platforms that share views on the Islamic identity of the state as a sacred feature of Islamocracy. Here we are not talking about a theocracy as the civil nature of the state has to be affirmed in constitutional terms. The role of religion in public life is cultural and social and the state has a duty to promote an enlightened view of Islam as a centrist way of life that seeks to achieve the happiness of man within the confines of its Divine morality. Islam would be advanced as a way of life that draws on the institution of justice in the community, something that dictates the activation of a set of moral values pertaining to freedom and accountability, equal participation in public decision making, and access to communication channels.

In Islamocracy, power is not concentrated in the hands of a single leader; though the leading figure could have credible powers vested in him/her by the constitutions in his/her capacity as the prime decision maker. Power separation is a defining feature of Islamocracy because it stifles authoritarian excesses and institutes a significant check-and-balances system of government. Everybody is subject to the rule of law. The executive branch is responsible for running the day-to-day affairs of the state in times of peace and war while the legislative, as a representative of the community, is entrusted with law-making in tune with Islamic morality and contemporary visions. Members of representative councils or assemblies are freely-elected by community members who have equal access to run for parliamentary seats. Minorities are represented in national assemblies either as part of institutionalized quota systems or within the overall equal-opportunity access to parliamentary bodies which have the power to enact new laws relating to political, economic and social matters within enlightened understandings of the Islamic moral values. The *Shura* Council has a binding legislative rather than a voluntary consultative jurisdiction when it comes to the regulation of community life at domestic and external levels. The state has a full responsibility for ensuring community members' access to ballot boxes and running for public offices under platforms compatible with Islamic morality.

Although separation of powers is a fundamental feature of an Islamocracy, one needs to understand the unique Islamic perspective on this matter. In classical Islamic political theory, there is no division between the state and the community as noted in Western political conceptions of the state and civil society. However, the community could generate new organizational structures with differentiated orientations seeking to provide alternative visions to carry out policies and decisions. These are civil society institutions playing a substantive role in the political process to ensure community welfare and identity. Because Islam is taken as a comprehensive way of life, the notion of separating religious morality from temporal life matters as in Western societies is unthinkable. Some scholars note that the separation between religion and state, or what is religious or sacred in the West and what is secular, is something that has its own historical roots (Philipp, 1988). For a considerable period of time, people used to consider the Church as an institution which at times aligned itself with the ruling elite and did not necessarily serve the interest of the masses. It was perceived by some people, especially in the 17th century, as an institution which had a strong desire for power, struggling with the ruling elite or the so-called temporal authorities. In an Islamocracy, the permeation of religious beliefs in community life should serve as a moral tool for bolstering the Islamocratic identity of the state and society rather than to blindly overstretch Islamic values and norms to accommodate new practices in the 21st century. As noted earlier, what matters in an Islamocracy is the maintenance of the Arab-Islamic identity of the state and the community regardless of the type of structures and procedures employed for Islam is intrinsically about values and norms rather than about formalities.

If Islamocracy is about the perpetuation of an Arab-Islamic identity on the state and society drawing on modern structures and procedures, then we are talking about a social and political system that maintains its unique cultural features while sharing significant matters with other societies. Identity here refers to the cultural, religious and social heritage that confers on the Arabian communities their unique character. Identity is viewed as a safe haven to which Arab communities go to keep their distinctive existence. In the age of globalization, it is cultural identity, more than politics or economics that forms the final frontier in the struggle for survival. Identity here is not about coercive imposition of old-fashioned life styles on modern living conditions; it is rather a window of opportunity for community members to understand themselves within historical social and cultural phases of their development and to express themselves as such. Since the late part of the 20th century, all Islamic (and Arab) societies have been facing a wide range of challenges; yet the most outstanding has been that of cultural identity. Arab states have to some extent succeeded in importing economic and political recipes into their communities; but have flagrantly failed on the cultural front simply because identity cannot be imported. It is the responsibility of an Islamocratic state to bolster the use of Arabic as the central incubator of Arab-Islamic identity and to safeguard and promote an enlightened and centrist vision of Islam as the main source of Arab identity. Other sources of Arab identity as derived from secular traditions are also of paramount significance and need to be preserved as part of the community heritage.

VII.2. A Proposed Arab-Islamic Public Sphere Perspective

The previous section notes that contemporary thinkers on Islam and politics have elaborated 'Islamocracy' or Islamic governance as a viable alternative defining political systems in Islamic societies. The boundaries of political power in Islam seem well-defined with leadership selected by popular community will to apply an Islamically-inspired constitution drawing on the cherished moral values of *Ibadah* (Worship in its spiritual and temporal manifestations), justice, equality, freedom, accountability, honesty, diversity and peaceful coexistence. There is no room for despotism or arbitrary government in Islam as executive, consultative (or legislative in some aspects) and judiciary organs operate in a spirit of transparency as integral parts of the community to whom they are accountable. Freedom of expression is a basic right in an Islamocracy; yet, individuals and the community at large have their constitutional rights to protect themselves against offensive forms of speech. In classical Arab-Islamic communication traditions, speech was an important communicative action that needs to be harnessed in our in the pursuit of advancing the preservation of religious beliefs, justice, equality, and community welfare. There is no room for freedom of speech and expression that desecrates religious beliefs and universal human ideals or leads to the spread of vice and evil in the community. Furthermore, in a

Muslim community, the division of society into state and civil society sectors is virtually non-existent simply because the state should reflect popular will and nothing else. If the state is an expression of collective community will, then the prescribed divisions between the state and community actors are less relevant. However, this should not suggest that the community could not generate alternative visions for handling pressing problems facing the *Umma*. On the contrary, it is incumbent on the community to ensure through rational debates that all problems are addressed in a manner conducive to the realization of community goals and missions.

The introduction of new media institutions into contemporary Arab societies in the post-colonial period has generated heated debates regarding the 'Islamization' of media systems to reflect traditional values and practices in Arab societies (Hamada, 2004). With the rise of political Islam following the Iranian Revolution in 1979, new trends emerged in the Arab World for Islamic revival in different life aspects, including communications. Over 50 books on Islamic media were generated in the 1980s alone, perhaps echoing soaring Islamic sentiments on the eve of the former Soviet Union's defeat in Afghanistan that was presented as yet another 'Islamic victory in a decade after the Iranian Revolution.'[53] While most of those works were rather descriptive and normative in their approach to the evolution of an Islamic media model, very few sought to tackle the issue within an elaborate systematic analytical context. It was noted in those works that Islamic media should serve to promote noble Islamic values and traditions and contribute to social harmony and stability. Some of those works even studied existing media institutions as 'living models' of Islamic media primarily because their charters incorporated references to moral Islamic values or because most of their content was heavily religious. Because they dwelled very much on historical research, they seemed to have lost sight of contemporary media realities and their implications for Arab societies. This book seeks to offer a new perspective on Arab-Islamic communication in a contemporary context that draws on both traditional and modern components of media values and practices.

On the other hand, beyond the Arab World, normative theorization about Islamic media models has produced some good works whose findings could be conveniently applied to Arab World settings. Those works are marked by their analysis of historical traditions and their syntheses with contemporary media practices and norms. Mowlana (1988: 139-140) notes that ethical thinking practices pertaining to communication in Islamic societies (including Arab societies) are based on religious and secular ethics. Discussions of the issue within the

---

[53] Examples include Hamza (1989); Imam (1985); Abu Zaid (1986); Khatib (1987); al-Amin (2003). In practice today there is no journalistic code of ethics based on the principles of Islam, and few scholars have attempted to define an Islamic framework for mass media ethics (For example, Siddiqi (1989); Al Seini (1986); Schleifer (1986).

normative religious dimension have taken place in the context of Islamic jurisprudence (*fiqh*) and have been based on ethical views enunciated in the *Qur'an* and the *Sunna*. They have also drawn on broader philosophical and theological debates pertaining to Arab-Islamic thinking on norms of morality. A good deal of emphasis has been placed on media as tools for the institution of justice and the exposure of human right violations in Muslim countries, especially as they pertain to Western domination of this area of the world. It has been noted that media in the Arab World, predicated on the Islamic model would be voices of reason and faith, combining metaphysical and existential morality to establish the rule of *Shari'a* law in an enlightened and open-minded fashion. Ayish (2003b) elaborated a normative Arab-Islamic communication perspective based on both secular and religious values and percepts that promotes communication as a social action drawing on a set of dichotomies of both form and substance. He notes that contemporary media systems in the Arab World have failed because they could not accommodate professional and cultural communication realities in the evolving regional and global systems.

The development of professional codes of communication ethics is central for the success of an Islamocratic public sphere. Media ethics from Islamic and Western perspectives have been topics of global debates in the past two decades. A conference held in Germany on media ethics in Western and Muslim communities in March 2001 concluded that despite the existing problems of foreign reporting, many notions of good or bad journalism are actually interchangeable between the West and Islam. 'Objectivity', 'truthfulness', the 'respect of privacy', and a dislike of 'sensationalism' are common norms that are often violated in practical journalism but could, nevertheless, provide a basis for transcultural professionalism (Hafez, 2003). Participants in the conference called for in-depth debate over the actual contents and meanings of abstract norms such as 'freedom of expression', which could mean very different things in different political and cultural contexts. Contrary to common wisdom, however, limits to freedom of expression in media are often not merely the result of censorship and autocratic information control, but of journalistic self-censorship, which makes the question of journalistic ethics one of utmost importance. Ayish and Sadiq (1997) observed that Arab-Islamic values of justice, mercy, community cohesion and belief in Allah shape the ethical foundations of communication in classical and modern Arab history. At no moment in recent history have those foundations come to clash with those in the West than in the publishing of cartoons offensive to Prophet Muhammad by a Danish newspaper in September 2005. The issue triggered global debates on issues of freedom and responsibility in media work, thus underscoring the need to bring about more harmony into diverse world ethical and cultural norms in communication.

As much as the public sphere seems indispensable to Western democratic politics, it is also central to running public affairs in Arab-Islamic communities and beyond; yet on terms different from those applied in Western settings. In a Muslim state, the public sphere is not a space for waging battles between the state and civil society groupings, but rather an arena for offering alternative visions for the conduct of public affairs in tune with Islamic morality. This is carried out within the ethical and cultural context of the public sphere as an incubator of rational, decent, scientific, and balanced exchanges that seek to advance the cause of justice in the community and beyond. The public sphere needs to be kept pure from pollutions, as a tool for empowering the institution of justice rather than the reinforcement of altruistic pursuits. In addition, while there seems to be a broad consensus on the centrality of public communications in managing community affairs, the problems associated with transferring foreign concepts and practices into different social and cultural settings remains an insurmountable challenge. Since the concept of the public sphere, in its basic configuration, embodies the very indispensable role of communication in creating sustainable human communities across time and space, then the big question confronting us relates to whether we could conduct our public affairs in a globalized world with no such social space available. If we believe that Western democratic politics is a stranger to our political and cultural traditions, then how are we going to make up for the missing space (if we can ever do that) in the presence of global media outlets that defy our capacity to absorb them. What the author offers in this chapter is an Islamocratic public sphere scheme that draws on new conceptions of politics and media as derived from Arab-Islamic traditions and contemporary practices. Because the scope of the prescribed public sphere is pan-Arab rather than state-based, it takes the Arab World as a geographical and cultural entity as its prime object of investigation. The transnationalization of media organizations combined with the relative homogeneity of Arab-Islamic culture renders the analysis more relevant. This section does not seek to reinvent the wheel; but to build on an accumulated heritage of Islamic morality as explained in Chapter III as well as contemporary political practices to generate new ideas that neither compromise the pillars of Islamic *beliefs* nor obfuscate the positive ingredients of modern political contributions.

Islamocracy denotes more than the institution of free representation, separation of powers and constitutional provisions. It rather embraces the full spectrum of education and socialization at family and community levels. Islamocratic culture, with its centrist visions of society and the state, is the cornerstone of the educational system that should promote values of moderation, tolerance, diversity, freedom, honesty, respect, and far more important, the sense of cultural identity and consciousness. Educational curricula should be developed on the basis of enlightened Islamic values and orientations and should have a strong global component that promotes community interactions with other cultures. Clearly enough, the institution of an enlightened Islamocratic culture in the Arab World suggests not only the development of a sound political scheme of governance at the institutional level, but the creation of a grassroots cultural environment conducive to the application of political, social and economic practices in the community. Leading cultural institutions like mosques, schools, universities, clubs, social forums, and the media should work in sync to foster Islamocratic culture as the defining feature of Arab World identity. Cognizant of the formidable challenges embedded in outdated and misconstrued components in our heritage, the author views Islamocratization as a long-term process of sweeping transitions into a new era of community life marked by a strong sense of identity drawing on the best and the brightest of modern political and communication practices. It follows that the main function of the public sphere is the consolidation of an Islamocratic culture that safeguards community identity and reaches out to contemporary political experiences.

VII.3. Arab-Islamic Public Sphere Features

The central question addressed by this book arises from the broader intellectual tradition of media role in politics and in social change in Arabian societies and how this issue has been approached by Western writers. It has been noted earlier that although the Arab region was traditionally viewed by Western intellectual scholarship as a cultural and political wasteland marked by savage authoritarianism, it was in the post-9/11 era that more aggressive research has come to emerge, something closely amounting to a sort of Neo-Orientalism, bent on the intellectual reinvention of the Arab World, this time with the full backing of crude force. Western, especially American political researchers and media analysts, have tended to approach the Arab World mainly on the basis of untested stereotypes and historical inaccuracies, thus doing an irreparable injustice to its universally-recognized morals and cultural values. It is certainly true that the 21st century has dawned on the region at its worst phase of development. More than ever before, the Arab World was politically divided, militarily abused, culturally disoriented, and economically incapacitated. But Western scholarship's obfuscation of the *Umma's* history as either irrelevant or subversive seems to echo real ethnocentric overtones. The Islamocratic system is both an expression of Arab-Islamic assertiveness and of intercultural openness. In building durable relations with the West, both sides are not running out of ideas for peaceful coexistence, but rather of good intentions to make dreams of coexistence come true. Within this context, this book offers this framework for a public sphere model that draws on the key moral Islamic values and contemporary political practices giving substance and shape to Islamocracy.

Following is an overview of prescribed features of the Arab-Islamic public sphere that draw on both Arab-Islamic moral values and modern communication practices.

VII.3.1. Intellectual Roots

If the existing public sphere in the Arab region draws on Western conceptions of the role of communication media in democratic politics as a fourth estate to counterbalance state political power and to promote free expression, its function in Arab-Islamic communities takes on a different slant. The intellectual foundations of the Arab-Islamic public sphere are based on the conception of communication as a social action pursued by Man as part of a grand Divine Mission assigned to him by Allah within the notion of *Ibadah* (worship in its spiritual and temporal sense). We do not communicate just to express ourselves freely and to affirm our individual orientations, but also to demonstrate our commitment to our identity and more values of justice, equality, community cohesion, and prosperity within boundaries defined by Islamic and widely-accepted secular traditions. Freedom is not a goal onto itself, but rather a means of promoting virtue and combating evil in the community. It is a tool of self-fulfillment that eventually contributes to advancing community values and norms in tune with enlightened interpretations of Arab-Islamic traditions. Communication is never conceived as a tool of oppression and control; but a tool of enlightenment and education, seeking to create public consciousness of issues bearing on community life. Freedom of communication is highly sanctioned in Islam as long as its practice is conducive to the institution of justice and the exposure of corruption and inefficiency. The author introduces the concept of 'freesponsibility' to denote freedom within responsibility in communication practices. There is no room for absolute freedom in the Islamocratic community as communicators should always heed individual and community rights in their media practices. These rights include the right to safeguard religious beliefs against offensive actions; the right to protect privacy against intrusions; the right to preserve *Umma* interests (including security interests); and the right to be represented in a fair and balanced fashion in public media.

The intellectual foundations for the public sphere in an Arab-Islamic community also assume the existence of a diverse global public sphere made up of heterogeneous actors. Debating other actors in the public sphere is based on good sound reasoning, shared beliefs, respectful argumentation, scientific and realistic advocacy, and commitment to justice, equality, and community interests. Debates in the prescribed public sphere preclude sensationalism in argumentation and promote symmetrical communication through exchanges of views on the basis of ethical and moral rather than altruistic considerations. This suggests that the proposed Arab-Islamic public sphere is not designed to reinforce domination and subjugation, but to establish solid grounds for rational, critical, interactive and transparent modes of discourse. However, it should be noted that an Arab-Islamic public sphere would develop more successfully in the context of shared recognition by different actors that such debate is central to creating community awareness of pressing issues and how to address them in the best interest of the

Umma. The basic foundation for constructively engaging others in fruitful debates is a mutual recognition of the other as a human being seeking to understand and to share rather than to dominate and coerce the other side into accepting ideas.

VII.3.2. Indigenous Genesis

If the evolving public sphere in the Arab World has come out as a prime function of global transformations in international power structures and communications technologies, in an Islamocratic system, it has to primarily arise out of local political and cultural developments. The Islamocratic public sphere has to take on genuine indigenous colorations in substance, form, actors, and orientations in order to serve as a true representation of community concerns and views. It has to grow out of the local political, cultural and social settings in order to be able to serve as an enlightened extension of those settings at regional and global levels. In this case, the community should establish appropriate social and political arrangements that ensure the unique cultural identity of the public sphere. In addition, the community should develop communications capacities, drawing on its heritage, to empower individuals and institutions to produce competitive arguments to counter those arising from the global public sphere. Communication channels need to act freely and responsibly in relaying community views either as alternative visions to supplement state views on issues and events impinging on community life or to engage global actors on issues relevant to community interests and concerns. In this case, the public sphere is viewed as a discursive zone for stimulating enlightened state and community visions to perpetuate Islamocratic culture and identity within the confines of modern political and social practices. The main point to be emphasized here is that the public sphere needs to be genuinely Arab-Islamic in its moral foundations and truly modern in its practices. It arises and evolves in response to indigenous needs and concerns rather than being imposed on the community by virtue of global political and technological developments. In this case, the public sphere needs to be a proactive initiative launched by the community rather than a reactive phenomenon created to address external transitions.

The achievement of an Islamocratic public sphere is unthinkable in the absence of egalitarian arrangements and solid economic conditions. True Islamocratic morality is likely to generate solid political systems capable of safeguarding cultural identity of society and the state. It would also promote protective legal safeguards that ensure constitutional protection for the free and responsible expression in public debates. Economic prosperity is also essential for inducing community members to take part in public debates on issuing bearing on their life. In this case, public sphere debate is expected to reflect domestic concerns by domestic actors with domestic visions for social and political change. Politically-disenchanted community members are less likely to be motivated to take part in public debates even if they are offered the chance to do so. Low trust in media discourse that fails to be translated into concrete political and social change could be a daunting factor dampening interest in being partners to public sphere exchanges. As noted earlier, the mere availability of media channels is of less relevance in the absence of solid community confidence in media potential to bring about positive changes in its living realities. Community members and civil society groups would be more pre-disposed to trust a promising public sphere role only when it embodies a strong sense of social and economic justice in the distribution of resources and the application of public laws.

VII.3.3. Economic Foundations

If media channels in the current Arab public sphere of the early 21st century survive on state subsidies or commercial funding, then communications in the Islamocratic public sphere, whether state-controlled or privately operated, need to ensure a sustainable financial base that would help them keep the finest professional standards. Media, as central public sphere institutions, should be empowered to serve as voices of justice and virtue with full financial and editorial independence. There is no room for censoring information that condones covering up on fiascos and other types of corruption. Media should be able to seek viable sources of funding while keeping their editorial integrity away from political and social pressures. Media could run advertisements and establish subscription services and even receive state subsidies without letting that impinge on their mission as instruments of enlightened cultural assertiveness. Even when media are sponsored by the state, they are not expected to give unconditional support to unjust and corrupt state practices. On the contrary, the public sphere, at least in its local dimension, should serve as an arena for exposing, within parameters of decency, pitfalls in existing policies and systems and should provide relevant advice to policy makers on how problems could be rectified. One thing that needs to be noted here is that the public sphere should not be polluted by excessive commercial interests and orientations. Clear-cult boundaries should be drawn between culturally and politically valuable content and commercial message with pure promotional values. The insulation of the public sphere against commercial intrusions has been a central universal question in democratic societies. As noted earlier in the book, the rise of commercial orientations in Western media development in the 20th century prompted Habermas to bemoan the deteriorating conditions of the public sphere. Tensions between media interests in survival and their concerns about commercial sustainability need to be reconciled.

VII.3.4. Media 'Freesponsiblity'

Media in the proposed Arab-Islamic public sphere operate within a context of full freedom to gather, produce, and impart information as long as that contributes to the institution of justice and the promotion of a unique cultural identity. Individuals enjoy full freedom of expression as long as that freedom serves to foster justice, equality, creativity, cohesion, understanding, and community interests. States have no monopoly over information distribution systems as long as they seek to advance the social and political interests of the Islamocratic community at domestic and global levels. The public sphere in this case is an egalitarian arena for contesting views by either offering alternative visions to existing policies and orientations or seeking to engage outside actors in rational debates pertaining to pressing issues of concern to Arab and global communities. Media enjoy full freedom of speech and expression; yet, they are also accountable for their communicative actions. In this case, the legal system should define opportunities and limitations pertaining to media work on the basis of Islamic moral considerations. Furthermore, the public sphere should offer actors with different orientations the right to express themselves at two levels: the national level whereby actors (individuals and groups) representing varied community interests offer alternative visions to state policies and perspectives, and the global level where diverse community actors with common grounds engage foreign actors on issues of global interest. In an Islamocratic public sphere, the state can never be an authoritarian force of repression because it is committed to total community welfare as defined by its democratically-represented political bodies and Islamic laws.

VII.4. Components

The proposed Islamocratic public sphere is an open arena harnessed for the institution of a unique cultural community identity drawing on an enlightened understanding of Islamic morality and modern communication and political practices. In an Islamocratic public sphere, the rules of intellectual engagement are designed both to safeguard basic sources of Islamic morality and to promote an active role for the community in running its own affairs in the age of globalization.

VII.4.1. Actors in the Arab-Islamic Public Sphere

The Islamocratic public sphere in the age of globalization is no longer confined to the geographical boundaries of the Arab World. It overlaps very much with other regional and global spaces as mass media continue to extend their global reach beyond their national frontiers. Actors in this case are expected to embrace a wide range of orientations and visions. At the national level, 'diversity within unity' is the defining concept of the Islamocratic theory: diversity in interpretations and insights pertaining to living realities and unity in adherence to the moral foundations of the Islamocratic system. In this case, we expect to see the state, civil community groups, regional and global actors making use of the public sphere in rational exchanges that would help reach a maximum level of consensus on issues of common concern. The multiplicity of actors in the Arab-Islamic public sphere is central to the enrichment of the discussion. While actors engaged in national debates seek to offer alternative interpretations of ideological and political policies and visions, those taking part in the global public sphere seek to demonstrate both the unity and diversity of perspectives marking community debates. The Islamocratic public sphere could not offer room for actors seeking to undermine the very foundations of the *Umma* by encouraging bigotry, inciting dissent and disobedience, or promoting communal or ethnic divisions. If the Islamocratic public sphere aims at promoting dialogue with the 'other', then it should provide relevant space for opposing views that do not impinge on the basic premises of Arab-Islamic morality. In this case, we expect private individuals, political and social groups, national and foreign government officials, intellectuals and international representatives to be part of the public sphere as long as they demonstrate a sense of recognition for the legitimacy of the Islamocratic state.

VII.4.2. Institutions

All media of communication are expected to serve as platforms of rational debates in the Islamocratic public sphere in its local, regional and global manifestations. There is no limitation, whatsoever, on the nature of media institutions involved in public sphere exchanges as they range from the press, to satellite television, to the World Wide Web, to telephony systems, to interpersonal communications. Here, what matters is not the type of media channel used in public sphere communications, but rather the content it seeks to deliver and the moral boundaries they operate within. In fact, actors in the Islamocratic public sphere are encouraged to harness different media channels to relay their messages to their audiences, especially media with effective reach and persuasive power. Television and the Web are particularly two important media of communication with a lot of impact due to their interactive features and global reach. Though the institution of the public sphere is expected to be affiliated with both government and community sectors, it lends itself much to moral Islamocratic principles governing community affairs.

VII.4.3. Discourse

The Arab-Islamic public sphere draws on the use of Arabic and foreign language media discourse that promotes the cultural identity of the Islamocratic community, and creates consensus on contested issues pertaining to living realities in the Arab region. A sound Arab public sphere discourse should reflect respect for others' ideological and religious orientations; should be realistic and simple; should avoid offensive and pompous expressions; should draw on rational argumentation; should derive from the core moral values of Islam which embrace justice, mercy, equality, *Ibadah*, 'freesponsibility', respect for the other, and community cohesion. The Arab-Islamic discourse should promote international and inter-religious understanding and harmony; should advance the cause of justice; and should create common grounds for further human interactions. This discourse synthesizes cherished Arab-Islamic moral values and contemporary political and communication practices to create new meeting grounds and melting pots based on sensitivity to others' concerns and recognition of differences as natural features of human societies. An Islamocratic discourse should drift way from fanaticism and bigotry; it should take on a more symmetrical approach to cotemporary global issues, drawing on religious and cultural heritage and contemporary realities to evolve relevant solutions. It also should emanate from the true spirit of Islam without breaking away from contemporary human traditions with broad universal acclaim.

VII.4.4. Effects

The ultimate goal of establishing an Islamocratic public sphere is to institute and foster a unique cultural identity for Arabian communities within the confines of Islamic morality and modern political and communication practice. The public sphere is expected to serve as a tool for the institution of social justice, equality, human understanding, collaboration, community cohesion, respect for others' beliefs and traditions, and not as an arena for clashing civilizations. The Arab-Islamic public sphere is harnessed as a tool for evolving national and global consensus based on unique Arab concerns and common universal orientations. It is an arena that seeks to achieve concrete outcomes on the ground in policies, attitudes, and even actions at different levels. The target audience of the public sphere could be states, NGOs, media, or the general public (*Umma*) who are supposed to be the movers and shakers of political structures in the Islamocratic system. The prime aim is to create maximum consensus on how to best serve Islamocratic interests, especially those relating to the preservation of cultural identity for society and the state through rational discussions and exchanges. The mass-mediated public sphere would supplement contributions from other institutions like cultural forums, educational sectors and other intellectual platforms seeking to perpetuate cultural identity as the final frontier for *Umma* survival in the age of globalization.

VII.5. Realizing an Arab Global Constructive Engagement

The issue of constructive engagement is highly central for the success of the public sphere at local and global levels. It is taken for a fact that Arabs at private and officials levels would not make significant advancements in communicating with others unless they master constructive dialogue among themselves. The experience of the past four decades has rendered all Arab endeavors to engage others in short-term or long term dialogues useless simply because Arabs themselves were not speaking in one voice. The Arab public discourse in the age of globalization and previous eras has often been taken to task for failing to effectively address non-Arab audiences with persuasive messages that convey the true cultural essence of Arab-Islamic morality. Such failure, among other things, has been conducive to the deterioration of Arab-Islamic images in different communities in the West, especially in the United States. Although this issue has been broadly debated at official and non-official Arab World circles, mainly driven by rising Arab and Muslim stereotypes as evident in public opinion surveys and media studies, not much has been done to redress this problem. While some researchers invoked the cultural clash thesis to explain Arabs' failure to create a lasting footprint on global public spheres, others found convenience in conspiracy theories that present Arabs as clear targets of systematic Western plots to 'undermine our cultural heritage and stifle our revivalism'. Yet, when some sought to blame the Arab side for this failure, they seemed to be shooting at the wrong target by claiming that the whole matter is reduced to the absence of Arab communication mechanisms through which Arabs could deliver their messages to the other side. Here, we see a good deal of the blame heaped on Arabs' failure to allocate resources needed for making communication with the West possible through the establishment of new print and broadcast structures capable of reaching out to Western audiences on a systematic basis. Unfortunately, numerous past experiences have clearly demonstrated that the whole issue is neither financial nor technological, but rather cultural, intrinsically emanating from Arabs' failure to evolve a discourse that truly reflects their concerns and aspirations while reaching out to the other for understanding.

A tragic conclusion flowing from the above comments suggests that Arabs seem to view the rules of engagement in crude 'bullet theory' or 'tit-for-tat theory' terms that assume conspiratorial and culturally-deadlocked relations with the other who historically has been the West, and most recently has been the United States. Advocates of conspiratorial thinking view American media and other cultural products as no more than spearheads for political and military domination of Arab lands and resources and for a pre-emption of Arab awakening.

Terms like media and cultural 'onslaughts', 'invasions', and 'blitzes' are often used to describe evolving communication situations in the Arab World as marked by Western domination of the media sphere. To face up to these challenges, it is often suggested that Arabs should develop their infrastructures, prepare their communicators, and draw out long-term strategies to eliminate potential threats. Scores of conferences on communication and culture in the Arab World have also called for solidarity among social and political institutions to stave off the incoming threats and defeat enemies of the *Umma* by showing more attachment to our cherished values and cultural traditions. Media institutions have also been encouraged to be part of this defensive strategy by fighting on two fronts: the domestic front through reinforcing a sense of community cohesion with no clear vision about its substance and form, and the external front by refuting claims harmful to our society and values without offering alternative competitive perspectives. This state of confusion has only contributed to the consolidation of conventional stereotypes about Arabs as cultural failures despite the possession of one of the richest moral arsenal in human history.

An overview of the current Arab discourse in the currently evolving public sphere suggests that it is grounded in myopic visions of the nature, parameters, values, dynamics, players, structures, and potential effects of the unfolding global intellectual engagement. Although it was noted in Chapter VI that the evolving Arab public sphere is embracing multiple discourses reflecting the ideological orientations of a range of actors, such visions continue to share significant features that warrant their analysis as a single entity. A problem plaguing these discourse orientations is that they fail to recognize the 'other' in a human and respectable form, always drawing on a sense of uniqueness and superiority despite the bitter realities into which Arab World situations have degenerated. Yet, the most serious problem facing Arab discourse at the global level is the absence of a solid and systematic local/national orientation that reflects clarity of vision on central spiritual, political and cultural issues. There is a wide range of ideological, ethnic, political, and religious divisions in the Arab World; yet there is no unifying intellectual umbrella within which those divisions could turn into a constructive mosaic that enriches the public sphere.
The author believes that a constructive Arab engagement in the global intellectual public sphere is not a function of mere resources, but of three broad variables: discourse quality, culture, and power politics.

VII.5.1. Discourse Quality

Arab discourse in the modern and post-modern eras has lent itself more to communication dichotomies noted in the classical Arab-Islamic public sphere in Chapter III. It is a discourse that thrives more on the transcendental than on the existential; on the intuitive than on the rational; on the patriarchal more than on the free; and on the collective more than on the individual. Arabic as the prime carrier of cultural discourse in the public sphere has been influential in this regard. It has been noted by some researchers that as much as language is a means of communication, it is also an incubator of cultural and moral values, a carrier of national identity in its broadest sense. Language, according to Tibi (2002) constitutes a reservoir in which the cultural heritage of a people, its songs, traditions, history, literature, religion and folk mythologies are preserved and handed down from generation to generation. Suleiman (2003) notes that language maintenance in the face of the challenges mounted against it either by the enemy outside, or the enemy within, thus becomes the best and perhaps the only effective means of cultural survival and continuity. It was observed in Chapter II that Arabic has thrived more on its oral rather than written usage, leading to the prosperity of impressive poetic and oratory traditions. With its musical features defining its structure, Arabic has historically been characterized as dwelling on formalistic rather than content-oriented features.

Suleiman (2003) notes that the treatment of language as the core ingredient and the most prominent manifestation of nationalism is characteristic of Arabic discourse on the topic. In spelling out the content of this position, the Arab nationalists adopt as an article of supreme faith the view that language is not just a means of communication, of conveying messages between interlocutors, 'but a most eloquent symbol of group identity and one whose ultimate strength lies in its ability to provide the cultural and instrumental backbone of the group's legitimate 'objective of furthering its ethno-cultural self-interest'. In the Arab nationalist discourse, the universal theme that language cannot be separated from culture, in the same way as culture cannot be separated from language, is imbued with meanings whose significance encompasses a broad spectrum of issues – particularly the role of the glorious Arab past, with its proud achievements in the human sciences. Accessing culture through language thus becomes an exploration of the contribution of the medium and an articulation of the very essence of its content. Arab nationalism as a modernizing force is dynamically and inextricably rooted in this conception of the role of language, according to Suleiman (2003) in the life of the people; it is thus equipped with the durable ability to transcend the vast fluctuations in political fortunes which have befallen it over the past few decades.

The challenge facing Arabs in the age of globalization is not emanating from language itself, but from its usage. Arabic discourse has been taken to task for being 'noisy' and full of hyperbole without being matched by concrete action on the ground. Speeches and talk shows are full of ornamental oratory features, but once you zoom in on their substance, you would not come up with anything significant. This suggests that Arabs have become captive to their intrinsic linguistic propensity to be formalistic and musical when in fact they should make use of the language potential to serve as an effective communication tool. This in fact has been a legacy of the oral traditions in classical and early Arab world history when speech was taken for an action; when words were having the effect of bullets, when the poet was the soldier defending the honor of the tribe and the nation. It is true that the value of speech should not be underestimated because it reflects precious ideas that are the driving force for social change. Yet, to take words as equivalent to action in the sense of failing to take action because some words were made in lieu of that action is a major alarming source of concern. Arab summits' speeches have always been rife with flowery phrases and zealous statements pertaining to national and pan-Arab issues; yet once the meetings were over, nothing significant would materialize. As noted earlier, this obsession with the overuse of language has caused Saudi intellectual and former diplomat Ghazi al-Ghussaibi to describe Arabs as no more than 'a noise phenomenon.'

The implications of viewing language as a shouting tool are numerous. On the one hand, deepening beliefs in the power of words to induce the intended effect has made the Arab public sphere cluttered with speeches and counter speeches and talk shows as well as editorial writings – all thriving on the musical features of Arabic. On the receiving end, audiences who subscribe to the 'noise phenomenon' thesis are more likely to be affected by the noise magnitude of the language (spoken) and its flowery nature (written). Both communicators and receivers would then find a convenient escape in using the language as a substitute for real life actions, thus leading to further detachment from existing realities that would experience transformations induced by external actors. On the other hand, the use of language or even the use of a mindset that thrives on language as a substitute for action (even if it is no Arabic) to address non-Arabic speakers with a tongue possessing a strong sense of reality would be problematic. It has been noted that in evaluating their communication performance with other foreign nations, many Arab World media usually draw on the number of broadcasting hours and print media pages produced. The notion of whether such media efforts had any effects on the intended audiences remains totally unrealized simply because it is erroneously believed that the mere launch of a communication action means its goals have been achieved.

VII.5.2. Islamocratic Culture

The concept of culture is used here to describe the knowledge, language, values, customs, and material objects that are passed from person to person and from one generation to the next in a human group or society. While a society is made up of people, a culture is made up of ideas, behaviors, and material possessions. Culture exists in society and organizations and can be a supportive force providing a sense of continuity – it can also be a force that generates discord, conflict and even violence (Bates and Plog, 1990). The author believes that culture, in its broadest sense, shapes our moral, political and social views and perceptions that consequently bear on public discourse. The problem with investigating Arab culture relates to the huge gap separating the normative components of this culture and practices on the ground. This schism has continued to be a rather confusing public sphere discourse because when coming under fire, Arabs tend to refer to the historical legacy of normative traditions as if they are fully applied in reality while neglecting existing real practices that are targeted by criticism. For example, when human rights records come under fire in some Arab countries, the response would invoke ideals of Arab Islamic morality as provided for in Scriptures and other traditions while keeping a closed eye on realities as if they do not exist. This in fact applies to a whole set of issues for which Arab societies are taken to task; they are handled through an escapist approach that shows no adequate recognition for realities.

Although culture in its broad sense embraces a wide range of features, it is identity that stands out as the most central. Identity is the prime cultural variable that sets Arab discourse in full motion. The absence of a single real-life frame of reference for Arab-Islamic identity is the major obstacle militating against the realization of a constructive Arab global engagement. In this increasingly complicated and diverse global environment, actors in the public sphere could not engage in communications with anonymous partners. If you would like others to initiate a dialogue with you or to respond to your initiative, you need first to identify yourself in clear and simple terms. If you don't subscribe to a well-defined identity, you are most likely to be viewed as an outcast with no room for you in the global discourse. In the Arabs' situation, the issue takes on more serious implications because they have left their identity to be misrepresented by 'the other' on its own terms, which are flagrantly negative. Hence, Arabs are faced with a two-faced challenge on this identity front: they have failed to present themselves as affiliated with a well-defined identity that could be integrated into the ongoing universal debate and they have also failed to detach themselves from decades of stigmatization and demonization in world public spheres. For both challenges to be adequately addressed, Arabs need to define themselves in terms highly comprehensible to 'the other'. That invites a whole set of competing questions regarding who we are, what we would like to be, and how do we relate to tradition and modernity. These questions have actually formed the basis for over two centuries of Arab World debates on the issue of *Nahda* (Renaissance); yet, nothing substantive has materialized.

The centrality of identity in Arabs' engagement in the global public sphere suggests that new social, cultural and political realities need to be brought about to create a solid basis for a constructive dialogue with others. It has been noted in this book that the public sphere has failed simply because Arabs have failed to develop viable social and political systems that lend themselves to both tradition and modernity. Tradition here does not refer to the tribal schemes of government that seem to define the current Arab World political regimes; it rather refers to genuine Islamic moral and cultural values that confer on Arab societies their distinctive identity. For two hundred years, Arab societies have been captive either to narrow-minded and fundamentalist interpretations of Scriptures or to authoritarian visions of socio-political systems. Both schemes have flagrantly failed because they could not pass the test of creating a balanced synthesis between true tradition and true modernity. By the end of the 1980s, it turned out that the whole discourse about development was no more than a set of euphemisms for legitimizing authoritarian control and stifling alternative social and political solutions. Tensions between Islamic and nationalist views of society and the state have been transformed into perennial confrontations between tradition and modernity, both presented as two mutually-exclusive concepts that defy any synthesis.

An important argument offered by the author is that a genuine Arab identity should lend itself to both Arab and Islamic traditions within the concept of 'Islamocracy'. The concept suggests that Islam, as the defining source of identity for Arabs, embraces a wide range of universal moral values that could serve as a basis for a new contemporary social and political system in the region. When combined with the formal practices of electoral democracy, Islamocracy would generate a new political vision with well-defined foundations that ensure community involvement in running its own affairs on egalitarian and equitable terms drawing on mutual coexistence, tolerance, accommodation and respect. Because Islam, as a social and cultural system embraces a wide range of spiritual and temporal life affairs, the view of it as just a spiritual religion would be rendered irrelevant. This means that the basic foundations of Islamic morality like *Ibadah*, honesty, justice, equality, freedom, responsibility, mercy, respect and tolerance will be visible in material life transactions. While spiritual rituals could remain a domain for the individuals' relationship with Allah, temporal life affairs are the concern of community in its state and civil society manifestations, though as noted earlier in Chapter III, both spiritual and temporal spheres of life are integral parts of the concept of *Ibadah* (Worship). Once these true moral Islamic values and norms are integrated into the individuals' life behavior at personal and collective levels, the identity of the community would be more recognizable to the other.

VII.5.3. Power Realities

Research works seeking to investigate communication in its broadest sense outside its social and political contexts have generally failed to produce convincing findings about the form and substance of the media phenomenon. The dominant paradigm in media research that defined Western functional media traditions since the mid 1940s was experiencing serious declines both in the United States and in Developing countries primarily because it fell short of accounting for the structural political and economic variables that bear on media processes and effects at national and international levels (McQuail, 1995). It was noted that in critical research traditions that media organizations could not be viewed as independent organizations given their organic structural connections with political and economic power institutions in society. According to these perspectives, media institutions do not operate outside existing power arrangements as they serve to perpetuate them in rather subtle ways. The general conclusion reached by researchers about media role in society is that communications at their best serve to support existing strategies and action programs, but cannot work in their absence.

The structural nature of the Arab public sphere demonstrates a clear symbiotic connection with state institutions in different ways. As noted earlier, the state is the prime player in the evolving public sphere in the region. But as the state continues to lose further ground in the 'Arab street', the credibility of its discourse remains at low ebb. In addition, as the Arab World remains politically and economically disintegrated with its declining leverage in regional and global politics, the efficacy of the public sphere is likely to stay murky. The hyperbolic and flowery language that could not be matched by concrete political imitative on the ground seems to deepen a sense of apathy, mistrust, and even frustration on the part of an Arab public getting increasingly disenchanted with its political leaders. Since the immediate post-colonial era, the Arab public sphere has been dominated by a monologist state discourse rife with flowery promises; most of them were never delivered. This has applied to discourse traditions on national development, pan-Arab unity, the Palestinian question and democratization. Accumulating frustrations among Arab publics have rendered all political discourse carried by state media no more than hollow euphemistic structures designed to create false public consciousness about living realities. By the late 1980s, failures on fronts of development, pan-Arab unity, Palestine liberation, and democratization marked a new phase of mistrust and suspicion between ruling elites and the masses that could not come to terms with successive state failures.

VII.6. Summary & Conclusion

It has been clear that the development of an Arab public sphere perspective could not be realized outside the intellectual boundaries of a political theoretical framework. In this chapter, the author proposed Islamocracy as the defining political and social context for the institution of a viable public sphere in the Arab World. The concept draws on enlightened visions of Islamic morality as well as on modern political procedures and structures to evolve a scheme of governance that both preserve the unique identity of the community and the openness to contemporary political practices. Islamocracy has nothing to share with theocracy because it is based on a written constitution, electoral representation and power separation. Within the system of Islamocracy, the public sphere is viewed as an open arena for free exchanges that seek to help the community to achieve common visions on matters of concern to its living realities. The proposed public sphere is intellectually grounded in Arab-Islamic morality and modern political practices; indigenously-induced; based on combined freedom and responsibility; and thriving on independent economic sustainability. Its main function is to foster the cultural identity of the community as the final frontier in its struggle for survival. It embraces a wide range of actors and institutions with varied intellectual and political orientations; yet with common values of respect and recognition of the other. Its discourse is enlightened, centrist, rational, and culturally sensitive. To realize a constructive media engagement at local and global levels, Arabs need to give more priority to the development of a sound discourse than to technological communication investments. It is suggested that a successful public sphere is one that draws on a balanced discourse; recognizes power relations; and promotes Islamocratic culture.

VIII
CONCLUDING REMARKS

There is a tension in the Islamic World between the desire for democracy and a respect for liberty. (It is a tension that once raged in the West and still exists in pockets today.) This is most apparent in the ongoing fury over the publication of cartoons of the Prophet Muhammad in a small Danish newspaper. The cartoons were offensive and needlessly provocative. Had the paper published racist caricatures of other peoples or religions, it would also have been roundly condemned and perhaps boycotted.
(Zakaria, 2006)

As 2007 came to a close, the Middle East was still grappling with a wide range of strategic political and cultural issues; the most outstanding of the former was the increasing murkiness of America's future in Iraq and the receding popularity of U.S.-sponsored democratization drives launched in the post-September 11 era. Frustrated by spiraling violence in Iraq, the United States was apparently resorting to its old Cold War vision of viewing the Middle East in economic and security terms as the best way to serve its strategic interests in the region. In the four decades preceding the demise of the former Soviet Union, oil and Israel were the most defining factors of the U.S. Middle East strategy; and when combined with the current global war on terror, they are most likely to maintain their centrality for decades to come. If those political developments would suggest anything, it is that democracy could never be imposed on other societies, especially the Arab World, where 200 years of modern foreign colonial and postcolonial encounters have failed to set off genuine and sustainable Western-style transitions. A strategy of creative chaos has added up to the complication of an already complex situation in a region that continues to struggle for survival in the midst of serious economic and political woes marked by deteriorating standards of living and increasing state authoritarianism. Enduring conflicts in Iraq, Palestine, Sudan and Lebanon have furnished further evidence that the whole region is set for further critical transitions in the years to come.

At the cultural front, the past three years have also witnessed 'wars of culture' in which Islam has been a major target. Remarks by the Pope of the Vatican about the Prophet of Islam and the honoring of the controversial Salman Rushdi by the Queen of England have added up fuel to the dormant volcano across the Muslim World that erupted over the publication in some European newspapers of 12 cartoons perceived in the Muslim World to be offensive to Prophet Muhammad. Among other things, the three incidents have revealed, more than ever before, the depth of the existing intellectual divide separating two cultures with seemingly two divergent worldviews: the Muslim culture and the Western culture. To a remarkable extent, the Danish cartoons debate has become truly global, pitting those in favor of showing respect for the sacred as a paramount cherished value against those who argue for post-modernist freedom of expression as a limitless norm. The way this issue has been addressed in national and global public spheres also underscored the need for deeper understanding between Muslim and European societies on issues often taken for granted within their specific cultural and intellectual boundaries. For Arabs as core actors in the Muslim World, the cultural debates have presented them with further challenges relating to communicating with what they widely perceived as their traditional antithetical ideological counterpart, the West, on terms of common understanding between two sides already alienated by deeply-engrained political and cultural disparities on many fronts. An interesting feature of the global debate on the issue has been the call for respecting freedom of expression while shielding religious beliefs and symbols against critical onslaughts because those symbols stand for highly-cherished cultural orientations that confer a specific identity on certain groups or peoples. Calls for enacting international legal and ethical frameworks incriminating offensive communications targeting religious beliefs have generated significant echoes at global levels, thus suggesting an outstanding success for a centrist discourse that draws on compromise and harmonization rather than on clash between world civilizations.

The offensive-cartoons debate in the Arab World came at a time when the whole region seems to be experiencing deep ferment in its social, political and even intellectual life in the age of globalization. The Middle East has increasingly come under global (especially American) pressures in the past few years because it is perceived as a breeding ground for regional and global instability and conflict. The 9/11 events seemed to have provided the U.S. with a new political and intellectual arsenal to justify the implementation of a new vision for reforming the Middle East and rid the region of the woes it seems to inflict on other nations. A clash of civilizations' thesis has come to gain some popularity as both sides seemed to have misplaced the arising conflict within historical religious frameworks of conflict. The U.S. use of crude force to carry out its 'vision of reform' was spearheaded by a sweeping intellectual drive to reproduce the social and cultural history and reality of the Arab World from an American perspective. Amounting to some form of a neo-Orientalism, U.S. intellectual approaches to the Middle East since the early 1990s, as espoused by a wide range of research centers and individual commentators, have represented the region as a wasteland of Islamic fundamentalism, terror, and incompatibility with contemporary world civilizations. On the other hand, American intellectual initiatives, drawing on ethnocentric views of the individual and society, have presented Western democracy as the sole universal recipe for Arab people, capable of ridding the region of its political and security woes. In most writings on this issue, the Middle East is promoted as a potential source of world instability and conflict, rife with religious lunacy, political adventurism, and cultural backwardness. The only solution to pre-empt another 9/11-style tragedy is to conquer the region and root out its militant orientations by applying Western 'democratic' standards to social and political life.

In significant ways, the aforementioned 'global-perspective' introduction to this concluding chapter in a book about the Arab mass-mediated public sphere seems highly relevant. If the emerging Arab public sphere owes its existence and development largely to exogenous political and technological transformations, then the global factor remains highly decisive in shaping the future of communication and politics in the region. On the other hand, the synthesist approach used in this book suggests giving equal weight to indigenous cultural and political elements in the analysis of the mass-mediated public sphere. Hence, the notion of 'Islamocracy' has been advanced to affirm the hybrid nature of the Arab public sphere in the age of globalization. The development of an 'Islamocratic' public sphere is meant to demonstrate the extent to which Arabs could reach out to harness contemporary political practices and structures without compromising their indigenous Arab-Islamic cultural identity. In the age of globalization, cultural identity remains the final sanctuary for self-assertiveness, and hence Arabs' right to this distinctive feature of their life is a sacred right as much as it is for the French, the Americans, the Chinese or the Indians. This statement is meant to pre-empt any misunderstandings of 'Islamocracy' as a hollow emulation of a Western-style political and social system. The West could provide the Arab World with the best proven political schemes and practices, but not moral values because Islamic morality is universal by default.

An important aspect of the arising Western 'neo-orientalism' accompanying the current conflict over 'reforming the Arab World' relates to advancing views that the region has already shown signs of reform; the most conspicuous of them are evident in the emergence of an Arab public sphere. Scores of research works produced by individual writers and think tanks have promoted the idea of the Middle East is opening up to democracy through the emergence of multiple media outlets with different political orientations, allowing for public debates of issues long considered as taboos in Arab-Islamic culture. These writings argue that the emerging public sphere in the Arab World is both a product of and a sustainer of ongoing U.S.-driven reform; and hence holds a great promise for the region. More media outlets are mushrooming in the region everyday with traditional government censorship taking up back-burner positions in the emerging public sphere as individuals, non-governmental organizations, and political parties try to get a fair share of this evolving communication pie. These intellectual drives preach the idea that this public sphere mobility will eventually lead to more tangible political and social shifts in Arab societies eventually bring about the institution of more participatory arrangements based on freedom of speech and the press, respect for human rights, and a more equitable distribution of resources.

It is inarguable that the rise of new media in the Arab World since the early 1990s has marked a significant shift in the evolving public sphere in the region which, for long, had been dominated by state machinations. The writer noted that developments in the Arab public sphere over the past two decades have been a function of combined exogenous and indigenous historical opportunities and variables, though domestic forces seem to have a rather reactive role. Transformations in the global political and technological environments as marked by the end of the Cold War, the growing prominence of political and economic liberalism, and the diffusion of new information and communications technologies, were bound to bear on Arabs' public handling of local, regional and international issues. New communications modes and tools have rendered state censorship useless; unleashing new public debates on issues long viewed as taboos in modern Arab history. More than ever before, the public sphere landscape has become more varied and bustling with a wide range of voices that had been previously denied access to public visibility, mostly for political reasons. Whether it is a stunning letter to a newspaper editor, a daring phone call to a live radio or television show, or a critical Weblog remark or chat conversation, what gets into the Arab public sphere has dramatically revolutionized political discourse in the region. When combined with the global American-led drive for political reform in the area, such transformations have been viewed as perfectly fitting the evolving vision of democratization. The historical convergence of politics and technology in the Arab World has been received with much fanfare among Western intellectuals who foresee the evolving public sphere as a forerunner for a Western-style Arab political system.

A central argument advanced by the author in this book is that while the Arab World has indeed been at the center of political and technological metamorphoses, the framing of intellectual debates on how the public sphere bears on Arab World politics has been flawed. The author notes that the Arab region, since the early 1990s, has been catapulted into the eye of a global political, economic and technological storm that has shaken up its political and cultural foundations, inducing deeper ferment in its intellectual and moral values, and unleashing a renewed quest for salvation out of this debacle. The evolving political communication arena (the public sphere) has been championed by Western intellectuals as a promising sign of political democratization and cultural liberalization in the region. A strong sense of historical determinism seems to inspire advocates of the Western-style public sphere in the Arab World who foresee the convergence of world social and political development processes on a globalized (Americanized) model. But as the globally-induced experience of the past two decades has shown, political and media developments that furnish the foundations for a genuine public sphere in the Arab World seem to have spawned far more frustrating realities on the ground. Apart from the ideological and political factors giving rise to the huge Western-generated fanfare associated with the evolving political and communications landscape in the Arab World, the writer argues that Western perspectives defining the emerging Arab public sphere continue to be obscured by cultural short-sightedness and ethno-centric biases.

Obviously a public sphere has started to take shape at different public levels in the Arab World, the most outstanding of which is the mass-mediated public sphere. The winds of the information and communications revolution have been deeply felt at different Arab World frontiers, leading to the rise of new transnational media outlets with global reach and Western-style formats. These new media, comprising mainly of satellite television and World Wide Web outlets, are promoted as the institutions of the promised emerging Arab public sphere. For the first time in the region's history, private individuals are empowered to voice their views and concerns on issues of community interest in public arenas, no longer daunted by traditional state censorship. Among other things, the Arab public sphere is presented in mainstream Western political communication literature as a launching pad for more informed and enlightened public opinion on national, regional and global issues bearing on community life. As externally-induced political reforms proceed forward in the Arab World in the direction of further democratization, the power of public opinion is viewed as gaining greater significance in influencing national and regional policies in the area. National governments as well as global powers are getting increasingly cognizant of the potential effects of public opinion in shaping issues relating to political reform, regional stability and national integration, terrorism, inequitable social conditions, and economic progress. Hence, the emergence of a mass-mediated public sphere is widely perceived as an instrumental variable in shaping future policies at national and global levels in the region.

As the Arab World drifts more closely towards exogenously-driven political reforms, the public sphere is no longer projected as a luxury; but rather as an imperative component of 'the evolving democratic politics' that bears on the evolution of participatory political schemes in the region. The evolution of the public sphere is seen as vital as the institution of civil liberties, the launch of civil society institutions, or the diffusion of cultural diversity and political pluralism. Some researchers metaphorically refer to the public sphere not only as a mere a social space; but as a breathing space for community members to voice their concerns and enjoy a say in shaping public policies on issues of interest to their communities. As noted earlier in this book, if democracy is likened to a train that transports passengers from one station to another, the public sphere is the atmosphere that makes the journey enjoyable and safe. It empowers passengers to identify with one another; to share ideas and concerns; and to collectively decide on how best those ideas would be carried out to ensure that the train arrives at its destination as planned.

The failing U.S. strategy in Iraq and the region at large and the renewed interest in strategies based on political and security considerations, coupled with slow democratic reforms on the ground, all seem to have generated a state of confusion with serious implications for the institution of a genuine public sphere. At the political level, the Arab World found itself in dire divisive conditions unprecedented since its independence from European colonialism in the 1950s and 1960s. Pan-Arabism has been on the decline, giving way to further global political, military and economic engagement, thus rendering concepts like Arab world integration, solidarity, national security, common destiny, brotherliness, unity, and even identity as parts of a flagrantly-outdated discourse. The demise of the former Soviet Union, coupled with Iraqi military adventurism and a more direct U.S. military intervention in the region have fostered the pursuit of individual state orientations in the conduct of external relations as perceptions of interest shifted from the regional to the global. Domestically, Arab states in the early 1990s were keeping intact their autocratic and authoritarian postures inherited from the post-colonial era. Failing democratization experiences in countries like Algeria, Jordan, Egypt, Yemen, Morocco and Bahrain were bound to overshadow optimistic prospects for genuine liberalization in the region. At the social level, the decline and subsequent diminution of the middle class in many Arab countries have widened the gap between the haves and the have-nots, giving rise to expanding impoverishment; raising social tensions; and spawning militant religious and political orientations. Over fifty years of developmental ideology in the Arab World culminated in gross failures in the 1990s as national economies, most of them surviving on external subsidies or oil resources, failed to cope with changing domestic social imperatives and global transformations.

There is no way to theorize about the evolving Arab public sphere apart from globalization. It is clear that while the Arab World continues to suffer from political fragmentation, cultural disorientation, social disintegration, and economic recession, globalization as a sweeping economic, social, political and technological force remains the prime 'Black Hole' into which the region is bound to dive, unless counter-initiatives are launched. Regardless of the validity of its deterministic connotations, the more extensive and deeper globalization gets, the fewer Arab World choices become. Shifting global and regional political loci of control have reduced the Arab world into a real periphery with total dependency on the United States as the sole 'global center' to reckon with in this phase of contemporary human history. In the era of Cold War politics, individual Arab states enjoyed some form of state sovereignty and independence; but in the age of globalization, the erosion of political boundaries and geographical distances has re-engineered the process of 'domestic' change in total tune with broader global socio-political, economic and cultural trends set by 'the Powers that Be'. Because the national ships of Arab states are navigated in the stormy waters of globalization by the few ruling political and economic elite (whose political, military and economic interest have been locked into those of the Center beyond the point of return), only a synthetic vision of politics and culture drawing on a combination of traditional moral values and contemporary practices would chart new courses in their cruise into a well-defined destination. The long-awaited difference in current Arab World history could only be made by this intellectual synthetic initiative as the 1990s generated no single piece of evidence that the soc-called 'democratic reform' could have any meaningful impact.

An important argument offered in this book is that the Western-style notion of the public sphere, in its Westphalian sense, is bound to fail in the Arab World, primarily because its theoretical foundations clash with the conceptual premises of public engagement in political discussions in Arab-Islamic traditions. This should in no way suggest ruling out the relevance of the public sphere for contemporary Arab societies; but rather should induce more endeavors for the development of more viable public sphere perspectives for the region. The advent of globalization with its political and economic might and communication pervasiveness has become a central variable shaping our theoretical thinking about media and politics in the Arab World. Hence, the intellectual challenge facing the development of contemporary Arab-Islamic public sphere depends on our capacity to generate new intellectual frameworks based on the eclectic integration of normative Islamic political theory and modern political and technological opportunities arising from globalization, referred to in this book as 'Islamocracy' or Islamic governance. As such, the author notes that the state of confusion and disorientation experienced by the Arab World since the early 1990s could not produce a genuine public sphere in the absence of basic conditions for participatory politics.

The appalling condition of Arab World as documented by national and international human rights and press freedom organizations seem to have a dampening effect on future public sphere perspectives. When pressured by the United States to bring about political reforms into their societies, Arab states respond with procrastinations, superficial changes, and even with more authoritarianism. They seem willing to introduce democratic formalities like elections, but were resilient in rejecting the institution of legal and political conditions central to the success of democracy. On the other hand, it is not the mission of this book to view the convergence of local oppression and global dependency as a historical determinism, but rather as an opportunity for a pan-Arab soul-search for new choices that are more viable, more relevant, more sustainable and more humane than those offered by what Egyptian novelist Edward Kharrat termed 'savage globalization'. An important premise of this book draws on refuting the fallacy of globalization as a historical determinism, as the final frontier of human development on which all tracks of history are bound to converge. There is no room for 'end-of-history'-oriented theses in this book as the writer believes in the everlasting cycle of human intellectual evolution as the only historical determinism which lends itself to true human nature. Throughout history, synthesis was the defining concept of distinctive cultural perpetuation. Great ideas always perish if they remain captive to their traditional confines. They could rather attain greater durability and prominence when they are married with other great ideas to produce a more sustainable synthesis.

As an intellectual exercise in intercultural synthesis, this book has sought to reinforce convictions in the inevitability of a successful Arab-Western coexistence despite growing mistrust between the two sides. Both civilizations possess the best of moral values pertaining to human existence, norms, and rights. It is the responsibility of intellectual communities on both sides to bridge gaps and narrow down differences rather than to serve as spearheads for domination and bigotry. On the other hand, this book also aims to foster hopes in the inevitability of a bright Arab World future drawing on creative interpretations and readings of over 1400 years of Arab-Islamic value systems and moralities, the very value systems and moralities that have conferred on us our peculiar cultural identity as members of the global community. Arabism and Islam have for centuries defined our region's quest for prosperity and welfare, with Arabism being its flesh and Islam its soul. As a comprehensive way of life, Islam extends its concerns to temporal and spiritual domains, drawing its morality from a superb interplay between man's spiritual loft mindedness and his inner urges to be part of this material world. Throughout Arab-Islamic history, keeping the balance between the spiritual and the temporal in the context of justice, equality, responsibility, freedom of choice, and community cohesion was conducive to unleashing Arabs' potential in all realms of life, including communication. Historical evidence points out that the Arab-Islamic civilization reached its full potential only when public arenas were established to attract diverse views and concerns bearing on community life. When leaders opted to monopolize views about community reality and future by excluding other voices, the nation was heading into dark times. By default, Islam is a public-sphere-oriented way of life, always giving weight to individuals' involvement in public discussions of community affairs and asserting the collective nature of the community. The seeds of public sphere are well-engrained in Arab-Islamic traditions. What is needed is a creative integration of core moral Arab-Islamic values and historical experiences into a contemporary framework of public debates within a synthesist democratic scheme of governance referred to in this book as 'Islamocracy.'

The prime challenge facing Arabs in the 21st century is not economic or technological; it is rather cultural, defined mainly in terms of their ability to significantly sustain a balanced identity that meshes with contemporary human mindsets. The Arab-Islamic intellectual heritage, as informed by over 14 centuries of religious, philosophical, political and cultural debates (in classical and modern periods), has provided the basis for discussions of politics, economics, philosophy, and sociology in contemporary Arab societies. From the very basic normative moral values and historical experiences associated with the *Qur'an*, the Prophet's *Sunna*, traditions of the Rightly- Guided Companions and latter Caliphs, Muslim scholars, Arab poets and men of letters, philosophers, 19th century Islamic revivalists, secular nationalists, media figures, sociologist, feminists, and political activists and thinkers, Arab thought in the age of globalization has at its disposal a precious goldmine to tap on. Since the advent of globalization as a sweeping political, economic, cultural, and technological phenomenon some 20 years ago, scores of Arab intellectuals with varied ideological orientations stood up to those transformations, addressing how they could bear on Arab societies in the 21st century and beyond.

The central concern shaping ongoing Arab World discussions relates to the long-addressed question of *Nahda* (Renaissance), a 19th century theme whose debate has spawned a wide range of perspectives. Some thinkers argued that *Nahda* failed to materialize in the Arab World because Arab societies have either been seduced or coerced by colonialist Western nations to relinquish their historical organic attachment to Islamic teachings as provided for in the *Qur'an* and the *Sunna*. Thus, a fundamentalist discourse espoused by a sizable segment of the Arab intellectual community placed 'classical heritage' as the anchoring point for achieving *Nahda*. On the other hand, another group of thinkers with secularist orientations promoted Western-style modernization as the panacea for contemporary Arab society woes. Between both Islamic and secular points of view stands an impressive group of thinkers who argued for an eclectic amalgamation of traditional heritage and modern culture to generate a new social choice that is neither detached from genuine elements of the past nor immersed in the totalities of Western modernism. The problem with this approach has been conspicuous in its failure to re-interpret traditional and modern values and norms as they were uncritically fitted into contemporary social arrangements. The end result has been an acutely dialectical system of thought, totally bogged down in a futile quest for harmonization.

Since the concept of the public sphere is not about mere communication channels and resources, but more about moral values and political practices on the ground, one needs to identify and explicate the indigenous secular and religious moralities and historical experiences embedded in classical and modern Arab-Islamic heritage. Classical Arab-Islamic heritage is defined as the combined religious and secular worldviews shaping social relations in Arabian lands from pre-Islamic periods to the late 18th century. Modern Arab-Islamic heritage, on the other hand, embraces intellectual accumulations generated from the time of Napoleon's expedition to Egypt in 1798 to the end of the 1980s. Classical and modern Arab-Islamic traditions in those two periods combined with new intellectual and political realities in the 1990s and beyond, are brought to bear in this book on the evolution of an Arab public sphere in the age of globalization. The writer argues here that despite major black spots in classical and modern Arab World political practices, Arab-Islamic culture, due to its built-in assimilative capacity and adaptability, could be successfully employed to generate new perspectives of communication and politics in the context of globalization. Arab-Islamic culture has been defined as intrinsically humanly-rooted, rationally-based; knowledge-driven; publicly-oriented and universally-appealing. It is a universal culture that emphasizes the value of justice as the pillar of community survival, equality, unity and freedom of choice within responsibility.

The development of an Arab public sphere in the age of globalization, as noted earlier, draws on the potential for re-interpreting Arab-Islamic values to be conveniently fitted into a contemporary framework of public communications. This book has offered a set of basic premises that define the parameters of the proposed public sphere within an integrated framework of Islamic morality and modern political practices referred to here as 'Islamocracy'. The proposed framework suggests that a genuine contemporary Arab public sphere is based on justice as a central social and political value; community as the incubator of social and political justice; and leadership as the initiator and implementer of social and political justice within the community and beyond. Three basic public sphere concepts are elaborated: justice, equality and 'freesponsibility' (freedom and responsibility). The framework is related to a proposed political perspective defining basic values and practices relating to participatory governance in contemporary societies. In the proposed Islamic theory of the public sphere, the public and private spheres directly feed into the individual's metaphysical sphere in which the individual is held accountable before Allah for his actions. This book has focused exclusively on the public sphere as the social space mediating between community members (individuals and groups), on the one hand, and the government, with its executive and legislative branches, on the other hand. *Shura* (seeking and giving advice) is the driving force that keeps the public sphere in ceaseless motion. A set of religious and ethical principles and norms define the parameters of the Arab-Islamic public sphere. Public debates take place among private individuals, civil community groups, representatives of religious institutions, government officials, professional associations and political parties on issues of common concern for the community. Agendas should be drawn up on the basis of pan-Arab concerns, always in tune with safeguarding Arab interests. It is true that globalization is defining the public agendas of communities around the world, but issues like cultural identity, social justice, resistance of foreign domination and occupation, and people's right to self-determination should also feature highly on pan-Arab agendas.

The proposed Arab public sphere could not function in a political or constitutional vacuum. Constitutionally-provided justice, freedom to seek and impart information, as well as accountability define the parameters of debates which should freely address issues while being mindful of the legal implications of potential violations of privacy, public decency, common taste, or national security. The notion of common good or community interest should be the defining value for what is being debated. Pompous television exchanges with sensational features are more likely to prompt public outcry, especially when no intellectually or politically tangible outcomes are produced. Likewise, debates drawing on false or unverified information seeking to defame or stigmatize private persons or even public figures to achieve narrow political purposes should be viewed with disapproval in the public sphere. Legal state-wide enforcement of constitutional provisions is essential for ensuring a sustainable public sphere. At the global level, legal arrangements should be bolstered to pre-empt the propagandistic use of the public sphere to inflict damage on transnational players. Media need to develop and enforce their professional codes of ethics to keep media practitioners aware of the legal and ethical implications of potential violations. Community public opinion should be empowered to bear on political processes by giving access to rational and balanced voices with enlightened platforms. The public should be educated on its constitutional rights and the division of power should be clearly demarcated among the three government bodies within the Islamocratic system.

Arab intellectuals' pre-occupation with the establishment of a public sphere that draws on competing Arab-Islamic values with significant universal extensions has always injected hope into the modern history relations with the West. Of course, in a world of globalized political and economic integration, Arabs' application of their peculiar cultural and social norms into their own public sphere is rendered totally unrealistic. As noted earlier in this book, the traditional boundaries separating the local and the global have all broken down, giving rise to a more integrative environment that derives its continuity and prosperity not from local sources, but from global forces. In another book (Ayish, 2003a), the author suggested the development of Robertson's notion of 'glocalization' to describe current transformations in the international arena. But one should also note that the local may cave in to the global if it lacks the ingredients of sustainability that would ensure its survival and competitive edge. Hence, when it was suggested earlier in this work that Arabs need to evolve their own perspective of the public sphere that would not concede pivotal values and norms to rival Western ones, the purpose was to engage in a selective process of historical search for the 'best and the brightest' values and norms that would be appealing to non-Arabs at a global scale.

Though globalization has been brought to bear on the construction of an Arab public sphere perspective, it is not presented as a deterministic process that is antithetical to all types of creative local developments. Since globalization may not necessarily be always tied to American-specific dynamics of change as it has come to include European, Japanese, Chinese, Korean, and Latin American players, its strong American dimensions should not be taken in deterministic terms. Rather, it should be viewed as an open arena for all nations, including Arabs, to offer their cultural and moral commodities to global customers. Hence, the ball is in the Arabs' court to develop a public sphere concept that would 'mesh in' with the revolving global wheel, thus contributing to its smoother movement and life span. As noted in the Chapter III, Arab-Islamic history may not reflect perfect relations and structures in real life situations, but there are normative principles and values that carry the promise of a universal acceptance once applied in maximum honesty and good intentions. The challenge here relates to whether we would like to take our cultural reservoir as an indivisible package or approach it on an eclectic basis not with the objective of excluding or debasing certain values, but with the understanding that those values were convenient for addressing issues of early Islamic days because they were specifically tailored to handle those issues.

On the other hand, the Arab-Islamic heritage is rich with universally appealing values that would contribute to the enhancement of a global public sphere. We need to note that the modern Arab world history of the latter part of the 20th century gave rise to a redefinition of traditional values based on a history of oppression, injustice, occupation, and discrimination. It would be morally wrong to argue that we need to build our public discourse on the antithetical relations with the West by developing competing values and norms that would necessarily clash with legitimate Western values of freedom, justice, and equality. In fact, Arab might think of redefining world understanding of such values to address their concerns. They can even enrich their own universally appealing morality that embraces community cohesion, brotherly relations, belief in knowledge diffusion, and subordination to one Allah. Of course, the problem is that such moral concerns have been trashed by the American power when it comes to dealing with Arabs, especially in the post-September 11 era.

This book has made it clear that one could not speak of an Arab public sphere without referring to the growing role of the United States as a public sphere player seeking to maximize its public diplomacy gains in the region. Washington policy makers have long recognized the implications of this new sense of the public in the Arab world well before the 11 September terrorist attacks. For them, it is recognized as the 'Arab street', a new phenomenon of public accountability, which had seldom been factored into Western projections of Arab behavior in the past. The information revolution, and particularly the daily dose of uncensored television coming out of local TV stations like al-Jazeera and international coverage by CNN and others, is shaping public opinion, which, in turn, is pushing Arab governments to respond. We do not know, and the leaders themselves do not know, how that pressure will impact on Arab policy in the future. But as noted in the book, all hopes for an effective U.S. influence of the 'Arab Street' are likely to be dashed simply because Arab publics are experiencing first-hand the agonies of American interventionism and double-standardism in many parts of the region, especially in Iraq and Palestine. Arab audiences have grown more sophisticated in dealing with U.S.-sponsored public diplomacy efforts that they could not dissociate their perceptions of the United States from its ongoing policies in the Arab World. By doing so, they have actually carried on a long tradition of mistrusting American government media since the launch of the Voice of America Arab service in the mid 1950s. The enduring message always voiced by Arab public opinion is that the people of the region need the United States to demonstrate a stronger sense of justice than a promotion of the virtue of democracy and freedom.

In order for Arabs to constructively engage in the evolving global public sphere, three conditions must be met. First, the quality of public discourse should reflect a deeper understanding of the contemporary human living experience as made possible through the rational, symmetrical, critical and objective use of Arabic language or using these qualities as the defining mindset for communication in other languages. Second, human dignity, the institution of true Islamocratic culture in the public sphere as based on *Ibadah*, diversity, tolerance, 'freesponsibility', and peaceful co-existence. Third, recognition of the proven facts about communication as reflecting power structures and relations rather than creating them. It is not enough for the public sphere to advance morally-sound arguments. They need to be grounded in solid power structures that would ensure a higher level of trust in public sphere efficacy.

To conclude, this book is meant to serve as a launching pad for more visionary intellectual initiatives about communication and politics in the Arab World as well as dialogue with the West. This work has elaborated a two-track approach to the concept of the public sphere: the national-regional and the global. The national-global public sphere reflects Arab World political and social realities which vary from one country to another, but are subject to continuous change with the launch of trans-national media outlets like *al-Jazeera* and *al-Arabiya*. The basic argument offered here is that the current national-regional Arab public sphere is viewed as a buffer zone in the absence of political and social arrangements based on 'Islamocratic' principle of justice, freedom, and community cohesion. Unless the Arab World becomes cognizant of its essential cultural Arab-Islamic identity and of contemporary global realities, its pursuit of a sustainable public sphere would be highly illusive. By embarking on this synthetic task of reconciling (though not compromising) Arab-Islamic morality with contemporary political practices, Arabs would be able to achieve two major goals: they would construct their national-regional public sphere on the basis of well-defined identities, moral foundations, and political mechanisms conducive to the establishment of a public arena that responds to the indigenous needs of community members. On the other hand, the establishment of solid political and social foundations in Arab World communities would also facilitate a more effective Arabs' role in the global public sphere. Arabs would be better positioned to engage more efficiently in global debates relating to cultural and political issues on which they have well-defined positions. Clarity of vision would also empower Arabs to advocate their rightly-founded attitudes and orientations on the basis of their sense of justice, freedom, community cohesion, and human rights. As it stands now, the Arab political and cultural discourse is fragmented, foggy, and bogged down either in historical trans-fixation or contemporary over-sightedness.

The central view about public sphere efficacy in the Arab World revolves around its perception as a mechanism for channeling official and grassroots public concerns over national and global issues bearing on community life seems enigmatic. It is true that countries and leaders seem always keen on utilizing available public spaces to address pressing issues with specific arguments because they 'care for public opinion'. But as the experiences of the past decades have shown, even governments with the best democratic practices have been able to co-opt an effective role for the public sphere in generating more transparent and democratic politics either through gagging media voices or inducing them closer to official stands. The case of the U.S. media performance before and during the invasion of Iraq testifies to how media organizations constructed a political discourse that promoted the Bush Administration's point of view, and hence circumvented genuine public discussions of the invasion rationale and potential consequences. When one speaks of a global public sphere with no institutional arrangements to hold media actors accountable for their communicative actions, the issue of efficacy gets more complicated. Though global players seem keen on voicing out their stands on different issues by engaging in public sphere debates, they also seem more inclined to resort to crude force methods to achieve their objectives. In this case, global actors are able to sideline public sphere channels with their rational and critical discourse to create short-cut methods of carrying out their strategies.

But regardless of its immediate trickle-down effects on political realities at Arab and global levels, the public sphere remains the most significant arena for Arabs to engage others, especially the West, in discussions on issues of interest to both sides. As noted earlier, there is no specific recipe for making such engagement fully efficient, but the burden of realizing that end seems to fall on both Arabs and the West. Arabs need to define their vision of identity in the 21st century and show how they could bring forth their genuine traditions with universal and human moral norms in tune with the best human contemporary practices of the 21st century. The issue here is not about speaking in one voice, but rather about creating a consensus on the substance and parameters of Arabs identity in the age of globalization. Should Arabs carry on their dialogue with other civilizations on a rather fragmented and disoriented fashion, they are most likely to end up, as they have, as the biggest losers. The writer believes that Arab-Islamic heritage carries a huge potential for universal accommodation, but what is needed is re-positioning of that heritage in a contemporary context without risking the loss of its fundamental premises. The permeating effects of globalization have made virtually impossible to theorize about any political or cultural system as an isolated entity that could survive on its own without references to ongoing transformations. On their part, Western intellectuals also need to cast off their stereotypical conceptions of the Arab World as a cultural wasteland, or a breeding ground for terror and religious militancy. They should reconsider their typical orientalist approaches to the study of Arab World problems from an exclusive Western perspective, thus rendering the region's 1400 years of cultural heritage as irrelevant to contemporary settings. To achieve this state of accommodation, political and intellectual leaders on both sides of the divide need to constructively engage in this endeavor.

REFERENCES

Abdallah, A. (ed.) (2004), Al Khaleej Conference on the Arab Press in a Changing World, Sharjah: al-Khaleej Press (in Arabic).

Abd al-Rahman, A. (1985), Studies in Contemporary Egyptian Press, Cairo: Dar Al-Fikr Al-Arabi (in Arabic).

Abd al-Rahman, A. (1995), The Arab Press: Confronting Dependency and Zionist Penetration, Cairo: Dar Al-Fikr Al-Arabi (in Arabic).

Abd al-Rahman, A. (2006), Despotism and the Rule of Power in Contemporary Arab Regimes, in: Aljazeera.net:
http://www.aljazeera.net/NR/exeres/F32CD8F1-B629-46BB-9E9B-4524DBB7A883.htm (in Arabic).

Abootalebi, A. (1999), Islam, Islamists and Democracy, in: Middle East Review of International Affairs, No. 1, pp. 14-24.

Abu Bakr, Y., Labib, S. and Kandil, H. (1985), Development of Communication in the Arab States: Needs and Priorities, Paris: UNESCO Press.

Abu Lughod, L. (1990), Anthropology's Orient: The Boundaries of Theory on the Arab World, in H. Sharabi (ed.), Theory, Politics and the Arab World: Critical Responses, New York: Routledge, pp. 81-131.

Abu Zaid, F. (1986), Press Systems in the Arab World, Cairo: Alam Al-Kutub (in Arabic).

Achilles, Z. and Miege, B. (1994), The Limits to the Adaptation Strategies of European Public Service Television, in: Media, Culture, and Society, No. 3, pp. 31-46.

Ajibola, W. (1978), Foreign Policy and Public Opinion: A Case Study of British Foreign Policy over the Nigerian Civil War, Ibadan Social Science Series No. 8, Ibadan: Ibadan University Press. .

al-Amin, A. (2003), Non-verbal Communication in the Holy Qur'an, Sharjah: Department of Culture and Information (in Arabic).

al-Bab (2005), New World Order: President Bush's Speech to Congress, in: http://www.al-bab.com/arab/docs/pal/pal10.htm.

al-Hamad, A. (2003), Globalization: Challenges and Responses in the Arab World, Paper presented at the 4th Global Development Conference, organized by the Global Development Network (GDN), Cairo, January 19-20.

Ali, A. (2003), Globalization and Inequality in the Arab Region, Paper presented at the 4th Global Development Conference, organized by the Global Development Network (GDN), Cairo, January 19-20.

al-Jaberi, M. (1982), Contemporary Arab Discourse: An Analytical-Critical Study, Beirut: Arab Unity Studies Center (in Arabic).

al-Jaberi, M. (1997), Globalization Targets the State, the Nation and the Homeland, in: Asharq al-Awsat, February 7, p. 10.

al-Jaberi, M. (2003), Historical and Cultural Roots of Intellectual Reconciliation, in: Islamic Encyclopedia:
http://www.balagh.com/mosoa/sirah/xp0nzws1.htm (in Arabic).

al-Jaberi, M. (2004), Ibn Rushd and Ibn Khaldoun: The Compound State, in: http://www.wajhat.com/ (in Arabic).

al-Karni, A. (1994), Arab Media Discourse in the Age of Satellite Broadcasting, Paper presented to the Conference on Direct Satellite Broadcasting and Reception in the Arab Gulf Region, Al Ain (UAE) May 8-10 (in Arabic).

al-Khayyat, A. (2004), The Political System in Islam, Cairo: Dar Al-Salam Publishing (in Arabic).

al-Maududi, A. (2004), Essential Features of the Islamic Political System, in: http://www.jamaat.org/.

al-Qadhi, O. (2005), From others' Denial to Self-denial: Dominant Intellectual Trends in the Islamic World, in: Intellectual Forum for Creativity:
http://www.almultaka.net/home.php?start_from=60&archive=&subaction=&id= & (in Arabic).

al-Seini, S. (1986), An Islamic Concept of News, in: American Journal of Islamic Social Sciences, No. 32, pp. 277-289.

Alterman, J. (1998), Mid-tech Revolution, in:
http://www.mafhoum.com/press/50T1.htm.

Alterman, J. (2004), Arab Satellite Television: Can it Rise above Spectacle?, in: Arab Reform Bulletin, No. 11:
http://www.carnegieendowment.org/publications/index.cfm?fa=view&id=16242

al-Umran, H. (1996), MMDS: The Cultural Alternative to DTH, in: Middle East Broadcast and Satellite, September, pp.19-24.

al-Wali, A. (2006), Despotism in Philosophical Thought, in Aljazeera.net:
http://www.aljazeera.net/NR/exeres/746D1AA2-CA24-4A5B-85ED-F6301E5DE33A.htm.

Amin, S. (1997), Capitalism in the Age of Globalization: The Management of Contemporary Society, London: Zed Books.

Amman Center for Human Rights Studies (2006), Summary of the Report on Freedom of the Media in the Arab Countries, Amman.

Anderson, J. (1995), Cyberites, Knowledge Workers, and New Creoles on the Information Superhighway, in: Anthropology Today, No. 4, pp. 13-15.

Anderson, J. (2003), New Media, New Publics: Reconfiguring the Public Sphere of Islam, in: Social Research, No. 3, pp. 887-906.

Arab Media Free Network (2005), Internet Censorship in Egypt: A New Ground for Repression, in Arab Press Freedom Watch:
http://www.apfw.org/indexenglish.asp?fname=news%5Cenglish%5C2004%5C12289.htm.

Arab States Broadcasting Union (ASBU) (2005), Description of Satellite Television Broadcasting in the Arab World, in ASBU:
http://www.asbu.net/www/ar/home.asp (in Arabic).

Arab Unity Studies Center (1998), Arabs and Globalization, Beirut: AUSC (in Arabic).

Arendt, H. (1958), The Human Condition, Chicago: University of Chicago Press.

Arendt, H. (1960), The Origins of Totalitarianism, New York: Meridian Books.

Arneson, R. (1989), Paternalism, Utility and Fairness, in: Revue Internationale de Philosophie, No. 170, pp. 409-23.

Asfaruddin, A. (ed.) (1999), Hermeneutics and Honor: Negotiating Female Public Space in Islamic Societies, Boston: Harvard University Press.

Askar, I. (1982), The Arab Press in Palestine, Jordan, Syria, and Lebanon, Cairo: Muassasat Sijl al-Arab (in Arabic).

Ayalon, A. (1995), The Press in the Arab Middle East, New York: Oxford University Press.

Ayish, M. (1986), The Voice of America between Diplomacy and Journalism: a Case Study of the VOA Arabic Service, Unpublished doctoral thesis, University of Minnesota, Twin-Cities.

Ayish, M. (1987), VOA Arabic Service: A Study of News Practices and Occupational Values, in: Gazette, No. 2, pp. 121-130.

Ayish, M. and Hijab, I. (1988), International Broadcasting in Arabic: a Comparative Exploratory Study of RMCME, VOA, BBC, RM, in: Abhath al-Yarmouk, No. 1, pp. 15-26.

Ayish, M. (1991), Foreign Voices as People's Choices: BBC Popularity in the Arab World, in: Middle Eastern Studies, No. 3, pp. 374-389.

Ayish, M. and Sadiq, H. (1997), The Arab-Islamic Heritage in Communication Ethics, in: C. Christians and M. Traber (eds.) Communication Ethics and Universal Values, Thousand Oaks: Sage Publications, pp. 105-127.

Ayish, M. (2000), Arab World Television in Transition: Current Trends and Future Perspectives, in: Orient, No. 3, pp. 415-434.

Ayish, M. (2003a), Arab World Television in the Age of Globalization: an Analysis of Emerging Political, Economic, Cultural and Technological Patterns, Hamburg: Deutsches Orient-Institut.

Ayish, M. (2003b), Beyond Western Media Theories: A Normative Arab Islamic Perspective, in: Javnost (the Public), No. 2, pp. 33-57.

Ayish, M. (2004), The Impact of Arab Satellite Television on Culture and Value Systems in Arab Countries: Perspectives and Issues, in: Transnational Broadcasting Studies, No. 9:
http://www.tbsjournal.com/Archives/Fall02/Ayish.html.

Awadh, M. (2006), Arab Handbook for Human Rights and Development, in:
http://www.arabhumanrights.org/dalil/start.htm.

Aziz, S. (1968), The Egyptian Press and its Position on the British Occupation, Cairo: Ministry of Culture (in Arabic).

Azzi, A. (1989), The Arab Press: An Evaluation of William Rugh's Trilogy of Arab Media Systems, in: al-Fikr al-Arabi, No. 58, pp. 169-183 (in Arabic).

Azzi, A. (1998), Mass Media in the Grand Maghrib: Morocco – Algeria – Tunisia, in: http://us.geocities.com/azzirah.geo/maghrib.htm.

Ba'alabki, M. (1980), Al-Mawrid Dictionary, Beirut: Dar al-Ilm lil-Malayin (in Arabic).

Badrkhan, A. (2004), The Press in Diaspora, in: al-Khaleej Conference on the Arab Press in a Changing World, Sharjah: al Khaleej Press, pp. 168-175 (in Arabic).

Barakat, H. (1985), Contemporary Arab Society: An Exploratory Social Study, Beirut: Arab Unity Studies Centre (in Arabic).

Barakat, H. (1992), Beyond the always and the never: A Critique of Social Psychological Interpretations of Arab Society and Culture, in: H. Sharabi (ed.), Theory, Politics and the Arab World: Critical Responses, New York: Routledge Press, pp. 132-159.

Bates, D. and Plog, F. (1990), Cultural Anthropology, New York: McGraw-Hill.

Bel-Qaziz, A. (1998), Globalization and Cultural Identity, in: Arab Unity Studies Center (ed.), Globalization and the Arabs, Beirut: AUSC, pp. 24-34 (in Arabic).

Bel-Qaziz, A. (2002), The State in Contemporary Islamic Thought, Beirut: Arab Unity Studies Center (in Arabic).

Bel-Qaziz, A. (2006), History of the Struggle for Reform in the Arab World, in: Al Khaleej, March 17, p. 10 (in Arabic).

Benhabib, S. (1992), Modes of Public Sphere, in: C. Calhoun (ed.), Habermas and the Public Sphere, Cambridge: MIT Press, pp. 73-98.

Bennabi, M. (1991), The Grand Issues, Beirut: Dar Al-Fikr (in Arabic).

Berjas, B. (1988), Arab Press Handbook, Kuwait: Kuwaiti News Agency (in Arabic).

Bishai, W. (1973), Humanities in the Arabic Islamic World, Dubuque: WM C. Brown.

Bishara, A. (1998), Civil Society: A Critical Study, Beirut: Arab Unity Studies Center (in Arabic).

Bliwi, S. (2005), The Role of Freedom of Expression in the Progress of Civilization, in: Journal of Social Affairs, No. 88, pp. 31-61 (in Arabic).

Boukhnoufah, A. (2001), Does Local TV have a Place on Arab TV Landscape?, in: Arab Broadcasting, No. 2, pp. 13-22.

Boulawali, T. (2005), Dialogue, in: Civilized Dialogue, No. 1079: http://www.ahewar.org/debat/show.art.asp?aid=29841 (in Arabic).

Boullata, I. (1985), Trends and Issues in Contemporary Arab Thought. New York: State University Press.

Boyd, D., Straubhaar, J. and Lent, J. (1989), Videocassette Recorders in the Third World, New York: Longman.

Boyd, D. (1999), Broadcasting in the Arab World: A Survey of Electronic Media in the Middle East, Ames: Iowa State University Press.

Boyd, D. (2001), Saudi Arabia's International Media Strategy: Influence through Multinational Ownership, in: K. Hafez (ed.) Mass Media, Politics & Society in the Middle East, Cresskill: Hampton Press.

Boyd-Barrett, O. (1995), Conceptualizing the 'Public Sphere', in: O. Boyd-Barrett and C. Newbold (eds.), Approaches to Media: A Reader, London: Arnold, pp. 230-234.

Burchart, G. and Older, S. (2004), The Information Revolution in the Middle East and North Africa, Washington, D. C.: Rand Corporation.

Calhoun, C. (1992), Introduction, in: C. Calhoun (ed.), Habermas and the Public sphere, Cambridge: MIT Press, pp.1-48.

Castells, M. (1997), The Rise of Network Society, 2nd ed., Oxford: Blackwell.

Cioeta, D. (1979), Ottoman Censorship in Lebanon and Syria: 1876-1908, in: IJMES, No. X, pp. 86-167.

Clarke, R.A. et al. (2004), Defeating the Jihadists: A blueprint for Action, New York: Century Foundation Press.

Center for Strategic Studies (CSS), (2005), Revisiting the Arab Street: Research from within, Amman: Center for Strategic Studies.

Crone, P. (2004), God's Rule – Government and Islam: Six Centuries of Medieval Islamic Political Thought, New York: Columbia University Press.

Cukier, W., Bauer, R. and Middleton, C. (2004), Applying Habermas' Validity Claims as a Standard for Critical Discourse Analysis, IFIP International Federation for Information Processing, Vol. 143, Boston: Springer.

Cull, N. (2006), Public Diplomacy before Gullion: The Evolution of a Phrase, Blog Notes, USC Center on Public Diplomacy.

Curran, J. and Seaton, J. (1988), Power without Responsibility, 3rd ed., London: Fontana.

Curran, J. (1991), Mass Media and Democracy: A Reappraisal, in: J. Curran and M. Gurevitch (eds.), Mass Media and Society, London: Arnold, pp. 82-117.

Dabbous, S. (1994), The Press in Egypt, in Y. Kamalipour and H. Mowlana (eds.), Mass Media in the Middle East: A Comprehensive Handbook, Westport: Greenwood Press, pp. 60-73.

Dahlberg, L. (2000), The Internet and the Public Sphere: A Critical Analysis of the Possibility of Online Discourse Enhancing Deliberative Democracy, Unpublished doctoral dissertation in sociology at Massey University.

Dajani, A. (1984), The Development of the Concepts of Democracy in the Modern Arab Thought, in: Arab Unity Studies Centre (ed.), The Crisis of Democracy in the Arab Homeland, Beirut: AUSC, pp. 107-126 (in Arabic).

Dajani, N. (2001), The Changing Scene of Lebanese Television, in: Transnational Broadcasting Studies 7:
http://www.tbsjournal.com/Archives/Fall01/dajani.html.

Da Lage, O. (2005), The Politics of al-Jazeera or the Diplomacy of Doha, in: M. Zayani (ed.), The Al Jazeera Phenomenon. Critical Perspectives on new Arab Media, New York: Pluto Press, pp. 49-65.

Dawisha, A. (2003), Arab Nationalism in the Twentieth Century: From Triumph to Despair, Princeton: Princeton University Press.

Dean, J. (2001), Cybersalons and Civil Society: Rethinking the Public Sphere in Transnational Technoculture, in: Public Culture, No. 2, pp. 243-265.

Debbagh, A. (2004), Despotism in the Arab World: Roots and Reproduction Mechanisms, aljazeera.net, December 7:
http://www.aljazeera.net/NR/exeres/087F2086-2ABF-4329-8A11-DB06C4C40A13.htm (in Arabic).

Digital Studio (2001a), Super Channel Facelift for Jordan Television, No. 2, p. 6.

Digital Studio (2001b), JTV Claims Revamp a Success, No. 9, p. 8.

Duri, A. (2005), Introduction to Early Islamic History. Beirut: Arab Unity Studies Center (in Arabic).

Eickelman, D. and Anderson, J. (1999) (eds.), New Media in the Muslim World: The Emerging Public Sphere, Bloomington: Indiana University Press.

Eickelman, D. (2002a), The Middle East and Central Asia: An Anthropological Approach, New Jersey: Prentice Hall, pp. 253 & 283.

Eickelman, D. (2002b), The Arab Street and the Middle East's Democracy Deficit, in: Naval War College Review, No. 4, pp. 39-48.

El-Aswad, E. (2001), Muslim Sermons: Public Discourse in Local and Global Scenarios, Paper presented at the AAA conference, San Francisco.

El-Nawawy, M. and Iskander, A. (2003), Al Jazeera: How the free Arab News Network Scooped the World and Changed the Middle East, Cambridge: Westview.

Emirates Center for Strategic Studies and Research (ECSSR) (2002), Globalization and its Impact on Society and the State, Abu Dhabi: ECSSR.

Emirates Center for Strategic Studies and Research (ECSSR) (2006), Arab Media in the Information Age, Conference Proceedings, Abu Dhabi: ECSSR.

Ermes, A. (2004), The Arab Media in Britain, in:
http://www.aliomarermes.co.uk/resources/view_article.cfm?article_id=15

Esposito, J. and Voll, J. (1996), Islam and Democracy, Oxford: Oxford University Press.

Ess, C. (2001), Theoretical, Ethical, and Political Dimensions of the Public Sphere in the Age of the Internet, at Public Privacy: http://www.scripps.ohiou.edu/PublicPrivacy/abstr_ess.htm.

Fakhreddin, J. (2006), Public Diplomacy 101: A Required Course for Karen Hughes, in: Transnational Broadcasting Studies, No. 15: http://www.tbsjournal.com/Fakhreddine.html.

Farooq, M. (2002), Islam and Democracy: Perceptions and Misperceptions, in: Message International: http://www.globalwebpost.com/farooqm/writings/islamic/democracy.htm.

Felski, R. (1989), Beyond Feminist Aesthetics: Feminist Literature and Social change, Cambridge: Harvard University Press.

Fernback, J. and Thompson, B. (1995), Virtual Communities: Abort, Retry, Failure?, in: http://www.well.com/user/hlr/texts/ VCcivil.html.

Fraser, N. (1990), Rethinking the Public Sphere, in: Social Text, No. 25/26, pp. 56-80.

Fraser, N. (1993), Rethinking the Public Sphere: A Contribution to the Critique of Actually Existing Democracy, in: B. Robbins (ed.), The Phantom Public Sphere, Minneapolis: University of Minnesota Press, pp. 1-32.

Fraser, N. (2005), Rethinking the Public Sphere: A contribution to the Critique of Actually Existing Democracy, in: Aleterity: http://www.zephoria.org/alterity/archives/2005/02/.

Freedom House (2005), Women's Rights in the Middle East and North Africa: Citizenship and Justice, in: http://65.110.85.181/template.cfm?page=148

Frey, F. (1973), Communication and Development, in: I. de Sola Pool et al. (eds.), Handbook of Communication, Chicago: Rand McNally.

Fuller, G. (2002), The Future of Political Islam, in: Foreign Affairs, No. 2, pp. 22-37.

Garnham, N. (1986), The Media and the Public Sphere, in: P. Golding, G. Murdock and P. Schlesinger (eds.), Communicating Politics, Leicester: Leicester University Press, pp. 45-53.

Gause III, G. (2005), Democracy, Terrorism and American Policy in the Arab World, Paper presented to the Conference on Assessing Middle East Security Prospects, University of Vermont, Ft. McNaire.

Ghalyoun, B. (1999), The Arab World vis-à-vis the Challenges of the 21st Century: Big Challenges, Little Determination, in: Al-Mustaqbal al-Arabi, No. 232, p. 14, quoted in M. Diab, Arabizing Globalization: A Critical Issue, in: Qadaya Muaasira (Decisive Issues), October, p. 151 (in Arabic).

Ghali, B. (1999), Peace, Development and Democratization, Lecture presented at the Japan Institute of International Affairs, Tokyo, December.

Ghazali, M. (2004), Reasons behind Muslims' Defeat, in: IslamOnline: http://www.islamonline.net/Arabic/contemporary/2004/10/article02.shtml.

Giddens, A. (1999), Globalization: An Irresistible Force, in: Daily Yoniuri, June 7: http://www.globalpolicy.org/globaliz/define/irresfrc.htm.

Gregory, B. (2005), Public Diplomacy and Strategic Communication: Cultures Firewalls, and Imported Norms, Paper presented at the American Political Science Association Conference on International Communication and Conflict, George Washington University and Georgetown University, Washington, D.C., August 31.

Habermas, J. (1970), Toward a Rational Society: Student Protest, Science and Politics, Boston: Beacon Press.

Habermas, J. (1974), The Public Sphere: An Encyclopedia Article, in: New German Critique, No. 3, pp. 43-55.

Habermas, J. (1989), The Structural Transformation of the Public Sphere, Cambridge: MIT Press (Originally published in 1962).

Habermas, J. (1992), Between Facts and Norms: Contributions to a Discourse Theory of Law and Democracy, Cambridge: MIT Press.

Hafez, K. (ed.) (2001), Media and Society in the Middle East, New York: Hampton Press.

Hafez, K. (2003) (ed.), Media Ethics in the Dialogue of Cultures: Journalistic Self-Regulation in Europe, the Arab World, and Muslim Asia, Hamburg: Deutsches Orient-Institut.

Hafez, K. (2006), Arab Satellite Broadcasting: Democracy without Political Parties?, in: Transnational Broadcasting Studies, No. 15: http://www.tbsjournal.com/Hafez.html.

Hale, J. (1975), Radio Power: Propaganda and International Broadcasting, London: Elek Publishers.

Hamada, B. (2000), Islamic Cultural Theory, Arab Media Performance and Public Opinion, in: S. Splichal (ed.), Public Opinion and Democracy, New Jersey: Hampton Press, pp. 55-81.

Hamada, B. (2004), Global Culture or Cultural Clash: An Islamic Intercultural Communication Perspective, in: Global Media Journal, No. 4: http://lass.calumet.purdue.edu/cca/gmj/OldSiteBackup/SubmittedDocuments/archivedpapers/fall2004/refereed/basyouni.htm.

Hamza, A. (1989), Communication in the Early Islamic History. Cairo: Dar al-Fikr al Arabi (in Arabic).

Hamza, D. and Noor, F. (2005), Malaysia: The 'non-debate' in the Muslim World – Revisiting the Ethics of Difference in Islam, in: http://www.svabhinava.org/MeccaBenares/FarishNoor/NonDebatePart1-frame.php.

Hamzawi, A. (2005a), The Tortuous Path of Arab Democracy, in: The Daily Star, April 2.

Hamzawi, A. (2005b), Understanding Arab Political Reality: One lens is not enough, in: Policy Outlook, No. 3, Washington, D. C.: Carnegie Endowment for International Peace.

Handwerk, B. (2003), Can Islam and Democracy Co-Exist? In: National Geographic News: http://news.nationalgeographic.com/news/2003/10/1021_031021_islamicdemocracy.html.

Hartley, J. (1997), The Sexualization of Suburbia: The Diffusion of Knowledge in the Postmodern Public Sphere, in: Visions of Suburbia, London: Routledge, pp. 180-216.

Hawthorne, A. (2004), Political Reform in the Arab World: A New Ferment?, Washington, D.C.: Carnegie Endowment for International Peace.

Hawwa, S. (1988), Jundu Allahi Takhtitan, Beirut: Dar Ammar (in Arabic).

Held, D. (1980), Introduction to Critical Theory: Horkheimer to Habermas, London: Hutchinson, pp. 13-28.

Held, D., McGrew, A., Goldblatt, D. and Perraton, J. (1999), Global Transformations: Politics, Economics and Culture, Cambridge: Polity and Stanford University Press.

Hitti, P. (1963), The Arabs: A Short History, Princeton: Princeton University Press.

Hjroto, A. and Olufsen, C. (2003), Islamic Democracy: Analysis and Development of a Model of Islamic Democracy Based on Islam. Unpublished Ph.D. thesis, Copenhagen: Copenhagen University.

Hourani, H., Hawatmeh, G. and Essoulami, S. (1998), The Media and Freedom of the Press in Jordan, Amman: Sindbad Publishing House. (in Arabic)

Hroub, K. (2006), Satellite Media and Social Change in the Arab World, in: Emirates Center for Strategic Studies and Research (ed.), Arab Media in the Information Age, Conference Proceedings, Abu Dhabi: ECSSR, pp. 99-126 (in Arabic).

Hudson, M. (2003), Information Technology, International Politics, and Political Change in the Arab World, Paper presented at the Conference on Transnationalism, Royal Institute for Interfaith Studies, Amman, June 10.

Hudson, M. (2006), Washington and al Jazeera: Face to Face: Competitive Structures to Create Middle East Realities, in: Emirates Center for Strategic Studies and Research (ed.), Arab Media in the Information Age, Conference Proceedings, Abu Dhabi: ECSSR, pp. 243-266.

Ibn Khaldoun (2002), Muqaddima (Introduction), Edited by Ahmad Zuby. Amman: Dar Al-Arqam (in Arabic).

Ibrahim, H. (2004), Revival of Despotism in Arab States, in: aljazeera.net, October 3:
http://www.aljazeera.net/NR/exeres/89CA389F-50D3-4979-910D-DB6B644316B0.htm (in Arabic).

Imam, I. (1985), Fundamentals of Islamic Communication, Cairo: Dar al-Fikr al-Arabi (in Arabic).

International Research and Exchange Board (IREX) (2005), Media Sustainability Index – MENA, Washington, D.C.: IREX.

Islamonline (2003a), The Purpose of the Islamic State, in:
http://www.islamonline.net/English/introducingislam/politics/Politics/article02.shtml.

Islamonline (2003b), Rights of Citizens in an Islamic State, in:
http://www.islamonline.net/english/introducingislam/politics/System/article04.shtml.

Ismael, T. and Ismael, J. (1997), Civil Society in the Arab World: Historical Traces, Contemporary Vestiges, in: Arab Studies Quarterly, No. 1, pp. 44-68.

Ismael, J. and Ismael, T. (1999) Globalization and the Arab World in Middle East Politics: Regional Dynamics in Historical Perspective, in: Arab Studies Quarterly, No. 3, pp. 129-144.

Jabra, J. (1988), Arabic Language and Culture, in: M. Adams (ed.), The Middle East, New York: Facts on File Publications.

Jamai, A. (2004), Still Shooting the Messenger in Morocco, in: Arab Reform Bulletin, No. 11.

Jameelah, M. (1967), Islam in Theory and Practice. Lahore: Mohammad Yusuf Khan.

Jarrar, F. (2000), Radio and Television in Jordan, Amman: Al-Mujamma Al-Malaki li-Buhuth Al-Hadara Al- Islamiya (in Arabic).

Kamalipour, Y. and Mowlana, H. (eds.) (1994), Mass Media in the Middle East: A Comprehensive Handbook, Westport: Greenwood Press.

Karthigesu, R. (1994), Broadcasting Deregulation in Developing Asian Nations: An Examination of Nascent Tendencies Using Malaysia as a Case Study, in: Media, Culture, and Society, No. 3, pp. 73-90.

Katz, J. (1997), Birth of a Digital Nation, in: Wired, No. 4, pp. 49-52.

Kazan, F. (1993), Mass Media and Modernity, New York: Greenwood Press.

Kellner, D. (1997), Habermas, the Public Sphere and Democracy: A Critical Intervention, in:
http://www.gseis.ucla.edu/faculty/kellner/papers/habermas.htm.

Khatib, M. (1987), Lights on Communication in Early Islamic History. Beirut: Risala Foundation for Printing, Publishing and Distribution (in Arabic).

Khlify, M. (2006), The Roots of Despotism in Contemporary Arab Life, in: al-jazeera.net: http://www.aljazeera.net/NR/exeres/9C45333B-4753-4F6C-B2C0-8AEBA614534D.htm (in Arabic).

Khouri, R. (2001), Jordan Re-examines Role of the State, in: The Daily Star Online. March 29: http://www.dailystar.com.lb/opinion.21%5F04%5F01%5Fc.htm.

Khouri, R. (2005), The Status of Democracy in the Arab World, in: The Daily Star Online, October 5: http://www.dailystar.com.lb/article.asp?edition_id=10&categ_id=5&article_id=18964.

Kirat, M. (1993), The Algerian Newspeople: A Study of their Backgrounds, Professional Orientations and Working Conditions, Algiers: Office des Publications Universitaires (in Arabic).

Kraidy, M. (2006), Reality Television and Politics in the Arab World: Preliminary Observations, in: Transnational Broadcasting Studies, No. 15: http://www.tbsjournal.com/Kraidy.html.

Kramer, M. (2003), Arab Nationalism: Mistaken Identity, in: http://www.geocities.com/martinkramerorg/ArabNationalism.htm.

Labib, S. (2000), Arab Satellite Television Channels: Politics or Trade?, in: al Khaleej, June 9, p. 11 (in Arabic).

Lerner, D. et al. (1958), The Passing of Traditional Society, New York: Free Press.

Lewis, B. (1996), Islam and Liberal Democracy: A Historical Overview, in: Journal of Democracy, No. 2, pp. 52-63.

Lewis, B. (2005), Freedom and Justice in the Modern Middle East, in: Foreign Affairs, No. 3: http://www.foreignaffairs.org/20050501faessay84305/bernard-lewis/freedom-and-justice-in-the-modern-middle-east.html.

Lindsey, U. (2006), TV versus Terrorism: Why this Year's Ramadan Shows Tackled one 'Controversial' Subject, but were Barred from Broaching others?, in: Transnational Broadcasting Studies, No. 15: http://www.tbsjournal.com/Lindsey.html.

Lyotard, J. (1984), The Postmodern Condition, Minneapolis: University of Minnesota Press.

Lynch, M. (1999), State Interests and Public Spheres: The International Politics of Jordan's Identity, New York: Columbia University Press.

Lynch, M. (2003), Beyond the Arab Street: Iraq and the Arab Public Sphere, in: Politics & Society, No. 1, pp. 55-91.

Lynch, M. (2003a), America is Losing the Battle for Arab Opinion, in: International Herald Tribune, August 23, p. 7.

Lynch, M. (2003b), Taking Arabs Seriously, in: Foreign Affairs, No. 5, pp. 81-94.

Lynch, M. (2004), Shattering the Politics of Silence: Satellite Television Talk Shows and the Transformation of Arab Political Culture, in: Arab Reform Bulletin 11:
http://www.carnegieendowment.org/publications/index.cfm?fa=view&id=16242

Lynch, M. (2005), Assessing the Democratizing Power of Satellite TV, in: Transnational Broadcasting Studies, No. 14:
http://www.tbsjournal.com/lynch.html.

Lynch, M. (2006), Voices of the New Arab Public: Iraq, al-Jazeera, and Middle East Politics Today, New York: Columbia University Press.

Lynch, M. (2006a), Reality is not Enough: The Politics of Arab Reality TV, in: Transnational Broadcasting Studies, No. 15:
http://www.tbsjournal.com/Lynch.html.

Mady, A. (2004), Islam, Justice and Democracy: A Conceptual and Comparative Study, Paper presented to the CSID conference on Defining and Establishing Justice in Muslim Societies, Washington, D.C., May 28-29.

Mahmoud, Z. (1977), Rational Aspects of the Classical Arabic Culture, in G. Atiyeh (ed.), Arab and American Cultures. Washington, D.C.: American Enterprise Institute for Public Policy Research, pp. 87-92.

Mazrui, A. (2005), Islamocracy: In Search of a Muslim Path to Democracy, Center for the Study of Islam and Democracy, in:
http://www.islam-democracy.org/mazrui_bio.asp.

McQuail, M. (1995), Mass Communication Theory. London: Sage Publications.

McDonagh, K. (2003), A Global Public Sphere, in:
http://www.inter-disciplinary.net/transform/McDonagh%20paper.pdf.

Melhem, H. (2005), Melhem: Should the Arab News Media Matter much for U.S. Public Diplomacy?, in APFW: http://www.apfw.org/indexenglish.asp?fname=news%5Cenglish%5C2004%5C12289.htm.

Mesallami, I. (n. d.) Media Legislations: A Critical Analysis of Constitutional and Legal Foundations Governing Media Performance, Cairo: Dar Al-Fikr Al-Arabi (in Arabic).

Miles, H. (2003), Al-Jazeera: The Inside Story of the Arab News Channel that is Challenging the West, London: Grove Press.

Mohamed (2005), Can Blogging be any Good?, Posted at the blogging site: From Cairo With Love, in: http://fromcairo.blogspot.com/2005/06/whats-wrong-with-egyptians.html.

Moore, P. (1994), The International Context of Liberalization and Democratization in the Arab World, in: Arab Studies Quarterly, No. 3, pp. 45-66.

Muruwa, A. (1961), The Arab Press: Origin and Development, Beirut: Al Hayat Bookshop (in Arabic).

Mowlana, H. (1988), Mass Media Systems and Communication, in: M. Adams (ed.), The Middle East: A Handbook, New York: Facts on File Publications. pp. 825-839.

Mowlana, H. (1993), The New Global Order and Cultural Ecology, in: Media, Culture and Society, No. 1, pp. 9-27.

Murdock, G. (1992), Citizens, Consumers and Public Culture, in: K. Schroder, and M. Skovmand (eds.), Media Cultures, London: Routledge, pp. 17-41.

Nabhan, M. (1974), Political System in Islam, Kuwait: Kuwait University Publications (in Arabic).

Nabulsi, S. (2001), Arab Thought in the 20th Century, Beirut: Arab Foundation for Studies and Publishing (in Arabic).

Nasr, S. (1981), Islamic Life and Thought, Albany: University of New York Press.

Nawar, I. (2000), Freedom of Expression in the Arab World, Arab Press Freedom Watch, in:
http://www.apfw.org/indexenglish.asp?fname=report\english\2004\spe1001.htm.

Nawar, I. (2003), The State of the Arab Media: The Fight for Democracy, Arab Press Freedom Watch, in:
http://www.apfw.org/data/annualreports/2003/english/2003annualreport.pdf.

Nooh, A. (2003), Al-Kawakbi: A Renaissance Voice, in: Arab Unity Studies Center, Readings in Arab Thought, Beirut: AUSC (in Arabic).

Pan Arab Research Center (PARC) (2006), Advertising Monitoring Report 2005, Dubai: PARC.

Pasha, S. (1993), Towards a Cultural Theory of Political Ideology and Mass Media in the Muslim World, in: Media, Culture and Society, No. 1, pp. 61-79.

Pask, K. (2004), The Bourgeois Public Sphere and the Concept of Literatur, in: Criticism, No. 2, pp. 241-256.

Patai, R. (1969), Society, Culture and Change in the Middle East, 3rd ed., Philadelphia: University of Pennsylvania Press.

Philipp, T. (1988), Nation State and Religious Community in Egypt: The Continuing Debate, in: Die Welt des Islams, No. 4, pp. 379-391.

Pollock, D. (1992), The Arab Street: Public Opinion in the Arab World, Washington, D.C.: The Washington Institute.

Poster, M. (1995), Cyber-Democracy and the Public Sphere, University of California, Irvine, at:
http://www.uoc.edu/in3/hermeneia/sala_de_lectura/mark_poster_cyberdemocracy.htm.

Pye, L. (ed.) (1963), Communications and Political Development, Princeton: Princeton University Press.

Qaradawi, Y. (1998), Contemporary Ijtihad between Control and Disorder, Beirut: Maktab Islami for Printing and Publishing (in Arabic).

Qaradawi, Y. (2004), Reform as Religious Obligation, in Islamonline:
http://www.islamonline.net/English/News/2004-08/27/article05.shtml.

Qutb, S. (1949), Social Justice in Islam, New Jersey: Islamic Publications International.

Qutb, S. (1966), Ma'alim fi Tariq (Milestones), in: http://www.bahrainonline.org/showthread.php?t=111021 (in Arabic).

Rabasa, A., Benard, C., Schwartz, L. and, Sickle, P. (2007), Building Moderate Muslim Networks, Santa Monica: Rand Corporation.

Rinnawi, K. (2002), The Internet and the Arab World as a Virtual Public Sphere, in: http://burdacenter.bgu.ac.il/publications/finalReports2001-2002/Rinnawi.doc

Rheingold, H. (1994), The Virtual Community: Homesteading on the Electronic Frontier, New York: Harper Perennial.

Ridolfo, K. (2005), Analysis: Arab Media Contribute to Instability in Iraq, March 10, in: http://www.iwar.org.uk/news-archive/2005/03-16-3.htm.

Robertson, R. (1992), Globalization: Social Theory and Global Culture, London: Sage.

Rodinson, M. (1981), The Arabs, London: Croom Helm.

Rogers, E. (1962), Diffusion of Innovation, New York: Free Press.

Rugh, W. (1979), The Arab Press: News Media and Political Process in the Arab World, Syracuse: Syracuse University Press.

Rugh, W. (2004) Arab Mass Media: Newspapers, Radio and Television in Arab Politics, Westport: Prager.

Rugh, W. (2005), Anti-Americanism on Arab Television: Some Outsider Observations, in: Transnational Broadcasting Studies, No. 15: http://www.tbsjournal.com/Rugh.html.

Safadi, M. (1999), The Role of Globalization in the Imperialism of the Absolute, in: Al-Wifaq al-Arabi, No. 2, p. 24 (in Arabic).

Safi, L. (2004), Ideology and Politics: A General Theory of the Islamic State. Damascus: Dar Al-Fikr.

Said, E. (2003), Orientalism 25 Years Later: Worldly Humanism v. the Empire-Builders, in Counter Punch, August 4: http://www.counterpunch.org/said08052003.html.

Said, A. (2003), The Arab Satellites: Some Necessary Observations, in: Transnational Broadcasting Studies, No. 11: http://www.tbsjournal.com/Archives/Fall03/Monem_Said.html.

Sakr, N. (2006), Commercial Interests in the Arab Media, in: Emirates Center for Strategic Studies and Research (ed.), Arab Media in the Information Age, Conference Proceedings, Abu Dhabi: ECSSR, pp. 71-98.

Saleh, S. (1995), The Crisis of Press Freedom in Egypt: 1945-1985, Cairo: Dar Nashr Lil Jama'at.

Sardar, Z. (1993), Paper, Printing and Compact Disks: The Making and Unmaking of Islamic Culture, in: Media, Culture and Society, No. 1, pp. 43-59.

Schramm, W. (1964), Mass Media and National Development, Stanford: Stanford University Press.

Schleifer, S.A. (1986), Islam and Information: Need, Feasibility, and Limitations of an Independent News Agency, in: American Journal of Islamic Social Sciences, No. 1, pp. 109-124.

Schneider, S. (1997), Expanding the Public Sphere through Computer-mediated Communication: Political Discussion about Abortion in a Usenet newsgroup, Unpublished Ph.D. thesis submitted to the Massachusetts Institute of Technology.

Sein, L. (2005), CSID Sixth Annual Conference Report: Democracy and Development: Challenges for the Islamic World, Washington D.C., April 22-23.

Shamsuddin, M. (2000), Between Jaheliyya and Islam. Beirut: International Foundation for Research and Publishing.

Sharabi, H. (1988), Neopatriarchy: A Theory of Distorted Change in Arab Society, New York: Oxford University Press.

Sharabi, H. (2004), The Political Impact of Arab Satellite Television on post-Iraq War Arab World, in: Transnational Broadcasting Studies, No. 11: http://www.tbsjournal.com/Archives/Fall03/Hisham_Sharabi.html.

Sharp, J. (2004), The Broader Middle East and North Africa Initiative: An Overview, CS Report for Congress, in: http://www.fas.org/sgp/crs/mideast/RS22053.pdf.

Siddiqi, D. (1989), Mass Media Analysis: Formulating an Islamic Perspective, Paper presented at the AMSS conference, SYNU, Rochester (USA), October 26-28.

Sowwani, Y. (2004), Arabs and Globalization: Challenges and Alternatives, in al-Tajdid al-Arabi, in:
http://www.arabrenewal.com/index.php?rd=AI&AI0=1364 (in Arabic).

Stone, A. (2002), Many in Islamic World Doubt Arabs behind 9/11, in: USA Today, February 27:
http://www.usatoday.com/news/sept11/2002/02/27/usat-poll.htm.

Suleiman, Y. (2003), Arabic Language and National Identity, Washington, D.C.: Georgetown University Press.

Sultan, S. (2004), Forming Islamic Democracy, in: Islamonline:
http://www.islamonline.net/English/introducingislam/politics/Politics/article04.s html.

Taki, M. (2005), Weblogs, Bloggers and the Blogosphere in Lebanon, Syria and Jordan: An Exploration, Paper presented at the International Conference on Online Journalism in the Arab World: Realities and Challenges, University of Sharjah (UAE), November 22-23.

Tamimi, A. (1997), Democracy in Islamic Political Thought, London: Institute of Islamic Political Thought, in:
http://www.ii-pt.com/web/papers/democracy.htm.

Tamimi, A. (2001), Rachid Ghannoushi: A Democrat within Islamism, Oxford University Press.

Tarabishi, G. (2004), Arab Intellectuals and the Discontents of Globalization, in: Regional Forum on the Arab World and Globalization, in:
http://www.lcpslebanon.org/web04/english/activities/1999/tunis/Tunis_report.pdf.

Tehranian, M. (1999), Global Communication and World Politics: Domination, Development and Discourse, Boulder: Lynne Reinner Publishers.

Tessler, M. (2002), Do Islamic Orientations Influence Attitudes toward Democracy in the Arab World? Evidence from Egypt, Jordan, Morocco, and Algeria, in: International Journal of Comparative Sociology, No. 3-5, pp. 229-249.

Thornton, A. (1996), Does Internet Create Democracy?, Unpublished Master's Thesis, University of Technology, Sydney, in: http://www.zip.com.au/~athornto/thesis2.htm.

Tibi, B. (2002), Islam between Culture and Politics, New York: Palgrave.

Toulouse, C. and Luke, T. W. (1997), The Politics of Cyberspace, London: Routledge.

United Nations Development Fund for Women (UNIFEM) (2004), Progress of Arab Women: One Paradigm, Four Arenas and more than 140 Million Women, Amman: Arab States Regional Office.

United Nations Development Program (UNDP) (2004), Arab Human Development Report, New York: UNDP Regional Bureau for Arab States.

United Nations Development Program (UNDP) (2006), Arab Human Rights Index, New York: UN.

U.S. Department of State (2005), Middle East Partnership Initiative, in: http://mepi.state.gov/mepi/.

Valiuddin, M. (2001), Mu'tazilism', in: M.M. Sharif (ed.), A History of Muslim Philosophy, Islamic Philosophy Online, in: http://www.muslimphilosophy.com/hmp/13.htm.

Van Dijk, J. (1999), The Network Society: Social Aspects of New Media, London: Sage.

Wallerstein, I. (1998), Utopistics: Or Historical Choices of the Twenty-First Century, New York: The New Press.

Ward, D. (2001), The Democratic Deficit and European Union Communication Policy: An Evaluation of the Commission's Approach to Broadcasting, in: Javnost (the Public), No. 1, pp. 7-31.

Werbner, P. (1996), Public Spaces, Political Voices: Gender, Feminism and Aspects of British Muslim Participation in the Public Sphere, in: R. Shadid and P. van Koningsveld (eds.), Political Participation and Identities of Muslims in non-Muslim States, Kampen: Kok Pharos, pp. 53-70.

Willard, R. (1991), The Challenges to Public-Service Broadcasting, Berlin: Aspen Institute Berlin.

World Bank Group (2002), Civil Society and Globalization, The Mediterranean Development Forum, Amman (Jordan), October 6-9.

Wright, R. (1992), Islam, Democracy, and the West, in: Foreign Affairs, No. 3, pp. 131-145.

Yunis, M. (2004), Islamic Discourse in the Arab Press, Dubai: Dar Al-Qalam (in Arabic).

Yom, S. (2005), Civil Society and Democratization in the Arab World, in: Middle East Review of International Affairs, No. 4, pp. 14-33.

Za'atreh, Y. (2006), Anarchy in Internet Arenas and its Offense to Islam and Muslims, in: Aljazeera.net: http://www.aljazeera.net/NR/exeres/6E716070-88C6-47CF-966F-39E4F3C598E8.htm (in Arabic).

Zaine, A. (1992), Communication and Freedom of Expression in Yemen: 1974-1990, Beirut: Contemporary Thought Press (in Arabic).

Zakaria, F. (2006), Islam and Power: Is President Bush's Plan to Spread Democracy Turning into a Fiasco?, in: Newsweek, February 13: http://www.fareedzakaria.com/ARTICLES/newsweek/021306.html.

Zarqa, M. (1976), The Islamic Concept of Worship, in: K. Ahmad (ed.), Islam, its Meaning and Message, London: Islamic Council of Europe, pp. 109-116 (in Arabic).

Zayani, M. (2005), The Al Jazeera Phenomenon: Critical Perspectives on New Arab Media, New York: Pluto Press.

Zebian, S. (2004), U.S. Reform Threatens Arab Identity, in: Aljazeera.net: http://english.aljazeera.net/NR/exeres/EB331031-8AD1-47BD-9046-A71F0902B2EF.htm.

Zunes, S. (2001), U.S. Policy toward Political Islam, in: Foreign Policy in Focus, September 12: http://www.alternet.org/story/11479/.

MEDIEN UND POLITISCHE KOMMUNIKATION – NAHER OSTEN UND ISLAMISCHE WELT / MEDIA AND POLITICAL COMMUNICATION – MIDDLE EAST AND ISLAM

(Die Bände 1–10 sind beim Deutschen Orient-Institut, Hamburg erschienen und über dieses und den Buchhandel zu beziehen.)

Band 11 Jamal Nazzal: Das palästinensische Rundfunksystem und die deutsch-palästinensische Medienkooperation. 340 Seiten. ISBN 978-3-86596-058-0. ISBN 3-86596-058-8

Band 12 Aydin Nasseri: Internet und Gesellschaft in Iran. Mit einem Vorwort von Katajun Amirpur. 198 Seiten. ISBN 3-86596-116-9

Band 13 Maria Röder: Haremsdame, Opfer oder Extremistin? Muslimische Frauen im Nachrichtenmagazin Der Spiegel. 160 Seiten. ISBN 978-3-86596-143-3

Band 14 Antje Glück: Terror im Kopf. Terrorismusberichterstattung in der deutschen und arabischen Elitepresse. 206 Seiten. ISBN 978-386596-157-0

Band 15 Muhammad I. Ayish: The New Arab Public Sphere. 254 Seiten. ISBN 978-3-86596-168-6

Band 16 Susan Schenk: Das Islambild im internationalen Fernsehen. Ein Vergleich der Nachrichtensender *Al Jazeera English*, *BBC World* und *CNN International*. 176 Seiten. ISBN 978-3-86596-224-9

Band 17 Jan Michael Schäfer: Protest in Ägypten. Wie Al-Jazeera und andere Medien die Kifaya-Bewegung möglich machten. 150 Seiten. ISBN 978-3-86596-219-5

Frank & Timme

MEDIEN UND POLITISCHE KOMMUNIKATION – NAHER OSTEN UND ISLAMISCHE WELT / MEDIA AND POLITICAL COMMUNICATION – MIDDLE EAST AND ISLAM

Band 18 Sarah Jurkiewicz: Al-Jazeera vor Ort. Journalismus als ethische Praxis. 140 Seiten. ISBN 978-3-86596-228-7

Band 19 Katharina Nötzold: Defining the Nation? Lebanese Television and Political Elites, 1990–2005. 376 Seiten. ISBN 978-3-86596-242-3

Band 20 Kerstin Engelmann, Friederike Günther, Nele Heise, Florian Hohmann, Ulrike Irrgang, Sabrina Schmidt: Muslimische Weblogs. Der Islam im deutschsprachigen Internet. 282 Seiten. ISBN 978-3-86596-239-3

Band 21 Carola Richter: Medienstrategien ägyptischer Islamisten im Kontext von Demokratisierung. 354 Seiten. ISBN 978-3-86596-361-1

Band 22 Douglas Reynolds: Turkey, Greece, and the "Borders" of Europe. Images of Nations in the West German Press 1950–1975. 558 Seiten. ISBN 978-3-86596-441-0

Band 23 Kai Hafez (Hg.): Arabischer Frühling und deutsches Islambild. Bildwandel durch ein Medienereignis? 154 Seiten. ISBN 978-3-86596-497-7

Band 24 Almut Woller: Transformation der Geschlechterverhältnisse in den Vereinigten Arabischen Emiraten. Eine feministische Diskursanalyse der Arbeitsmarktintegration emiratischer Frauen. 234 Seiten. ISBN 978-3-7329-0015-2

Band 25 Margret Müller: The World According To Israeli Newspapers. Representations of International Involvement in the Israeli-Palestinian Conflict. 286 Seiten. ISBN 978-3-7329-0286-6

Frank & Timme